Year-Round Developmental Activities for Preschool Children

Year-Round Developmental Activities for Preschool Children

JoAnne Carswell Calvarese
Charron Carlson Sundman

THE CENTER FOR APPLIED
RESEARCH IN EDUCATION
West Nyack, New York 10995

10   9   8   7   6   5   4   3   2   1

Library of Congress Cataloging-in-Publication Data

Calvarese, JoAnne Carswell, 1949–
    Year-round developmental activities for preschool children /
JoAnne Carswell Calvarese, Charron Carlson Sundman.
        p.   cm.
    "The Center for Applied Research in Education."
    ISBN 0-87628-984-7
    1. Education, Preschool—United States—Activity programs–
–Handbooks, manuals, etc.   2. Creative activities and seat work–
–Handbooks, manuals, etc.   3. Child development—Handbooks, manuals,
etc.   I. Sundman, Charron Carlson, 1952–   II. Center for
Applied Research in Education.   III. Title.
LB1140.35.C74C35   1990
372.5—dc20   90-30537
                                                                CIP

ISBN 0-87628-984-7

**THE CENTER FOR APPLIED
RESEARCH IN EDUCATION**
BUSINESS & PROFESSIONAL DIVISION
A division of Simon & Schuster
West Nyack, New York 10995

Printed in the United States of America

To Sted and
Lauren and Alison

To Rick and
Katie and Eric and Michael
and Thomas

Acknowledgments

We would like to thank . . .

. . . Our editors Evelyn Fazio and Win Huppuch who encouraged and supported us through many months of hard work.

. . . Moocho Salomon for explaining Jewish customs and traditions.

. . . Russ and Anita Bonnevie, Jim Ross, Ellen Morrow, and Harry Hikel for their advice in their fields of expertise.

. . . Irma Haggerty for patiently reviewing our writing.

. . . Employees of the Littleton Public Library and the Village Book Store for their invaluable help in researching children's literature.

And finally we would like to recognize the Mother Goose and other traditional nursery rhymes, stories, and finger plays for which no authors have been found.

ABOUT THE AUTHORS

Charron Carlson Sundman, B.A., Mount Holyoke College, has been actively involved in education for more than 15 years, beginning as a substitute teacher at Holyoke High School, Holyoke, Massachusetts. After completing courses in Early Childhood Development and Elementary Education at Mount Holyoke College, she received a New Hampshire teacher's certificate in elementary education in 1980 and served as assistant teacher, then director/head teacher, of the Toddler Program at The Children's House Montessori School in Littleton, New Hampshire. Mrs. Sundman also taught a six-week course, "Making Your Own Learning Games for Children," at the School for Lifelong Learning, University of New Hampshire.

JoAnne Carswell Calvarese has been working with young children for over 14 years in various day care and toddler programs. Her experience includes six years as director/head teacher of the Toddler Program at The Children's House Montessori School, Littleton, New Hampshire, and two years as assistant in the same program. She has also served as the summer director, R.L.D.S. Campgrounds, Onset, Massachusetts, and as a substitute teacher at Whitefield, New Hampshire, Elementary School. Mrs. Calvarese is currently completing her B.P.S. in Child Development and Early Childhood Education at the School for Lifelong Learning, University of New Hampshire. JoAnne has studied string bass at the Conservatory of Music in Kansas City and the University of South Florida. She played a season with the Florida Gulf Coast Symphony in Tampa.

ABOUT THIS TEACHER'S RESOURCE

Year-Round Developmental Activities for Preschool Children gives teachers of young children a unique store of stimulating developmental activities with which to build basic learning skills related to all curriculum areas. Included are over 300 enjoyable learning experiences conveniently organized into 10 monthly sections and presented in the same subject order each month: Art, Music, Movement, Language, Nutrition, Science/Nature, Math, Social Studies, and Health/Safety.

For easy and effective use, each activity is spelled out in a step-by-step format and provides all the details and directions you need for a complete, well-organized lesson plan. It includes a descriptive title . . . specific skills/concepts covered . . . suggested age levels for use . . . length of time required . . . materials needed . . . introduction . . . procedure . . . closure . . . and follow-up suggestions. Where appropriate, activities also include directions "For Adult to Do Ahead." Moreover, the introduction, procedure, and closure for each activity are written in language you can use just as it is to present the activity to children.

Also included in this resource are the following special aids:

- "Stages of Child Development," a description of children's normal growth patterns in each of these areas: gross motor skills, fine motor skills, language skills, and self-help skills.
- "Chronological Sequence of Skill Development," a chart depicting children's growth from 18 months through 5 years.
- "Suggested Toys for Preschool Children," including toys for toddlers (18 months to 3 years) and toys for 3-, 4-, and 5-year-olds.
- "Directions for Making Your Own Teaching Tools," including a flannel board, parquetry or tangram pieces, and "Cuisinaire-like" rods
- "Guidelines for Taking a Field Trip" with a sample emergency card and permission slip

In addition, a brief preface entitled "How to Use This Resource Most Effectively" precedes the monthly activity sections. This explains the thematic nature of each month's activities and provides brief descriptions of the nine subject categories in each section.

All the learning experiences in this collection of *Year-Round Developmental Activities* have been used successfully with children in a variety of preschool settings. We hope they will work with equal or greater success with the children in your own program.

JoAnne Carswell Calvarese
Charron Carlson Sundman

STAGES OF CHILD DEVELOPMENT

As a child grows, he or she passes through many stages of development. This resource specifically addresses the toddler (18 months to 3 years old) and the preschool or nursery school-aged child (3 to 5 years old).

The toddler stage of development is an exciting period of growth for a child. There is exploration of the environment using all five senses (often without discrimination!). Each child is the center of his or her universe around which the world revolves. The child delights in learning how daily interaction with this universe effects change.

As the child enters the renowned "terrible twos," he or she need not turn into an uncontrollable terror! This stage of development can be seen as one in which the child is beginning to explore how much he or she controls this universe—what the limits are. With gentle guidance from you, the adult, the child can form limits of control that are compatible with the needs of others as well as his or her own.

Learning for a toddler often occurs when an activity can be repeated over and over. For example, a child will turn a bowl of cotton balls over and then pick them up one by one, replacing them in the bowl. At this point, an adult would place the bowl of cotton balls back on the shelf; not so the toddler! The child is then apt to turn the bowl upside down and empty its contents once again. The toddler does not view this as a task of cleaning up a spill, as an adult might. Rather, he or she sees it as a game in which the dumping out and the picking up are equally important components. For this reason, a child can repeat this series of actions over and over without tiring. These simple movements are a challenge, and the child is striving to master them. There is delight in every accomplishment.

At 3, 4, and 5, the child becomes more autonomous. Improved fine and gross motor skills allow the child to meet many of his or her needs with little help from an adult. Dressing, undressing, using the bathroom, and eating are some of the activities in which the child is able to take an active role or possibly handle completely.

The typical 3-, 4-, or 5-year-old will spend most waking hours at play. Play is extremely important to their development. Especially enjoyed is group play with peers or involvement in dramatic play. Play also offers an excellent opportunity for language development.

Sand, water, rhythm instruments, and art materials provide a great variety of creative activities for a child at this stage of development. They allow the child a chance for free expression, to experiment, and to stretch the imagination.

During each stage of development, the child works on a set pattern of skills which eventually will be mastered. This book provides myriad activities that specifically foster the development of four major skill areas: gross motor, fine motor, language, and self-help.

FINE MOTOR SKILLS

Fine motor skills involve the refined use of fingers, hands, and feet. Manipulatives such as puzzles, pop beads, and pegboards aid the child in becoming better able to gain control of small muscle groups. Clay, crayons, and finger paints are useful tools for further fine motor development.

A toddler has already begun to use simple hand-eye coordination, as in sucking the thumb, picking up toys, or handling finger foods. Rolling rubber balls and tossing bean bags are great activities to encourage continued development of hand-eye coordination.

All these skills will be used in the future for zipping, buttoning, holding a pencil (fork or spoon), and other activities using the fingers.

GROSS MOTOR SKILLS

Walking, running, climbing, jumping, pushing, pulling, throwing, catching, and carrying are examples of gross motor skills which employ the use of the entire body—especially the arms and legs.

A typical 18-month-old child has already developed many gross motor skills, such as crawling and walking. At this point, it is important to gain better control of these movements through repetition. As the child masters these skills, he or she will gradually become more rhythmic and coordinated in movements.

By ages 3, 4, and 5, the child may use stairs, swings, jungle gyms, and balance beams to develop further the newly acquired gross motor skills of running, hopping, and jumping, activities of which a child never seems to tire.

LANGUAGE SKILLS

The development of language actually begins at birth and continues at a rapid rate until approximately age 4. By age 4, the average child is able to form complete sentences.

Language development follows a set pattern. The progression of language acquisition is from the simple to the complex. A child begins with individual sounds and soon moves on to syllables. Next, there is an attempt at one-word sentences, followed later by two- and three-word sentences. By ages 4 and 5, the child is able to use more complex sentences.

No amount of repeated drill will change the progression of this development. It is important to remember that each child will progress as he or she is developmentally able, and that there is a wide range of individual variation in the area of language development.

The adult can best encourage the child's language development by talking, singing, and reading to the child from infancy. Toddlers enjoy picture books, nursery rhymes, and books with one or two sentences to a page. Three-, 4- and 5-year-olds have a longer attention span. They prefer longer stories, rhyming words and poems, songs, and silly jokes.

SELF-HELP SKILLS

One of the best ways to help your child become an independent, questioning individual is to scale the world around down to the child's level so that he or she may interact with this environment, master it, and thereby gain self-confidence as well as gradual independence.

Here are a few suggestions for scaling down a classroom or home environment for the toddler through the 5-year-old child:

- Place toys on a few shelves within the child's reach rather than in an overflowing toy box.
- Provide a kitchen corner complete with low table (a box will do in a pinch), some plastic bowls and cups, wooden spoons, and other nonbreakable items.
- Mount plastic hooks (with rounded edges) low on the wall of a child's bedroom or classroom and encourage the child to hang his or her clothing on them.
- Hang a mirror at the child's level in the bedroom or bathroom. Place the child's comb and a box of tissues within reach, and encourage their use.

CHRONOLOGICAL SEQUENCE OF SKILL DEVELOPMENT

The accompanying chart shows skills for children 18 months through 5 years of age. The skills are arranged in groupings of several months at a time and are meant to be used as a guide rather than as a rigid timetable. This information will help you to anticipate stages of normal child development in the areas of fine motor, gross motor, language, and self-help skills.

Each child will acquire these skills at his or her own pace. Some children develop them more quickly in one area and more slowly in another. Check with a pediatrician if you are concerned about the progress of a child.

CHRONOLOGICAL SEQUENCE

*The following books were used as resources for determining average skill abilities for each age group: Frank and Theresa Caplin, *The Second Twelve Months of Life* (New York: Bantam Books, 1977); Theresa and Frank Caplan,

	18-20 MONTHS	21-24 MONTHS	25-30 MONTHS
GROSS MOTOR SKILLS	• Walks with feet wide • Jumps with both feet off floor • Kicks a large ball • Runs stiffly • Walks up and down stairs with help • Pushes and pulls large toys or boxes around • Climbs on a low step or table	• Walks more rhythmically • Moves easily from standing to running • Goes up and down stairs alone • Stands on either foot—holding on to something • Jumps in place • Pedals a small tricycle • Throws an object overhand • Alternates quickly between sitting and standing • Walks a few steps on tiptoe	• Runs without losing balance • Jumps from low bottom step to floor • Turns around • Kicks a ball • Climbs stairs unaided • Throws an object haphazardly and retrieves it • Avoids obstacles while walking
FINE MOTOR SKILLS	• Scribbles in circular motion • Holds two objects in one hand • Throws a small rubber ball • Fits objects together (simple puzzle pieces, pegs in holes, nesting cups, rings on poles)	• Establishes left or right handedness • Enjoys tactile books like *Pat the Bunny* • Strings several large beads • Builds a tower with 6 cubes or more • Makes a train with blocks • Draws crude picture using multiple and single lines	• Builds a tower with more than 6 blocks • Strings a whole lace with beads • Take the lid off a jar • Draws a vertical line • Turns pages of a book one at a time
LANGUAGE SKILLS	• Points to own body parts when asked • Attempts to sing • Understands simple questions • Points to pictures of familiar objects • Responds to speech with speech • Enjoys listening to nursery rhymes • Labels actions • Attempts to talk in sentences (subject/verb) • Uses expressive vocabulary of 15 or more words.	• Enjoys listening to simple stories • Follows directions • Asks for things by name • Echoes words and inflections of adults • Associates names with most familiar objects • Uses expressive vocabulary of 50 or more words	• Uses expressive vocabulary of 50 to 300 words • Begins to use pronouns especially mine, me, you, I • Acquires many more verbs in vocabulary • Uses the word "no" often • Enjoys books and listening to stories • Sings phrases of simple songs
SELF-HELP SKILLS	• Undresses self • Handles spoon well • Unzips zipper • Asks for food and drink • Washes and dries hands • Pours water from one cup into another • Helps pick up toys and put away with adult assistance • Likes to fetch and carry	• Wants to "Do it myself." • Has short attention span—flits from activity to activity • Handles spoon and cup well—holds cup in one hand • Participates in washing and drying self • Likes to sweep, mop, dust, hammer, shovel, scoop, and rake • Turns doorknobs and opens doors • Undresses without help • Helps dress self—but doesn't differentiate front from back or right from left • Picks up toys and puts them away with verbal encouragement	• Holds a glass securely • Grasps an object without dropping it • Begins "potty" training • Begins eating at the family table • Likes to wash hands—doesn't like face washed • Starts learning to brush teeth

OF SKILL DEVELOPMENT *

The Early Childhood Years (New York: Bantam Books, 1983) and Rosalind Charlesworth,
Understanding Child Development (New York: Delmar Publishers Inc., 1983).

31-36 MONTHS	3-3½ YEARS OLD	3½-4 YEARS OLD	4-5 YEARS OLD
• Begins to turn somersaults • Runs, but is not able to start and stop quickly • Hops on one foot for 2 or more hops • Masters riding a small tricycle • Walks upstairs using alternate feet • Walks down stairs alone	• Stands on toes • Climbs up an inclined board or small slide • Climbs on a jungle gym • Walks in a straight line • Gets up from squatting position without help • Catches a large ball with arms extended in front • Pedals and steers a small tricycle • Gallops, walks, runs, and jumps to music	• Runs smoothly • Tiptoes for a long distance • Walks on a balance board • Jumps high • Tries catch and throw ball games • Steers tricycle so it doesn't bump into things	• Hops on one foot 4-6 hops • Runs, rolls, and climbs • Sits with knees crossed • Swings and twirls on a swing set • Somersaults • Uses hands to catch a ball • Makes a U-turn on a tricycle • Walks upstairs one foot to a step
• Moves fingers independently • Builds a tower of 8 blocks • Enjoys experimenting with clay, sand, or fingerpaints • Draws a horizontal and a vertical line • Strings macaroni, beads, and buttons with large holes • Matches jigsaw puzzle piece to the shape of the hole	• Has increased control of fingers • Picks up small objects • Improves control of pencil • Places round, square, and triangular blocks in form board • Builds a tower with 9 small blocks	• Begins to use small scissors • Traces diamond shape on a piece of paper • Uses thin, uncertain lines in his drawings • Draws a circle and a square	• Uses blunt nosed scissors • Cuts on a line with scissors • Draws a human figure with head, body, arms, and legs • Strings a set of small beads
• Averages 50 new words a month to expressive vocabulary • Uses sentences containing 3 or more words • Asks questions—What?, Why?, Where? • Enjoys picture books with several sentences on each page • Sings entire short song	• Uses expressive vocabulary of 900 words • Uses language to get what is wanted • Asks how and when questions • Responds to more difficult directions • Remembers many songs • Uses plurals	• Makes up new words • Uses longer sentences • Uses average vocabulary of about 1,500 words by age 4 • Understands the concepts of on top of, under, beside, etc. • Enjoys listening to stories for period of 15-20 minutes • Loves silly rhymes and rhyming words	• Uses a vocabulary of about 1,900 words by age 4½ • Says hello, goodbye, please, thank you • Says his own first and last names • Uses sentences of 5 to 6 words • Asks the meaning of words • Identifies 10 objects from a picture • Enjoys jokes, funny, and silly books
• Finishes "potty" training (usually by age 3) • Eats without much spilling • Takes off and puts on shoes—can't tie (velcro shoes at this time aid independence.) • Undresses completely • Begins to select own clothing.	• Uses both hands to pour from pitcher into a cup—with little spilling • Holds cup by handle • Puts on shoes, slacks, and underpants with little help • Buttons some buttons • Zips once zipper is started	• Helps with household chores • Uses toilet unassisted • Puts shoes on correct foot	• Washes hands, face, and brushes teeth with supervision • Handles a spoon and fork • Pours milk from a pitcher without spilling • Dresses and undresses

SUGGESTED TOYS FOR PRESCHOOL CHILDREN

The following lists offer suggestions for toys appropriate for toddlers (18 months to 3 years) and for 3-, 4-, and 5-year-old preschoolers. These lists suggest basic items for providing your day care center or preschool with an adequate supply of materials that will encourage a child's development. They contain the basics. A visit to a good children's toy store and your own imagination can supplement this list.

TOYS FOR TODDLERS

Small building blocks
Large stringing beads with shoelace for stringing
Hammer and pegboard
Kitchen set (unbreakable dishes, pots and pans, etc.)
Child-sized hand broom and mop with handle cut off
Dolls
Doll bed and carriage
Dress-up clothes (simple pull-on clothing, no buttons or zippers)
Water play materials (plastic spoons, cups, pitchers, funnels)
Soft animals
Sand play materials (shovels, pails, spoons, sieves, molds)
Small combination climbing stairs and slide (appropriate height)
Simple shape sorter box (three shapes)
Art supplies: paper, crayons, big brushes, poster paints, fingerpaints, paste, scraps of material, yarn, colored construction paper, white painting paper
Rocking toy (boat or plastic teeter-totter)
Rhythm instruments
Big balls
Cloth balls

TOYS FOR 3-, 4-, AND 5-YEAR-OLDS

Large building blocks
Stringing beads
Lacing cards or boot
Zipper and button frames
Kitchen set with pots, pans, and plastic child-sized dishes
Broom, brush, dustpan, mop, duster, rake, shovel (all child-sized)
Doll, doll clothes, carriage, bed, and high chair
Dress-up clothing (may include clothing that zips and buttons)
Tree stump with hammer and big nails
Spray bottle with cloth for shining and polishing
Sand play materials (shovels, pails, molds, sieves, sifters, spoons, plastic spoons, cups, and pitchers)
Water play materials (plastic spoons, cups, pitchers, sieves, funnels, food colors for colored water)
Climbing and sliding areas (height appropriate for this age child)
Swings
Shape sorters up to seven or eight different shapes
More complex puzzles (up to ten pieces)
A rocking toy
Balance beam
Tumbling mat
Wagon
Dump truck
Musical toys (xylophone, toy piano)
Rhythm instruments
Mirror
Stacking toys
Nesting toys
Hand puppets
Large interconnecting plastic blocks
Peg boards
Parquetry pieces (see p. xv)
Cuisenaire rods and inch blocks (see p. xvi for making your own)
Large nuts and bolts—2' diameter
Flannel board (see p. xv)
Art supplies: paper, crayons, brushes, watercolors, poster paints, fingerpaints, painting paper, paste, scraps of material, yarn, paste, construction paper, moist clay, small scissors, glue, dried noodles, dried peas and beans
Games or puzzles for color, size, and shape identification

DIRECTIONS FOR MAKING YOUR OWN TEACHING TOOLS

The following provides detailed directions for making three useful teaching/learning devices: a flannel board for displays, parquetry or tangram pieces for exploring geometric shapes, and "Cuisenaire-like" rods for investigating number relationships.

HOW TO MAKE A FLANNEL BOARD

A flannel board is a necessary item for any preschool program. Flannel boards can be purchased from educational supply catalogs or made at home.

Materials:
1. One piece of lightweight board (pegboard or panelling) cut to the desired size.
2. A piece of dark or light blue flannel or felt fabric large enough to cover the board you have cut. *Note:* Allow the fabric to be approximately 2–3 inches larger on all sides than the cut board.
3. Duct tape, glue gun, or staples.

Procedure:
1. Lay the flannel fabric on a table.
2. Place the cut board in the center of the fabric.
3. Tape, glue, or staple the edges of the fabric to the back of the board.

Construction of Flannel Board Pieces:
1. Cut out pictures of something you plan to discuss (e.g., farm animals) and glue a large piece of flannel on the back OR
2. Draw pictures on construction paper and glue a piece of flannel on the back OR
3. Draw pictures of the objects right on the pieces of flannel and cut out shapes. Use several colors of clothing on people or trim on buildings and glue them on to the largest piece.

HOW TO MAKE PARQUETRY OR TANGRAM PIECES

Parquetry/tangram pieces are thin wooden or posterboard pieces cut in geometric shapes. These pieces can be used by the child as a manipulative material to investigate geometric forms and explore patterns, designs, and colors. They can be purchased from educational supply catalogs (Cuisenaire Co. of America, Inc., 12 Church Street, Box D, New Rochelle, New York 10802) or made at home.

Here are directions for making parquetry/tangram pieces.

Materials:
1. Posterboard (several different colors).
2. Clear contact paper.
3. Pencil.
4. Ruler.
5. Sharp scissors.

Procedure:
1. Draw five or six copies of each shape on the posterboard.
2. Cover the posterboard with clear contact paper.
3. Cut out the parquetry pieces.

Place the parquetry pieces in a special box or basket. This will help keep the pieces from being lost. It also makes the setup and cleanup of this material easier for the child.

HOW TO MAKE "CUISENAIRE-LIKE" RODS

Cuisenaire rods are wooden or hard plastic rods of different lengths. They encourage children to explore number relationships by fitting the rods together in a variety of ways. They also serve as a concrete number line. A rod which is 5 units long and another rod 5 units long is the same length as a rod 10 units long.

Cuisenaire rods can be purchased from educational supply catalogs or from Cuisenaire Company of America, 12 Church Street, Box D, New Rochelle, New York 10802. They can also be made at home. Following are instructions for making them. Using the materials listed here, you will make five sets of rods measuring 1 inch to 5 inches in length.

Materials:
1. Two pieces of ¾-inch × ¾-inch × 48-inch baluster stock (found at lumberyards or supply stores).
2. Ruler.
3. Pencil.
4. Hand saw.
5. Sandpaper.
6. Spray paint.

Procedure:
1. Mark the baluster stock at 1-inch intervals five times. Mark the stock at 2-inch intervals five times. Mark the stock at 3-inch intervals five times. Mark the stock at 4-inch intervals five times. Mark the stock at 5-inch intervals five times.
2. Cut the stock at the marked intervals.
3. Sand the rough edges. (Children could help with the sanding.)
4. Paint the rods different colors. Any color of paint may be used as long as each size group is the same color and each color is distinct. The following colors are suggestions:

   - Leave the five 1-inch rods a natural color.
   - Paint the five 2-inch rods red.
   - Paint the five 3-inch rods blue.
   - Paint the five 4-inch rods yellow.
   - Paint the five 5-inch rods green.

TAKING A FIELD TRIP

Taking a field trip with preschoolers (3 to 5 years old) can be great fun if you are organized and prepared and have enough chaperones. First, you should contact the place you will be visiting at least one to two weeks in advance. Let them know how many children, what their ages are, and how many chaperones will be attending. Indicate what you would like the children to view as well as any hands-on activities you wish. Tours should be limited to 10 minutes. An activity in which the child participates can be 10 to 15 minutes long depending on the attention span of the children and the number of chaperones helping. You know best the attention span of your children. We recommend a ratio of one adult to three children for chaperoning purposes.

The following are some essentials you should have with you:

1. A signed Field Trip Permit, or permission slip, for each child.
2. A completed Emergency Card for each child. *Note:* Samples of the Field Trip Permit and Emergency Card are found on the next page.
3. Diapers.
4. Wipes.
5. Small first-aid kit.
6. Extra clothing.
7. Plastic bags (for wet clothing or used diapers).
8. Tissues.
9. Small snack.
10. Books and toys for car.
11. Water and paper cups.

Cars used for transportation should have personal as well as collision insurance. There should be a seat belt and a car seat for each child as required by your state.

Although planning for a field trip with preschoolers takes a little extra thought and preparation, the opportunity for new experiences and for learning makes your efforts well worthwhile!

FIELD TRIP PERMIT

_____ is hereby given permission

to take a field trip to _____

Transportation will be by _____ Date of trip _____

Time of departure _____ Estimated return _____

Lunch _____

Cost per child _____ Adult(s) in charge

_____

_____

_____
Signature of parent or guardian

- -

EMERGENCY CARD

Name of child _____

Name of parent _____ Phone (home) _____

Phone (work) _____

Name of person who may be contacted in case of emergency or illness if you cannot be reached:

Name _____ Phone _____

Name of local physician _____ Phone _____

In the event of an emergency, if I cannot be reached, _____
has my permission to authorize treatment for my child.

Signature of parent or guardian _____

Date _____

HOW TO USE THIS RESOURCE MOST EFFECTIVELY

This resource contains ten sections corresponding to the months of the school year, September through June. Each month offers a theme or focus. To encourage exploration of each theme from different perspectives, activities relating to music, language, art, math, and other subjects are included. Special days, holidays, or red letter days are also approached from several perspectives.

Activities in the ten monthly sections are identified by Subject found in the upper right–hand corner of each page. The nine subject categories included provide numerous activities geared specifically to the 18 months to 5-year-old child. For example, Subject: Art means that the activity is an art activity.

Following are descriptions of the nine subject categories in each section.

1. ART

Although young children must be closely supervised during art activities, the need for extra supervision invites an opportunity for quality time with each child. This time allows for activities that not only develop gross and fine motor skills, but also provides opportunities for the insightful teacher or parent to further their understanding of each child.

Art activities should allow time for the child to experiment with many different mediums. Drawings should never have adult expectations placed on time. To a child, each work has a definite meaning.

In the preschool years, the child proceeds through several developmental stages in art. These stages include random scribbling, creating definite shapes, combining two or more shapes to produce a design, and drawing a picture which an adult can recognize. Most toddlers spend their time creatively producing works that exemplify the first three stages. By the age of 5, most children will draw a very primitive picture using the shapes they have practiced.

2. MUSIC

Music is a very important part of classroom or at-home activities. A child should experience many forms of musical expression. There should be times for movement to music, singing, playing rhythm instruments, as well as listening to a variety of musical styles.

3. MOVEMENT

Ideas for organized games that encourage exercise and development of gross and fine motor skills are included in this section.

4. LANGUAGE DEVELOPMENT

Language development activities are a blend of several areas: poetry, fingerplays, literature, speech, and vocabulary development.

Memory as well as fine and gross motor skills can be developed through the repetition of short poems, rhymes, and songs that are accompanied by finger and body motions. Finger play provides the child with an action activity that is a quiet contrast to the gross motor activities found under Movement.

Poetry is a link between music and literature. It encompasses the brevity and rhythm of songs along with the expressions of ideas found in stories. Selected poems have been chosen for their relevance to the theme or special days of each month.

Speech and vocabulary activities offer experiences which will help expand a child's growing language skills.

Reading to a child is an excellent activity for broadening knowledge of the world as well as expanding vocabulary. An exciting story encourages a child to sit and listen for a longer length of time. It is also a great quiet time activity, versatile enough to interest a large group of children or provide quality time with a single child. Selections listed in each monthly section are pertinent to the theme, special days, and season of that month.

5. NUTRITION

The child's sense of taste continues to develop during the toddler and preschool years. Introduction of new and varied textures and tastes encourages the child to try new foods. The child also learns to compare and contrast foods.

6. SCIENCE/NATURE

Interaction between a child and nature stimulates the child's curiosity about his or her environment. Discovering the results of these interactions is an exciting event that provides a basis for future science experiences.

7. MATH

One of the most important skills to be developed for math readiness is the ability to classify. Many of the activities in this area give the toddler the opportunity to move and sort things according to size, color, and shape.

8. SOCIAL STUDIES

The social studies activities introduce the toddler to the world and different people. Ideas for enrichment activities, field trips, and extracurricular activities are also provided.

9. HEALTH/SAFETY

The activities in this category encourage the toddler or preschooler to become more aware of health and safety in all aspects of daily life. Hygiene, kitchen safety rules, and crossing the street are some of the many topics covered in the various activities.

CONTENTS

About the Authors • vii

About This Teacher's Resource • viii

Stages of Child Development • ix
    Fine Motor Skills • ix
    Gross Motor Skills • x
    Language Skills • x
    Self-help Skills • x

Chronological Sequence of Skill Development (Chart) • xi

Suggested toys for Preschool Children • xiv
    Toys for Toddlers • xiv
    Toys for 3-, 4-, and 5—Year-olds • xiv

Directions for Making Your Own Teaching Tools • xv
    How to Make a Flannel Board • xv
    How to Make Parquentry or Tangram Pieces • xv
    How to Make "Cuisenaire-like" Rods • xvi

Taking a Field Trip • xvii
    Sample Field Trip Permit and Emergency • xviii

How to Use This Resource Most Effectively • xix

Monthly Activity Outline • xxi

SEPTEMBER ACTIVITIES—Theme: Animals—Special Day: Rosh Hashanah • 1

ART: Little Brown Squirrel (2) • Apple Prints (2) • Mixing Colors (4) MUSIC: Three Little Ducks (5) • Those Silly Animals (7) • Bingo (8) MOVEMENT: Vegetable Toss (8) • Walk Like an Animal (9) • Rolling a Ball (11) • LANGUAGE: Open, Shut Them (12) • Up and Down (12) • The Apple Tree (13) NUTRITION: Harvest Vegetable Platter with Dip (14) • Apples Dipped in Honey—Rosh Hashanah Snack (14) • Lion Salad (15) SCIENCE/NATURE: Drying Apples (16) • Baby Animals and Parents (for toddlers) (17) • Matching Baby Animals and Parents (Ages 3 through 5) (17) • Harvest the Garden (18) MATH: Animal Crackers—Edible Math (Ages 2 and 3) (19) • Animal Crackers—Edible Math (Ages 3 through 5) (19) • Five Little

Monkeys (20) SOCIAL STUDIES: The Fall Season (21) • Let's Go to the Zoo (22) • What Is My Name? (23) HEALTH/SAFETY: Field Trip to the Dentist (23) • Fire Drill (24) • Crossing the Street with an Adult (25)

OCTOBER ACTIVITIES—Theme: Fall—Special Day: Halloween • **26**

ART: Leaf Prints (27) • Stenciled Jack-o-Lanterns (27) • Tissue Paper Ghosts (28) MUSIC: Halloween Is Here (30) • Little Brown Squirrel (31) • Rhythm Instruments (31) MOVEMENT: Trees Swaying to Music (32) • Walking Slowly and Walking Quickly (33) • "Witchy Whiz" (33) LANGUAGE: Five Little Jack-o-Lanterns (34) • Halloween (35) • In, Out (36) NUTRITION: Apple-Cheese-Coconut Snacks (36) • Roasted Pumpkin Seeds (37) • Baked Pumpkin (38) SCIENCE/NATURE: Nature Walk (38) • Carve a Pumpkin (39) • Autumn Tree (40) MATH: Matching Game (41) • Collecting and Sorting (41) • Memory Game (42) SOCIAL STUDIES: Growth Chart (43) • Let's Go to the Country (43) • Who Is That? (44) HEALTH/SAFETY: Let's Wash Up (45) • Stop, Drop, and Roll (45) • Trip to/or Visit from the Fire Department (46)

NOVEMBER ACTIVITIES—Theme: Family—Special Day: Thanksgiving • **48**

ART: Crayon Melt Picture (49) • Cornstarch Beads (49) • Hand Turkeys (50) MUSIC: Over the River (52) • Sleep, Baby, Sleep (53) • My Bonnie (53) MOVEMENT: Toe-Heel Dance (54) • Walk/Run (55) • Reach for the Sky (56) LANGUAGE: Tell Me a Story (56) • Mr. Turkey (57) • The Indians (58) NUTRITION: Peanut Butter Raisin Bread Sandwiches (58) • Warm Apple Cider Punch (59) • Dairy Products (60) SCIENCE/NATURE: Loud and Soft (60) • Magnets (for 3–5 years old) (61) • What Would Happen If? (62) MATH: More or Less (62) • Parquetry Shapes (63) • Turkey Tail Matching Game (64) SOCIAL STUDIES: My Family (64) • Let's Go Visit the Grocery Store (66) • Family Party (67) HEALTH/SAFETY: Running Indoors (67) • Sneezing (68)

DECEMBER ACTIVITIES—Theme: Holiday Traditions—Special Days: Hanukkah, Christmas • **69**

ART: Stenciled Candle (70) • Christmas Trees (71) • Potato Print Bells (72) MUSIC: We Wish You a . . . (72) • Christmas Bells (73) • The Lights (74) MOVEMENT: Following the Leader (75) • Log Rolling (76) • Push/Pull Box (76) LANGUAGE: Here's a Cup (77) • Make a Rhyme (77) The Night Before Christmas (78) NUTRITION: Paintbrush Cookies (79) • Milk Punch (79) Potato Latkes (80) SCIENCE/NATURE: Sense of Touch (81) • Feed the Birds (82) • Reflections (83) MATH: Building with Inch Cubes (84) Advent/Hanukkah Calender (84) • Sorting By Number (85) SOCIAL STUDIES: Pinata (86) • Who Am I? (86) • Let's Have a Holiday Party (87) HEALTH/SAFETY: Let's Eat (88) • Cover Your Mouth (88) • Rub-a-Dub (89)

JANUARY ACITIVITIES—Theme: Winter—Special Day: New Year's Day • **90**

ART: Clay Play (91) • Snowflakes (91) • Sponge Print Snowpeople (92) MUSIC: Marching Bank (93) • The North Wind Doth Blow (93) • Snowflakes (94) MOVEMENT: Toss (95) • Let's Pretend to Skate (96) • Mitten Scramble (96) LANGUAGE: Mittens, Hats, and Boots (97) • The Chimney (98) • A Winter Poem (98) NUTRITION: Popcorn (99) • Bread and Cereal Group (100) • Peanut Butter Crackers (101) SCIENCE/NATURE: Me and My Shadow (101) • Winter (102) • What Should I Wear in the Winter? (103) • Pine Bough Potpourri (103) MATH: Counting Raisins (104) • Shapes (105) • Block Building (106) SOCIAL STUDIES: Growth Chart (106) • A Trip to Kindergarten (107) • Let's Go to the Mountains (107) HEALTH/SAFETY: The Police Officer (108) • I Have a Healthy Body (108)

FEBRUARY ACTIVITIES—Theme: Nursery Rhymes—Special Day: Valentine's Day • **110**

ART: Lambs (111) • Heart Collage (112) • Spiders (112) MUSIC: Baa, Baa Black Sheep (113) • Mary Had a Little Lamb (114) • Tiddley Winky (115) • Twinkle, Twinkle Little Star (116) MOVEMENT: London Bridge (116) • Pat-a Cake (117) • Ring Around the Roses (118) LANGUAGE: Feelings (118) • Little Miss Muffet (119) • Goldilocks and the Three Bears (119) NUTRITION: Meat, Fish, and Chicken (120) • Valentine's Party Drink (122) • Gingerbread Cookies (122) SCIENCE/NATURE: Melting (123) • Sense of Smell (124) • A Nest for the Birds (124) MATH: Matching Hearts (125) • Counting and Clapping (126) • One, Two Buckle My Shoe (126) SOCIAL STUDIES: Learning Names (127) • Having a Puppet Show (128) • A Trip to the Library (128) HEALTH/SAFETY: Scissors (129) • Rest Time (130) • Walking Up and Down Stairs (131)

MARCH ACTIVITIES—Theme: Weather—Special Day: St. Patrick's Day • **132**

ART: Shamrock Potato Prints (133) • Paper Bag Windsocks (133) • Kits (134) • MUSIC: The Weather Song (136) • Rain, Rain Go Away (137) • Mr. Sun (137) MOVEMENT: Obstacle Course (138) • Lion Hunt (139) • Hop Across the Stream (140) LANGUAGE: My Hat (141) • The Weather (142) • The Robin (142) NUTRITION: Food Groups—Fruits (143) • Measuring (144) • Fruit and Vegetable Salad (145) SCIENCE/NATURE: Weather Calendar (146) • Seasons (147) • Sense of Taste (147) MATH: Sequencing (148) • Some, None (148) • Halves and Wholes (149) SOCIAL STUDIES: What Would You Wear? (150) • Tea Party (150) • The Veterinarian (151) HEALTH/SAFETY: Washing Your Hands (152) • Combing Your Hair (152)

APRIL ACTIVITIES—Theme: Spring—Special Days: Easter, Passover • **154**

ART: Easter Bunny Finger Puppet (155) • Eggshell Mosaics (155) Watercolor Painting (157) MUSIC: Ham and Eggs (157) • Spring Time is Here! (158) • It Rained a Mist (159) MOVEMENT: Egg Toss (160) • Egg Hop Game (160) • Hide the Egg (161) LANGUAGE: The Rain (162) • I Saw a Little Bunny (162) • Spring (163) NUTRITION: Egg Salad Sandwiches (164) • Spring Bunny Salad (165) • Charoset, a Passover Snack (166) SCIENCE/NATURE: Spring Tree (166) • Sense of Hearing (167) • Nature Egg Dyes (168) MATH: Box Building (169) • Eggs in a Basket (169) • Matching Shapes (170) SOCIAL STUDIES: Field Trip to The Greenhouse/Florist (171) • Baby Face (171) • Growth Chart (172) HEALTH/SAFETY: Cleaning Up Spills (173) • Brush Your Teeth (173)

MAY ACTIVITIES—Theme: Plants and Flowers—Special Days: May Day, Mother's Day • **175**

ART: Butterflies (176) • Clay Play (176) • Paperweights (178) MUSIC: Planting Song (179) • Oats, Peas, Beans, and Barley (180) • Flowers (180) MOVEMENT: The May Pole (181) • Heads, Shoulders, Knees, and Toes (182) • Follow That Line! (183) LANGUAGE: Be a Clown (183) • The Butterfly (184) • Colors (185) NUTRITION: Food Groups, Vegetables (185) • Oatmeal Raisin Cookies (186) • Kitchen Rules (187) SCIENCE/NATURE: Flower Parts (188) • Let's Plant (189) • Floating Garden (189) MATH: Cuisenaire Rods (190) • Tall and Small (191) • Seed and Plant Game (191) SOCIAL STUDIES: Body Tracings (192) • Neighborhood Walk (193) • Let's Go to the Lake (194) HEALTH/SAFETY: Stop, Look, and Listen (194) • Kitchen Safety (195)

JUNE ACTIVITIES—Theme: Transportation—Special Days: Father's Day, World Environment Day • **197**

ART: Sand Pictures (198) • School Bus (198) • Clay Chimes (200) MUSIC: The Train (201) • Trucks, Cars, and Buses (202) • Canoe Song (202) MOVEMENT: Row Your Boat (203) • Riding Toys (204) • Airplains (204) LANGUAGE: Banbury Cross (205) • Cars and Trucks Maze (205) • Transportation (206) NUTRITION: Cucumber Canoes (207) • Strawberry Milk Shakes (207) • Food Identification (208) SCIENCE/NATURE: Prisms (209) • World Environment Day (June 15) (209) • Sense of Sight (210) MATH: Right Hand, Left Hand (210) • Same or Different (211) • Is It Full or Empty? (212) SOCIAL STUDIES: Here Comes the School Bus (212) • Let's Go to the City (213) • What Color Is? (214) HEALTH/SAFETY: Seat Belts for Safety (214) • Wipe Your Face (215) • Picking Up Toys (215)

SEPTEMBER ACTIVITIES

THEME: *Animals*
SPECIAL DAY: *Rosh Hashanah*

ART:	Little Brown Squirrel
	Apple Prints
	MIXING COLORS
MUSIC:	Three Little Ducks
	Those Silly Animals
	Bingo
MOVEMENT:	Vegetable Toss
	Walk Like an Animal
	Rolling a Ball
LANGUAGE:	Open, Shut Them
	Up and Down
	The Apple Tree
NUTRITION:	Harvest Vegetable Platter with Dip
	Apples Dipped in Honey—Rosh Hashanah Snack
	Lion Salad
SCIENCE/ NATURE:	Drying Apples
	Baby Animals and Parents (for Toddlers)
	Matching Baby Animals and Parents (Ages 3 Through 5)
	Harvest the Garden
MATH:	Animal Crackers—Edible Math (Ages 2 and 3)
	Animal Crackers—Edible Math (Ages 3 Through 5)
	Five Little Monkeys
SOCIAL/ STUDIES:	The Fall Season
	Let's Go to the Zoo
	What Is My Name?
HEALTH/ SAFETY:	Field Trip to the Dentist
	Fire Drill
	Crossing the Street with an Adult

LITTLE BROWN SQUIRREL

Purpose:	To paint and paste a squirrel.
Skills/ Concepts:	To use fine motor skills in holding a paintbrush. To use fine motor skills in painting.
Ages:	18 months (with help); 2 through 4 years old.
Length of Activity:	Allow a minute or so for painting and a minute or so for pasting.

Materials:		
	Squirrel pattern (body)	Paintbrush
	Squirrel pattern (tail)	Dark brown fake fur
	White construction paper	Easel
	Dark brown tempera paint	Paste

For Adult to Do Ahead:	Purchase fake fur fabric from any store that sells fabric. Trace the squirrel pattern on the following page onto white construction paper. Cut out the shape and clip it to the easel. Cut the tail for the squirrel out of fake fur.
Introduction:	Introduce this activity by saying to the children, "We're going to paint this shape fastened to the easel."
Procedure:	Have the children cover the shape with brown tempera paint, then allow the paint to dry. Ask if the children have ever seen a squirrel swish its tail. Show the tail pieces. Let the children hold the tail, and talk about the softness of the fur. "Let's paste the tail to the squirrel shape we painted."
Closure:	End the activity by saying, "Let's tape our picture to the wall so it will dry."
Follow-up Activity:	See October Activities for the song "Little Brown Squirrel."

APPLE PRINTS

Purpose:	To print on paper using an apple as the stamp.
Skills/ Concepts:	To use fine motor skills (holding the apple and pressing it in paint and on paper). To transfer a pattern to paper.
Ages:	18 months (with help); 2 through 4 years old.
Length of Activity:	Allow 3 minutes.

Materials:		
	Apples, cut in half	Saucer or small dish
	Tempera or fingerpaint	Light-colored or white construction paper

For Adult to Do Ahead:	Cut the apples in half and put the paint in the saucer.
Introduction:	Begin by saying, "You've eaten apples, but have you ever painted with an apple?"

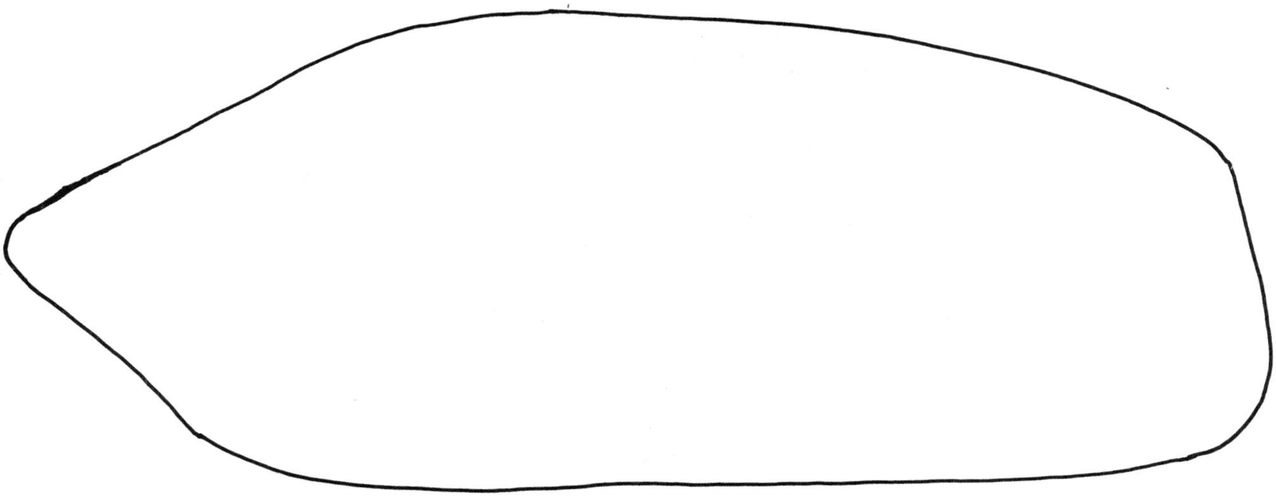

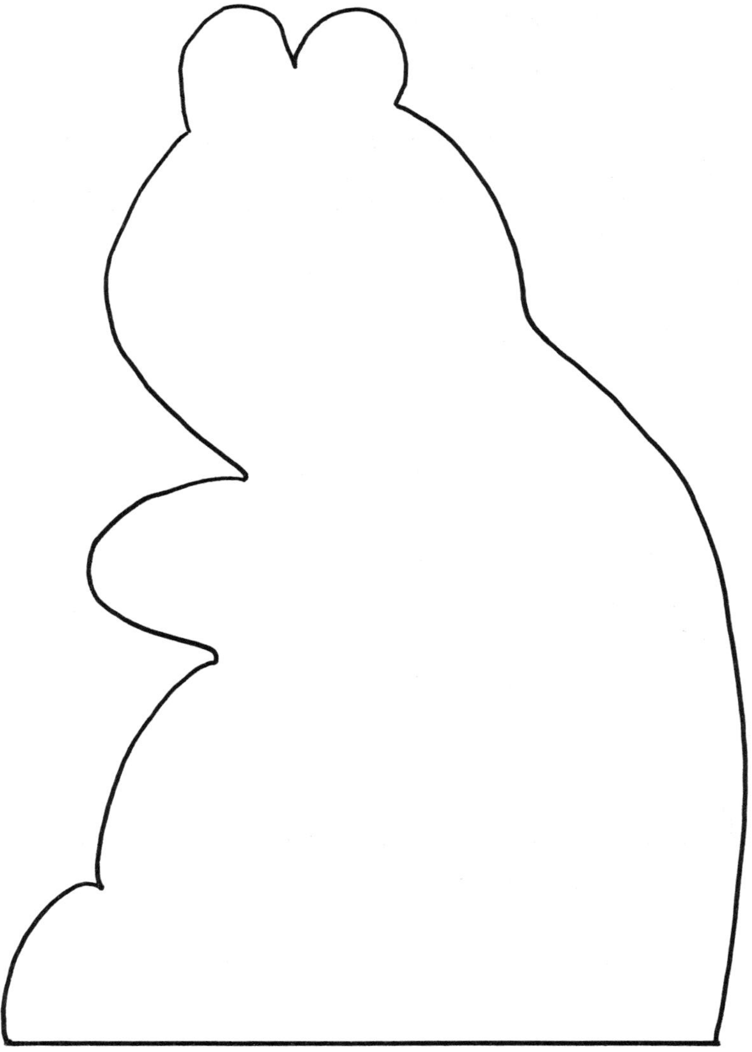

Procedure: Show the child that you dip the apple into the paint, and then you press the apple onto a piece of paper. Let children experiment with pieces of apple, pressing them several times into the paint and then onto the paper. Tell the children, "See what happens if you don't press the apple into the paint?" (The pattern should be lighter.)

Closure: Ask, "Did you enjoy using an apple instead of using a paintbrush?" The child may want to do more than one picture.

Follow-up Activity: Try printing with other vegetables. Celery, carrots, potatoes, and peppers will work well.

MIXING COLORS

Purpose: To experiment with colors.

Skills/ Concepts: To show how primary colors change when mixed.
To identify colors.
To develop small muscle groups by using eye dropper.

Ages: 3 through 5 years old.

Length of Activity: Allow 5 minutes.

Materials: Styrofoam egg carton, one carton per child   Warm water
Eye dropper, one per child   Red, green and blue crepe paper

For Adult to Do Ahead: For each color you need several yards of crepe paper, warm water in a glass and a baby food jar with lid.
—tear each color of crepe paper into small pieces and put into glasses of warm water. (one color per glass) Let sit 5–10 minutes.
—squeeze crepe paper and throw away.
—pour crepe colored water into baby food jars to store.

Introduction: Commence by saying, "Let's go outside and experiment with colors."

Procedure: Young children will need close supervision so they do not drink the colored water. Give each child an egg carton and an eye dropper. Fill half of each compartment with warm water. "Can you put several drops of the red color in the water?" (children add red to one of their compartments) "Now let's add some blue to the red water and see what happens." (it turns purple) "Let's fill the next compartment with some red and then add some yellow. What happens?" (it turns to orange) Continue by filling two compartments with blue and adding red to one and yellow to the other. And finally fill two with yellow and add red and blue. Encourage children to continue to mix colors and see what happens each time.

Closure: You might conclude by saying, "Which of the colors did you like the best?"

Follow-up Activities: Use the "crepe colors" as paint. Provide white paper towels for the children to use as paper. Brush on the "crepe colors."
Read *Mouse Paint* by Ellen Stoll Walsh, New York: Harcourt, Brace, Jovanovich, 1989.

THREE LITTLE DUCKS

Purpose:	To sing a song using hand and arm movements.
Skills/ Concepts:	To memorize a simple song. To use fine and gross motor skills.
Ages:	18 months through 5 years old.
Length of Activity:	Allow 2 minutes.
Materials:	Song
Introduction:	Ask, "What sound do ducks make when they "talk" to each other?" Quack. "Let's sing a song about three little ducks."
Procedure:	As you sing the song, the children will quickly join in the "quack, quack, quack" chorus.
Closure:	You may close by asking, "How many little ducks did we sing about? What did the little ducks say to each other? Where did the little ducks go?"
Follow-up Activity:	A duck stick puppet is simple to make and a great way to accompany the "Three Little Ducks" song. Cut the duck pattern out of white construction paper. The children should color the shape with crayon or markers. The entire body may not be covered or filled in. Each duck should look individual. Tape or glue the duck to a craft stick. Read *Have You Seen My Duckling?* by Nancy Tafuri (New York: Greenwillow, 1984).

Three Little Ducks

Traditional

Three lit-tle ducks that I once knew, Fat one, skin-ny one, they were two. But the one lit-tle duck with the fea-ther on his back, He ruled the o-thers with a quack, quack, quack, quack, quack, quack, quack, quack, quack, quack | He ruled the o-thers with a quack, quack, quack!.

2. Down to the river they would go
Wibble, wobble, wibble, wobble to and fro
But the one little duck with the feather on its back
He ruled the others with a quack, quack, quack,
Quack, quack, quack, quack, quack, quack.
He ruled the others with a quack, quack, quack.

3. Home from the river they would come
Wibble, wobble, wibble, wobble, ho-ho-hum.
But the one little duck with the feather on its back,
He ruled the others with a quack, quack, quack,
Quack, quack, quack, quack, quack, quack,
He ruled the others with a quack, quack, quack.

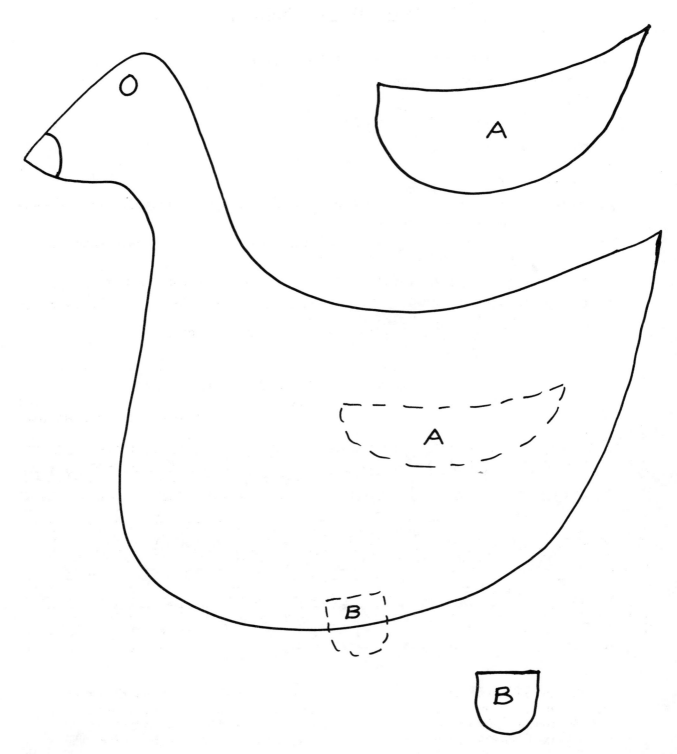

THOSE SILLY ANIMALS

Purpose:	To sing a song with a chorus and verses.
Skill/ Concept:	To memorize a simple song.
Ages:	18 months through 5 years old.
Length of Activity:	Allow 2½ minutes
Materials:	Song
Introduction:	Begin by saying, "I know a song about some silly animals. Part of the song goes like this _____." Sing the chorus.
Procedure:	Invite the children to join in singing the chorus. Ask them to listen while you sing about the animals and then repeat the chorus.
Closure:	Ask, "Can you think of any other animals we could sing about in our song?"
Follow-up Activity:	Do a movement exercise while singing "Those Silly Animals." Hold hands and go around in a circle while singing the chorus. Act out each verse. Read *Noah's Ark* by Peter Spier (NY: Doubleday, 1977).

Those Silly Animals

Traditional
Words by—JoAnne Calvarese

Ducks in the din-ing room sip-ping soup. Ducks in the din-ing room sip-ping soup, Ducks in the din-ing room sip-ping soup. Ducks in the din-ing room sip-ping soup. Oh dear, what will I do? Oh dear, what will I do? Oh dear, what will I do? Sill-y-y an-i-mals what to do?

2. Pigs in the parlor having tea.
   Pigs in the parlor having tea.
   Pigs in the parlor having tea.
   Pigs in the parlor having tea.

   Chorus

3. Bears in the bathtub scrubbing their toes.
   Bears in the bathtub scrubbing their toes.
   Bears in the bathtub scrubbing their toes.
   Bears in the bathtub scrubbing their toes.

   Chorus

BINGO

Purpose:	To sing a spelling song.
Skills/ Concepts:	To memorize words and melody. To clap rhythmically.
Ages:	18 months through 5 years old. The 18-month-old to 2-year-old will enjoy the repetitiousness of the song and may clap throughout the entire song.
Length of Activity:	Allow 2 minutes.
Materials:	Song
Introduction:	Say, "I know a song about a farmer who had a dog. The dog's name was Bingo."
Procedure:	"As we sing this song, we will come to a part that spells the dog's name: B-I-N-G-O. Each time we sing the song, we will drop one letter of Bingo's name and clap in its place. We will continue to drop and clap until all of the letters of Bingo's name are silent and we are clapping out Bingo's name. Let me show you what I mean." Sing the song through twice and the second time leave out the "B" and clap. "Now let's start the song again."
Closure:	Ask, "What do you think might be a good name for a dog?"
Follow-up Activity:	Make a pet book. Help the children collect pictures of pets. Paste the pictures onto colored construction paper and bind one side with yarn. Let the children name each pet as you print the name under each picture in lowercase letters.

© 1990 by The Center for Applied Research in Education

Bingo

American Folk Song

There was a farm-er had a dog and Bing-o was his name-o, B-I-N-G-O, B-I-N-G-O, B-I-N-G-O and Bing-o was his name-o.

VEGETABLE TOSS

Purpose:	To throw and retrieve an object.
Skills/ Concepts:	To develop gross motor skill of throwing. To identify vegetable shapes visually. To retrieve an object. To throw an object at a target.

Ages: 18 months to 2 years old: will be able to place or drop an object into a basket; 3 through 4 years old: will be able to toss an object into a basket at a short distance.

Length of Activity: Allow 2 to 5 minutes.

Materials: Vegetable bean bags (see "For Adult to Do Ahead")
Laundry size basket

For Adult to Do Ahead: Cut shapes out of felt using the patterns on page 10. Stitch vegetable shapes using a ½-inch seam; leave an inch opening. Fill vegetable shapes with dried beans or uncooked rice. Complete stitching the shapes.

Introduction: Begin by saying, "Look what I have in my basket." Give children an opportunity to look, touch, and identify vegetable bags. "Let's play a game with these shapes."

Procedure: The younger children may only be interested in placing the bags into the basket and then picking them up again. For older children, place two strips of masking tape 2 feet apart on the floor. Place the basket on one strip and have the children put their feet on the second strip. Have the children take turns tossing or throwing the bean bags into the basket.

Closure: When the children tire of tossing or placing the bags into the basket, suggest that the bags be stored in the basket and be played with at a later time.

Follow-up Activity: Play hide the vegetable. Have the children leave the room, and then "hide" the vegetable bags in obvious spots. Call the children back into the room and ask them to find the vegetable bags. When they are found say, "Now it's my turn to leave the room and Allison may hide the vegetables." Don't be surprised if the child "hides" the bags in the same spots you did.

WALK LIKE AN ANIMAL

Purpose: To imitate different animal walks using the whole body.

Skills/ Concepts: To walk on a line.
To practice the gross motor skills of crawling, walking, and flapping.
To use memory to recall how certain animals walk or move.

Ages: 18 months to 5-year-olds.

Length of Activity: Allow 5 minutes.

Materials: Animal pictures (dog, duck, bird, snake, etc.)

For Adult to Do Ahead: Collect pictures of familiar animals. For durability, these can be mounted on heavy paper and covered with contact paper. This is an activity that is appropriate for indoors or outdoors. If used outdoors, draw or paint a line in the shape of a circle on the sidewalk or driveway. If used indoors, put a masking tape circle on the floor.

Introduction: Ask, "Can you walk this line?" Start the children walking around the circle.

Procedure: Then proceed by saying, "What nice walking I see." Show the children an animal picture, such as a dog. Ask the children, "What animal is this? Yes, it's a dog. I wonder how this dog would walk around our circle?" Join the children crawling on all fours around the circle. Continue until all pictures have been shown and the children have moved or walked like each animal.

Closure: Close by asking, "Which animal walk did you enjoy most? Would you like to try moving like that animal again?"

Follow-up Activities: Tape the animal pictures to a wall or door in an open area where the children can see the pictures and have space to imitate the walks.

Play selections from the record *Walk Like the Animals* by Georgiana Liccione Stewart. The record is available through Kimbo Educational, P.O. Box 477, Long Branch, New Jersey 07740.

ROLLING A BALL

Purpose: To teach a simple game that can be played alone, in pairs or with a group

Skills/ Concepts: To roll a ball
To develop hand, arm and shoulder muscles
To aim a ball

Ages: 18 months through 5 year olds

Length of Activity: Allow 5 to 10 minutes

Materials: A soft ball that rolls

Introduction: Begin by saying, "Rolling a ball can be lots of fun. Who would like to play with me?"

Procedure: FOR ONE CHILD: Child sits on the floor. Set an object (block) up about two feet away. Ask the child to roll the ball towards the object. Move the object further away to increase the challenge. Let child retrieve ball and move object each time. Soon he or she can play on their own.
FOR TWO CHILDREN: Children sit apart facing each other with legs spread apart. They take turns rolling the ball back and forth to each other.
FOR A GROUP OF CHILDREN: Children sit side by side in a circle and roll the ball across the circle trying to aim at a different child each time.

Closure: Conclude by saying, "Let's be sure to put our ball away in a safe place so that no one will trip over it."

Follow-up Activity: Try the same games using a balloon instead. A single child can toss balloon high up in air and catch it as it floats down. Two or more children can gently punch balloon back and forth.

OPEN, SHUT THEM

Purpose: To memorize a simple fingerplay.

Skills/
Concepts: To repeat a fingerplay.
To use hand and finger movements (fine motor skills).

Ages: 18 months through 5 years old. (This is a very appealing fingerplay for the younger child.)

Length of
Activity: Allow 2 minutes.

Materials: Fingerplay

Introduction: Ask, "Can you open and shut your hands? I know a fingerplay we can sing using our hands."

Procedure: Sing the fingerplay. Encourage the children to join you in singing the fingerplay a second time.

Follow-up
Activity: Play a simple "follow the leader" game. Ask children to open their mouths. Ask children to close their mouths. This can be repeated several times. Then ask children to open their eyes. Ask children to close their eyes. This may also be repeated several times. Older children will enjoy taking turns at being the leader.

Open, Shut Them

Traditional

O-pen, shut them. O-pen, shut them. Give a lit-tle clap. O-pen, shut them. O-pen, shut them. Fold them in your lap. Creep them, creep them, creep them, creep them, right up to your chin. O-pen wide your lit-tle mouth, but do not let them in.

UP AND DOWN

Purpose: To teach the opposites up and down.

Skills/
Concepts: To discriminate up and down visually.
To follow simple directions.

Ages: 18 months through 5 years old.

Length of Activity:	Allow 5 minutes. (The younger child, 18 months to 2 years old, may participate in this game for a shorter length of time.)
Materials:	None needed.
Introduction:	While standing, legs together straight, ask the children, "Can you stand up like I am standing?" Sit down and ask, "Can you sit *down* like I am sitting?" Emphasize the words *up* and *down*.
Procedure:	Tell the children, "We are going to play a game. When I say 'up' we will stand up and when I say 'down' we will sit down." Repeat the words "up" and "down" at random. An older child may want the opportunity to be the leader.
Closure:	Before the children have tired of the game, ask one last time, "Can you show me 'up'? Can you show me 'down'?"
Follow-up Activity:	Use this as an outdoor activity. A small hill or pile of sand can be used to walk "up" and "down."

THE APPLE TREE

Purpose:	To learn a poem about an apple tree.
Skills/ Concepts:	To repeat a simple poem. To use finger, hand, and arm movements to accompany the poem (fine and gross motor skills).
Ages:	18 months (will enjoy listening to and watching the activity); 2 through 5 years old.
Length of Activity:	Allow 2 minutes.
Materials:	Poem A basket or bowl of apples
Introduction:	Hold up an apple. Encourage children to identify the apple. Tell the children, "I have a poem about an apple tree I'd like to teach you."
Procedure:	Have children repeat each line of the poem after you. Say the poem several times.

Way up high in an apple tree,	(Raise hands overhead.)
Two little apples looked at me.	(Keep arms overhead. Make two circles using forefingers and thumbs.)
I shook that tree as hard as I could.	(Make two fists and place them on top of each other. Hold them in front of you and shake.)
Down fell the apples.	(Raise hands and bring down in front of your body.)
Um-m they were good.	(Rub stomach with one hand.)

Follow-up Activity:	Mix vanilla yogurt with a little cinnamon and use as a dip for apple slices.

HARVEST VEGETABLE PLATTER WITH DIP

Purpose:	To enjoy the vegetables harvested from the garden.
Skills/ Concepts:	To identify vegetables. To use fine motor skills for stirring and spooning.
Ages:	18 months through 5 years old.
Length of Activity:	Allow 15 to 20 minutes.

Materials:

Bowl	3 oz. whipped or softened cream cheese
Spoon	⅓ cup peanut butter
Platter	Milk
Sliced vegetables	

For Adult to Do Ahead:	Cut and slice the vegetables.
Introduction:	Begin by saying, "I'm going to prepare a snack using the vegetables we picked in our garden. Would you like to help?"
Procedure:	Help the children arrange the vegetables on the platter. Encourage them to identify the vegetables as they are placed on the platter. Place the cream cheese and peanut butter in the bowl. Help the children identify the ingredients using sight and smell. Blend the ingredients adding milk until the mixture is a sour cream–like dipping consistency. Provide a small cup or container for children to spoon their own serving of dip. This discourages the spread of germs.
Closure:	Review by asking, "Can you remember what ingredients were used to make the dip?" Help with small hints when needed. "Can you remember what vegetables we ate with the dip?" Help again when needed.
Follow-up Activities:	To extend this activity, provide three or four distinctly different vegetables such as carrots, cucumbers, celery, and broccoli. Provide a separate plate or bowl for each vegetable and let the child sort the vegetables into the bowls before the snack. After the snack let the children help with clean up. Fix warm water for the children to wash the plastic bowls, spoons, plates, and measuring cups.

APPLES DIPPED IN HONEY—ROSH HASHANAH SNACK

Purpose:	To acquaint children with a snack typically eaten during Rosh Hashanah.
Skills/ Concepts:	To differentiate between a "whole" apple and a "slice" of apple. To develop fine motor skills used for spooning. To develop eye-hand coordination in dipping.
Ages:	18 months through 5 years old.
Length of Activity:	Allow 10 to 15 minutes.

Materials:

Apples, one per child   Knife
Honey   Spoon
Paper plates, one per child   Napkins

For Adult to
Do Ahead:

Wash and dry the apples.

Introduction:

Introduce the lesson by saying, "The Jewish people celebrate Rosh Hashanah each fall. For them it is a time to be thankful for all the food they have harvested or taken from their fields. Apples are one of these foods. Today we are going to prepare a special snack made with apples."

Procedure:

Show the children a whole apple. Ask them, "What is this?" If children do not identify the apple, offer help. Ask a child to feel and look at the apple. Cut a slice of an apple. Give this to a child and say, "This is called a slice of apple." Let the child hold and feel the apple slice. You can continue slicing the apple and giving each child a slice. Don't be surprised if the child pops the slice into his mouth.

While you hold the honey jar, tell the children to place a spoonful of honey on their plate. It may be helpful to demonstrate this for the younger, 18 month or 2-year-old. Once children see you complete this task, they should be able to follow your verbal instructions.

Next tell the children, "We are going to 'dip' the apple slice into the honey." The children should be eager to follow your lead. Finally, "the best part—eating!" Continue until all the apples are eaten.

Closure:

Ask, "What did you enjoy most while we prepared this snack: the spooning, the dipping, or the eating?"

Follow-up
Activity:

Be sure children throw away their paper plates and napkins. Supply damp sponges so children can wash their spot at the table. This is a good opportunity to practice hand and face washing.

LION SALAD

Purpose:

To provide a nutritious snack or lunch that complements this month's focus on animals.

Skills/
Concepts:

To identify foods.
To develop fine motor skills in placement of facial features.
To develop fine motor skills in putting together lion head.
To develop eye-hand coordination.
To follow verbal directions.

Ages:

18 months to 2 ½ years (with verbal help);
3 through 5 years old (independently).

Length of
Activity:

Allow 15 minutes.

Materials:

Picture of a lion   Grapes, sliced in half, no seeds
Canned peach halves, one per child   Lettuce leaves
Shredded cheese   Plates, one per child
Raisins   Bowls to hold ingredients
Can of Chinese noodles

Introduction: Show the children the picture of the lion and ask, "Can you tell me what animal this is? Yes, this is a lion. Sometimes the lion is called 'King of the Jungle.' I have a special lion treat for us to prepare today."

Procedure: Show the children the bowls of ingredients. Encourage the children to identify the foods. Talk about the shapes and colors. The children should be able to prepare their own lion salads by following these verbal directions:

Place a leaf of lettuce on plate.
Place a peach half in center of lettuce.
Sprinkle shredded cheese around head to form mane.
Use raisins for eyes.
Use grape half for nose.
Use a Chinese noodle for mouth.

Three to 5-year-olds can often complete their salads by looking at a sample salad.

Closure: Ask, "Does this animal face look familiar to you? What type of animal did we make this salad look like?" The salad may look like a different animal to each child.

Follow-up Activity: After eating the lion salad, ask the children to help clean up. Give each child a damp sponge. Have the children wipe the table surface where the salad was prepared. Show the children how to hold a bucket at the edge of the table to catch the crumbs. Though many crumbs will fall on the floor initially, with practice the children will perfect their cleanup skill.

DRYING APPLES

Purpose: To dry apples to be eaten for a snack.

Skills/ Concepts: To use fine motor skills for stringing.
To use observation skills for daily comparisons.

Ages: 18 months to 5 years old.

Length of Activity: Allow 10 minutes to string apples and 1 week to dry apples.

Materials:
Apples (one per child)	Heavy string
Cookie sheet	Thumb tacks or nails

For Adult to Do Ahead: Core and peel all but one apple. Slice apples into rings and place on cookie sheet.

Introduction: Ask children, "What kind of fruit is this?" Hold up the apple.

Procedure: Say to children, "Look what I did with all of the apples. Do you know what I did? I peeled the apples. I cored the apples (took out the middle), and I cut the apples into rings. We are going to put these apple rings on a string and let them hang in the air." Encourage children to string the apples. You may need to hold the string or wrap the end of the string with masking tape to form a needle. When the apples are all strung say, "Now we will hang up the apples." Tie string to nails or thumb tack to wall so apples are suspended in the air. "As the apples dry they will look different."

Closure: Close by saying, "Each day we will check our strings of apples to see how they have changed. In a few days we will be able to eat the apple rings for a snack."

Follow-up Activity:
September 26 is Johnny Appleseed's birthday. Make felt board figures to use as you tell the story of Johnny Appleseed. A simple story might only use the figures of Johnny (with a pan on his head), a tree, and apples. The children will enjoy telling this story while using the felt board.

BABY ANIMALS AND PARENTS
(for toddlers)

Purpose:
To identify baby animals and their parents.

Skills/ Concepts:
To identify baby animals visually.
To identify adult animals visually.

Ages:
18 months through 2 years old.

Length of Activity:
Allow 2 to 5 minutes.

Materials:
Pictures of baby animals and their parents

For Adult to Do Ahead:
For better durability, pictures can be mounted on construction or heavy-weight paper and then covered with contact paper.

Introduction:
Say to children, "I have some pictures for you to see."

Procedure:
Place a few of the pictures in front of you at a time. Give the children time to study the pictures and offer comments. Children may identify the animals by name. If not, then you should give the name of the animal. Encourage the children to give you information about the pictures. Separate the pictures into two groups, one for animal babies and one for adult animals.

Closure:
At the conclusion, tell children, "We'll put these pictures away and look at them another time."

Follow-up Activity:
Make an animal baby and parent book. Collect extra pictures of animals. Mount the pictures on construction paper and punch holes at one side of the construction paper. Help the children lace yarn or ribbon through the holes and tie.

MATCHING BABY ANIMALS AND PARENTS
(Ages 3 through 5)

Purpose:
To match baby animals with their parents.

Skills/ Concepts:
To identify baby animals visually.
To identify adult animals visually.
To match baby animals with their parents.

Ages:
3 through 5 years old.

Length of Activity:
Allow 2 to 5 minutes.

Materials: Pictures of baby animals and their parents

For Adult to Do Ahead: For better durability, pictures can be mounted on construction or heavy weight paper and then covered with contact paper.

Introduction: Tell the children, "I have some pictures for you to see."

Procedure: Place several pairs of pictures in front of you. Ask the children, "Can you match the baby animals with their parents?" If children have trouble help identify the animals by name, and then help place the baby and adult animals in pairs. Continue the game until all of the cards have been matched.

Closure: Conclude by saying, "Would you like to mix the cards up and match them again?"

Follow-up Activity: After children have mastered matching the animal pairs, use the cards to play a memory game. Mix the cards up and place them in front of the children picture side down. Have the children turn over two cards at a time trying to match pairs. If the pair does not match turn the cards picture side down again and turn over two more cards. Continue until all pairs have been found. (You may also sort cards into piles of baby animals and parent animals.)

HARVEST THE GARDEN

Purpose: To pick and use vegetables planted during May in gardens or pots.

Skills/ Concepts: To identify ripe vegetables.
To use fine motor skills for picking vegetables.

Age: 2 through 5 years old.

Length of Activity: Allow 10 minutes.

Materials: Basket
Knife (for adult if needed)

Introduction: Begin by saying, "Let's go for a walk in the garden" or "Let's check the vegetables we planted in our pots."

Procedure: As you check the plants some questions to ask the children might be, "What vegetables are these?" "Do you think these vegetables are ready to pick?" "What color do these vegetables need to be?" Help the children to identify the ripe vegetables. Help children to pick vegetables, using the knife if needed.

Closure: Say, "Now we'll take the vegetables inside and wash them."

Follow-up Activity: Make a salad with the vegetables gathered from the garden, or clean the vegetables and eat them raw with a dip.

ANIMAL CRACKERS—EDIBLE MATH
(Ages 2 and 3)

Purpose:	To provide a tactile and tasty twist to counting.
Skills/ Concepts:	To count in sequence to 3. To repeat a counting sequence. To understand the concept of 3.
Ages:	2 through 3 years old.
Length of Activity:	Allow 5 minutes.
Materials:	2 small plastic bowls 6 animal crackers
For Adult to Do Ahead:	Place three animal crackers in each bowl.
Introduction:	"Let's do some counting before we have a little snack. Can you help me?"
Procedure:	Place the bowls in front of the children. Take one cracker at a time out of one of the bowls. As you lay each cracker down say, "One, two, three." Point to each cracker on the table and say, "One, two, three. I have three crackers for my snack. Would you like to count out three crackers for your snack?" Encourage children to take the crackers out of the bowl one at a time and to count out loud as they do. "Let's check and see if we each have the same number of animal crackers." Help children count your crackers and then count their crackers. If the children eat the crackers before they are counted, replace the three crackers and start again.
Closure:	Say, "Now that we've counted our crackers, let's eat them!"
Follow-up Activity:	Help children to sort crackers into groups of lions, tigers, bears, and so on.

ANIMAL CRACKERS—EDIBLE MATH
(Ages 3 through 5)

Purpose:	To provide a tactile and tasty twist to counting.
Skills/ Concepts:	To identify numbers. To develop fine motor skills through use of thumb and first finger. To understand the sequence of one, two, three. To repeat a counting sequence.
Ages:	3 through 5 years old.
Length of Activity:	Allow 5 minutes.

Materials: Posterboard   Small plastic bowl
Markers   Animal crackers
Clear contact paper

For Adult to Do Ahead: Using the Magic Marker, divide the top half of the posterboard into three sections, as shown in diagram. Label the first section on the left "1," label the middle section "2," and label the remaining section "3." Cover the board with clear contact paper to keep the numbers from smudging, and so the board may be wiped with a damp sponge when needed. Place six animal crackers in the bowl.

1	2	3

Introduction: "Let's do some counting before we have a snack. Can you help me?"

Procedure: Point to the number 1 on the board. Ask the children, "What number is this?" Offer help as needed. Point to the number 2 for the children to identify and then to the number 3 for the children to identify. Next place the bowl of animal crackers near the bottom half of the board. Ask the children to take one animal cracker from the bowl and place it in the section marked 1. Ask the children to place two crackers in the section marked 2 and then three crackers in the section marked 3. Ask the children to count the crackers in each section. Provide verbal assistance as needed.

Closure: Conclude by saying, "Let's eat our animal crackers now. This is certainly a delicious way to learn our numbers."

Follow-up Activities: Use the board to count other objects such as small cars or people.
Read *A Peaceable Kingdom* by Alice and Martin Provensen (NY: Puffin 1981).

FIVE LITTLE MONKEYS

Purpose: To learn a counting rhyme.

Skills/ Concepts: To develop fine motor skills through use of hands and arms.
To repeat a fingerplay.
To count to 5 by rote.

Ages: 18 months through 5 years old.

Length of Activity: Allow 1 to 2 minutes.

Materials: Fingerplay

Introduction: Begin by saying, "I know a fingerplay about five little monkeys and an alligator."

Procedure: Children will join in as you repeat the verse of the fingerplay.

Five little monkeys sitting in a tree, Teasing Mr. Alligator,	(Left arm is tree, hold up five fingers to be monkeys.)
Can't catch me!	(Move pointer finger back and forth in front of body.)
Along comes Mr. Alligator Quiet as can be . . .	(Hands together pointed away from body, weave back and forth.) (Clap hands together while holding wrists together. The alligator has gotten a monkey.)
Four little monkeys sitting in a tree, Teasing Mr. Alligator,	(Left arm is tree, hold up four fingers to be monkeys.)
Can't catch me!	Continue motions as above.
Along comes Mr. Alligator Quiet as can be . . .	
Three little monkeys sitting in a tree, Teasing Mr. Alligator, Can't catch me! Along comes Mr. Alligator Quiet as can be . . .	(Hold up three fingers.)
Two little monkeys sitting in a tree, Teasing Mr. Alligator, Can't catch me! Along comes Mr. Alligator Quiet as can be . . .	(Hold up two fingers.)
One little monkey sitting in a tree, Teasing Mr. Alligator, Can't catch me! Along comes Mr. Alligator Quiet as can be . . .	(Hold up one finger.)
No more monkeys sitting in a tree, Teasing Mr. Alligator, Can't catch me!	(Hold up fist.)

Closure: Conclude by saying, "Those little monkeys teased that alligator too often."

Follow-up Activity: Cut flannel board pieces of the tree, monkeys, and alligator. Children can place and remove the pieces as the fingerplay is repeated.

THE FALL SEASON

Purpose: To acquaint children with the season of fall.

Skills/ Concepts: To learn how the fall season brings about change.
To expand vocabulary.
To begin the study of geography.

Ages: 3 through 5 years old.

Length of Activity: Allow 5 to 10 minutes, depending upon participation and attention span.

Materials: Two or three pictures of harvesting (e.g., apple picking, gathering corn, harvesting vegetables from a garden or farm)
Pictures of leaves changing in different parts of the country
Pictures of children going off to school

Introduction: Begin by telling students, "Fall is a special time of year. School begins in the fall. In some places, leaves turn bright colors and then fall to the ground. Many people pick fruits and vegetables in the fall. Let's look at some pictures showing fall in different parts of our country."

Procedure: Show the children pictures you have gathered and ask questions about what is seen in the pictures. Some questions to ask might be:
What do you see in the picture?
Are there people in the picture?
What are the people doing?
Are there animals in the picture?
What kind of animals are in the picture?
What are some of the colors you see in the picture?
For the older child, let each child pick a picture and talk about what is in the picture.

Closure: Conclude by saying, "Can you remember what kinds of vegetables we harvested from our garden?"

Follow-up Activity: Cut out and paste onto construction paper pictures of the foods harvested from your garden. Help the children to identify the different vegetables.

LET'S GO TO THE ZOO

Purpose: To acquaint children with a zoo and some of the animals found in it.

Skills/ Concepts: To expand vocabulary.
To identify animals.

Ages: 18 months through 4 years old.

Length of Activity: Allow 5 to 10 minutes.

Materials: Zoo animal flannel board pieces
Flannel board
Pictures of a zoo

For Adult to Do Ahead: Prepare zoo animal flannel board pieces (see p. xv).
Pictures of the zoo may be pasted on construction paper.

Introduction: Ask, "Does anyone know what a zoo is? A zoo is a place to go and see animals."

Procedure: Continue with, "I wonder what kinds of animals we might see at the zoo?" Allow the children time to name as many animals as possible. Place pictures of the zoo in front of children. Ask the children what they see in the pictures. "Today let's pretend the flannel board is a zoo. Would you help me fill the zoo with animals?" As children arrange the flannel board animals on the board, ask them to name each animal. Have the children describe what each animal looks like. Ask the children what sounds the animal might make. Ask the children what movements the animal might make.

Closure: Conclude by saying, "The zoo looks like a fun place to visit. Do you think it would be a noisy place to visit?"

Follow-up Activities: Make arrangements to visit a local zoo or a petting zoo.

Read the poem "At the Zoo," from *Poetry in Motion* by Rae Pica (available through Front Row Experience, 540 Discovery Bay Blvd., Byron, California 94514).

Play the selection "Goin' to the Zoo" from *Singable Songs for the Very Young* by Raffi (produced by Raffi with Ken Whitely, 1976, Troubador Records, Ltd. available through Columbia House, CBS Records, New York, New York 10019).

WHAT IS MY NAME?

Purpose: To help children learn first and last names.

Skills/ Concepts: To memorize name.
To recall name.
To begin social introductions

Ages: 2 through 4 years old.

Length of Activity: Allow 2 minutes.

Materials: Song "What Is Your Name?" from *Learning Basic Skills Through Music* by Hap Palmer, Educational Activities, Inc. Freeport, New York 11520
Record player

Introduction: Introduce yourself by saying, "My name is *(adult or teacher's name)*. What is your name?"

Procedure: Have children repeat their first and last names. Continue with, "Now I am going to play a song about names. This song will ask for your name. When I point to you, tell me your name." Play the record.

Closure: Conclude by saying, "Now can you tell me my name?"

Follow-up Activity: Ask each child to identify the child sitting next to him or her. In the case of older children, ask if they can remember the first and last names of all of the children sitting in the group.

FIELD TRIP TO THE DENTIST

Purpose: To introduce children to the dentist and dentist's office in a casual, friendly way.

Skills/ Concepts: To feel comfortable with the dentist.
To learn how to brush teeth.

Ages: 3 through 5 years old.

Length of Activity: Allow 1 hour.

Materials: Permission slips, one per child
Chaperones, one adult for every three children

For Adult to Do Ahead: Reread page xvii about taking a field trip. Contact the dentist or the dentist's office Let the dentist know

1. How many children are coming.
2. What you want to see.
3. What you want him or her to talk about.
4. The children's attention span.
5. Can each child take home a toothbrush.

Arrange for transportation and chaperones.

Introduction: Open the lesson with "Today we're going to visit Dr. _____. Dr._____ is a dentist. We'll see the dentist's office and learn how to brush our teeth correctly."

Procedure: When you arrive at the dentist's office, make introductions. Before the tour or talk, it may be helpful to remind the children to keep their hands by their sides or in pockets. Tell the children, "The dentist uses special tools and instruments and we don't want to disturb them."

Closure: Conclude by saying, "Thank you very much, Dr. _____. Today we've learned a lot about keeping our teeth healthy."

Follow-up Activities: Have the children practice brushing their teeth. A mirror mounted on the wall in front of the sink will help in this assignment.
Teach the song "Brush Your Teeth" from *The Book of Kids Songs by* Nancy and John Cassidy (Palo Alto, California: Klutz Press).
Send thank you note, decorated by children, to the dentist.

FIRE DRILL

Purpose: To teach children to evacuate a building quickly, but safely in case of a fire.

Skills/ Concepts: To listen to directions.
To walk quickly.
To follow directions.

Ages: 18 months through 5 years old.

Length of Activity: Allow 10 minutes each month.

Materials: Fire alarm or a bell

Introduction: Always begin by saying, "Today we are going to have a fire drill. First, we are going to hear a loud noise. This noise may frighten you, but it is just a noise. Are you ready? The noise will sound like this (make the alarm go off or ring the bell, briefly). That sound will tell us that it is time to do a fire drill. When we hear that sound we leave what we are doing and go quickly to the door. We will walk quickly, with our hands by our sides, out the door and to the (name an area such as the swings). Wait there until I come out and call your name."

Procedure: Continue with, "Let's first practice walking quickly. This is how to walk quickly." Show children a quick walk. "Stand behind me and let's see if we can walk quickly together. Remember we aren't running, we are walking quickly. You are doing a great job of walking quickly. Let's try our fire drill now. Go back to playing, when you hear the loud noise go quickly to the door so we can walk quickly outside to the _____. Don't forget to wait for me." Ring alarm or bell and help children walk through the fire drill.

Closure: Conclude by saying, "You did a great job of walking quickly out to the _____. Let's go back inside and find something to play with."

Follow-up Activity: Show children alternative exits in case the first one is blocked by fire. Practice using the alternative exits.

CROSSING THE STREET WITH AN ADULT

Purpose: To teach children how to cross the street with an adult.

Skills/ Concepts: To listen to directions.
To follow directions.
To look both ways before crossing the street.
To cross within the crosswalk.
To "stop, look, and listen."

Ages: 2½ through 5 years old.

Length of Activity: Allow 15 minutes.

Materials: None needed.

Introduction: Begin by saying, "Today we are going for a walk. We will be crossing the street. Before we cross the street, we need to "STOP, LOOK, and LISTEN". That means we will stop at the street, look both ways to make sure there are no cars coming, and listen for any sounds of cars or honking horns."

Procedure: Continue by asking, "What are we going to do when we reach the street?" Encourage the children to respond, "Stop, look, and listen." "Don't forget we need to hold hands." Take children on a short walk that involves crossing a quiet street. A 10- or 15-minute round trip is suggested for 2 ½- to 3-year-olds. Four-year-olds can walk a bit farther, especially if you have a specific destination in mind that interests them.

Closure: Conclude by saying, "We certainly had a good walk. Fresh air and exercise are very good for your body. Does anyone remember what to do before you cross the street? That's correct, you stop, look, and listen."

Follow-up Activity: Help the children to plan another walk.

OCTOBER ACTIVITIES

THEME: *Fall*
SPECIAL DAY: *Halloween*

ART:
    Leaf Prints
    Stenciled Jack-o-Lanterns
    Tissue Paper Ghosts

MUSIC:
    Halloween Is Here
    Little Brown Squirrel
    Rhythm Instruments

MOVEMENT:
    Trees Swaying to Music
    Walking Slowly and Walking Quickly
    "Witchy Whiz"

LANGUAGE:
    Five Little Jack-o-Lanterns
    Halloween
    In, Out

NUTRITION:
    Apple-Cheese-Coconut Snacks
    Roasted Pumpkin Seeds
    Baked Pumpkin

SCIENCE/NATURE:
    Nature Walk
    Carve a Pumpkin
    Autumn Tree

MATH:
    Matching Game
    Collecting and Sorting
    Memory Game

SOCIAL STUDIES:
    Growth Chart
    Let's Go to the Country
    Who Is That?

HEALTH/SAFETY:
    Let's Wash Up
    Stop, Drop, and Roll
    Trip to/or Visit from the Fire Department

LEAF PRINTS

Purpose:	To produce a printed outline of a leaf.
Skills/ Concepts:	To use fine motor skills for pressing. To use gross motor skills for painting. To identify colors. To identify leaves.
Ages:	18 months through 5 years old.
Length of Activity:	Allow 5 minutes.

Materials:

Leaves	White construction paper
Paintbrush	Newspaper
Paint (water colors or tempera)	

For Adult to Do Ahead:	Gather leaves of different varieties. Tape newspaper to the top of the table you will be using.
Introduction:	Open by saying, "I have several different leaves." Show the children the leaves. "Let's make some leaf prints with these leaves."
Procedure:	As you point to each leaf say, "This one is from a _____ tree, this is from a _____ tree, and this one is from a _____ tree. Which leaves would you like to work with?" Children should pick several leaves. Children should pick a color of paint and using the brush paint the back of the leaf. Each leaf may be painted in a different color. "Now you are going to place the white paper on top of the painted leaves and press down with your hands." Gently help the children lift the white paper from the leaves. If the leaves stick let the child remove them from the paper.
Closure:	Conclude by saying, "Look at the prints you made. You can see the outline of the leaf on the paper."
Follow-up Activity:	Teach the fingerplay "The Leaves":

Falling, falling from a tree.	(Flutter fingers down in front of body.)
Leaves are falling down on me.	(Palms down, move hands back and forth in front of body.)
See them flying through the air.	(Brush hands quickly in front of body.)
Flutter softly everywhere.	(Flutter fingers up in front of body.)

STENCILED JACK-O-LANTERNS

Purpose:	To stencil a jack-o-lantern face.
Skills/ Concepts:	To use fine motor skills for pasting. To identify colors visually. To use fine motor skills for tearing paper.
Ages:	18 months through 5 years old.

Length of
Activity: Allow 15 minutes.

Materials:
White posterboard   1-inch paintbrush
Orange tissue paper   Craft knife
Black tempera paint   Newspaper
White glue   Sponges (cut in small pieces, 2″ × 2″)

For Adult to   Cut white posterboard into two 6-inch circles. Thin down the white glue with water.
Do Ahead: Cut a jack-o-lantern face out of one of the 6-inch circles with the craft knife (see the
                accompanying pattern). Tape newspaper to the area you will be using. Orange tissue
                paper may be torn into pieces or left for the child to tear.

Introduction: Begin by saying, "I'm going to make a smiling jack-o-lantern. Would you like to make
                one too?"

Procedure: If the children are going to tear paper, give each a piece of tissue paper to tear into
                small pieces. "After you have torn some tissue paper, we are going to glue it to this
                circle." Show children the posterboard circle. Ask, "What color is the tissue paper?"
                Show children how to place the tissue paper on the circle and apply glue with the
                paintbrush. Continue until the circle is covered with orange tissue paper. When the
                tissue paper has dried say, "Now our pumpkin needs a face." Place the jack-o-lantern
                stencil over the orange circle. Tape the stencil to the table. Ask the children what color
                the paint is. Show the children how to dip the sponge into the black paint and dab over
                the openings cut in the stencil. Carefully remove the stencil.

Closure: Close by asking, "Do you think this jack-o-lantern is happy or sad?"

TISSUE PAPER GHOSTS

Purpose: To create a simple Halloween decoration.

Skill/   To use fine motor skills for crushing paper into a ball.
Concept: To practice tying (for the older child).

Ages: 18 months through 5 years old.

Length of   Allow 5 minutes.
Activity:

Materials: White tissue paper, 2 pieces per ghost
                String or yarn per ghost 1 piece 12 inches long
                Black Magic Marker

For Adult to   Cut the string or yarn into 12-inch pieces.
Do Ahead:

Introduction: Begin by saying, "Let's decorate the room for Halloween. I'll show you how to make a
                friendly ghost."

Procedure: Have children crush one piece of paper into a ball shape. Place the paper ball into the
                center of the second piece of paper. Let the children help pull the sides of the paper up
                toward the center and grasp hold of the ball from the outside. Tie with the piece of
                string. Assist children in drawing eyes on the ghost with the marker.

Closure: Conclude by saying, "Let's hang our ghosts from the ceiling so they can fly above us." Black thread may be drawn through the top of the ghost's head with a needle. Knot the thread and use to tack to ceiling or hang from the window.

Follow-up Activity: Use the ghost as a kite. Children could fly the ghost inside or outside. Indoors play the song "In the Hall of the Mountain King" (from Grieg's *Peer Gynt*) from *More Fiedler's Favorites for Children* (Fiedler/Boston Pops, RCA, 1971).

HALLOWEEN IS HERE

Purpose: To sing a Halloween song.

Skill/ Concept: To sing a simple song.

Ages: 18 months through 5 years old.

Length of Activity: Allow 1 minute.

Materials: Song

Introduction: Begin by saying, "I have a Halloween song to sing for you."

Procedure: Sing song and then ask, "Would you like to sing along with me?"

Closure: Ask older children, "Do you think the song sounds happy or sad?" The song is written in a minor key, so it has a sad, mysterious sound.

Follow-up Activity: Provide the children with a variety of "dress-up" clothing. Some good items are shawls, blouses or shirts, scarfs, hats, beads, aprons, shoes (not too big), and gloves.

Halloween

Words and music by:
JoAnne C. Calvarese

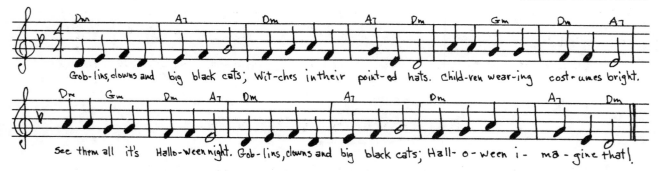

LITTLE BROWN SQUIRREL

Purpose:	To sing a song.
Skill/ Concept:	To memorize a simple song.
Ages:	18 months through 5 years old.
Length of Activity:	Allow 2 minutes.
Materials:	Song
Introduction:	Begin by saying, "The squirrels have been busy gathering nuts and food for the winter. I know a song about a little brown squirrel."
Procedure:	Sing the song. Invite the children to join you singing it again.
Follow-up Activity:	Hide walnuts in a room. Give children baskets or small buckets and let them gather walnuts.

Little Brown Squirrel

Words and music by:
JoAnne C. Calvarese

RHYTHM INSTRUMENTS

Purpose:	To familiarize younger children with basic rhythm instruments
Skills/ Concepts:	To use basic instruments for "making music." To listen to the sounds the instruments make.
Ages:	18 months through 5 years old.
Length of Activity:	Allow 5–10 minutes.

Materials: Set of basic rhythm instruments such as

Jingle bells	Rhythm sticks
Handle bells	Tambourine
Wrist bells	Wood blocks
Triple bells	

Introduction: Begin by saying, "Today we are going to 'make music.'" Show the children the instruments.

Procedure: Give an instrument to each child. Let children experiment with the instruments. Encourage the children to turn the instruments and look at all sides. Show the children how to use the instrument properly. For example, shake the bells or tap them in the palm of your hand. Say, "Let's try to make music with our instruments." Shake, strike, and play instruments. Continue to encourage the children to experiment with the instruments.

Closure: Conclude by saying, "We've had a good time making music. Now it's time to put the instruments away."

Follow-up Activity: Play a favorite record or tape and encourage the children to play along with the music.

TREES SWAYING TO MUSIC

Purpose: To listen to the rhythm of a song and move in time to it.

Skills/ Concepts: To listen to music.
To use gross motor skill of raising arms over head.
To use gross motor skill of swaying back and forth.

Ages: 18 months through 5 years old.

Length of Activity: Allow 2 minutes.

Materials: Battery operated tape recorder or musical instrument
Slow musical tune such as Rimsky-Korsakov's "Song of India" from *More Fiedler Favorites for Children* (Fiedler/Boston Pops, RCA, 1971)
Picture of a tree that shows the trunk, branches, and twigs

Introduction: Ask children, "Can you tell me what is in this picture?" Point to the trunk. "Do you know what this part of the tree is called?" If there is no response, say, "This is the trunk of the tree." Point to the branches and say, "What are these big arms that stretch out from the trunk called?" If there is no response say, "They are the branches." Point to the twigs of the tree. "Do you know what these are?" If there is no response say, "These are the twigs. They are attached to the branches of the tree. Let's go outside and pretend that we are trees."

Procedure: Once outside, say, "We're going to pretend that we are trees. Our bodies will be the trunk of the tree. Let's stand up straight and tall. Next we'll raise our arms up over our heads and reach for the sky. Our arms will be the branches of the tree, so spread them wide. Our fingers will be the twigs. Wiggle those little twigs. Now let's sway our bodies and arms back and forth as if a breeze is blowing. Very good. Let's flop over and hang our arms down and shake them out to relax them. Now I'm going to play some music. First, I want you to listen to the music. . . . Now let's try to sway our bodies or tree trunks back and forth to the music. Now raise those branches, spread out your twigs and sway to the music. . . . Very good. Now let's flop over and shake out our arms and fingers."

Closure: Ask, "Do trees move quickly or slowly? I wonder what makes the trees move their branches? Can you remember?"

Follow-up Activity: Look around outside for different types of trees, bushes, or flowers that move with the wind. Try to imitate these things.

WALKING SLOWLY AND WALKING QUICKLY

Purpose: To practice walking slowly and quickly.

Skills/ Concepts: To understand the difference between slowly and quickly.
To develop gross motor skill of walking.
To listen and follow directions.

Ages: 2 through 5 years old.

Length of Activity: Allow 2 to 5 minutes.

Materials: None needed.

For Adult to Do Ahead: Paint or draw a line on sidewalk or driveway.
If this game is played inside, put a masking tape line on the floor.

Introduction: Begin by saying, "Let's go outside and play a follow the leader game."

Procedure: Then ask, "Can you put your feet on the line and turn toward me?" Stand perpendicular to the line. "I want you to watch me before you move. First, I am going to walk *slowly*. Can you walk slowly too? . . . Now please put your feet back on the line. I am going to walk quickly. Can you walk quickly? . . .Great! Put your feet on the line and listen for me to say the word *quickly* so you can walk quickly or the word *slowly* so you can walk slowly." Do this several times. Ask the children, "Would you like to say the words *quickly* or *slowly* while I put my feet on the line and do what you say?"

Closure: Conclude by saying, "Would you like to try doing something else quickly and slowly?"

Follow-up Activity: Try other activities quickly and slowly such as clapping, marching, blinking, and waving.

"WITCHY WHIZ"

Purpose: To pretend to ride a witch's broom to the accompaniment of music.

Skills/ Concepts: To move to music.
To glide around the room.
To pretend to hold a broom.

Ages: 18 months through 5 years old.

Length of Activity:	Allow 3 minutes.
Materials:	Selection "Witchy Whiz" from the record *Tickly Toddle* by Martha and Hap Palmer, Educational Activities, Inc., Box 390, Freeport, New York 11520. Record player Broom with a long handle
Introduction:	Begin by saying, "When I think of Halloween, I think of jack-o-lanterns, ghosts, black cats, and witches. Let's pretend we're witches today."
Procedure:	Continue with, "Witches are supposed to be able to ride on broomsticks, and fly through the air. We can't fly, but we can pretend to be witches. Watch and I'll show you." Hold broomstick between legs and glide around the room. "Now we'll pretend we are holding a broomstick and 'fly' around the room." Play record and encourage children to glide and hop around the room pretending to hold a broomstick between their legs.
Closure:	Conclude by saying, "It's time to put our broomsticks away."
Follow-up Activity:	Play an identification game with flannel shapes and the flannel board. Cut shapes of pumpkins, ghosts, and black cats and have the children identify them as they are placed on the flannel board.

FIVE LITTLE JACK-O-LANTERNS

Purpose:	To learn a counting poem about Halloween.
Skills/ Concepts:	To memorize a poem. To use fingers for actions. To understand the meaning of the terms first, second, third, fourth, fifth.
Ages:	18 months through 5 years old. (The 18-month to 2-year-old child will probably enjoy listening to the poem more than acting or speaking it.)
Length of Activity:	Allow 1 minute, once a day for two or three weeks before Halloween.
Materials:	Poem Real jack-o-lantern or a picture of a jack-o-lantern
Introduction:	Ask the children, "Do you know what a jack-o-lantern is? Here is a jack-o-lantern." Show a real jack-o-lantern or a picture of one. "This is a pumpkin with a face carved in it. Let's learn a counting poem about five little jack-o-lanterns."
Procedure:	Say poem for children and then invite them to join in repeating it.

Five little jack-o-lanterns sitting on a gate.	(Hold up five fingers.)
The first one said, "My it's getting late."	(Hold up one finger.)
The second one said, "Who's out there?"	(Hold up two fingers.)
The third one said, "There are witches in the air!"	(Hold up three fingers.)
The fourth one said, "Let's run, let's run!"	(Hold up four fingers.)
The fifth one said, "It's only Halloween fun."	(Hold up five fingers.)

Then poof went the wind	(Move hands in front of body left to right.)
And out went the lights,	(Clap hands together.)
And the five little jack-o-lanterns	(Hold up five fingers.)
Jumped out of sight.	(Put hand behind back.)

Closure: Conclude this activity by asking, "How many fingers did we hold up? Let's count them."

Follow-up Activity: Cut five jack-o-lantern shapes out of orange felt. Children can place cutouts on flannel board as they say the poem. Teach five children the five jack-o-lantern parts. As the five children recite their parts, the rest of the group fills in the remainder of the words to the poem.

HALLOWEEN

Purpose: To introduce children to words commonly used during Halloween.

Skills/ Concepts:
To identify objects visually.
To identify objects verbally.
To expand vocabulary.

Ages: 18 months through 5 years old.

Length of Activity: Allow 3 to 5 minutes.

Materials:

Picture or construction paper cutouts of	
pumpkin,	ghost,
jack-o-lantern,	bat,
black cat,	witch

Introduction: Begin the activity by saying, "Halloween is coming soon. Many children wear costumes on that day. Many people decorate their homes and schools with Halloween pictures. I'm going to show you some Halloween decorations."

Procedure: As you show the children each picture ask, "What is this?" or "Do you know who this is?" If the children do not answer, help the children to identify the picture. Talk about the colors black, orange, and white and have the children find objects which are these colors.

Closure: Conclude by saying, "I wonder if you will dress up in a costume for Halloween?"

Follow-up Activities: Teach the jack-o-lantern poem.

A jack-o-lantern is big,	(Hold arms in a circle over your head.)
A jack-o-lantern is round,	(Hold arms in a circle in front of your body.)
A jack-o-lantern has a great big smile,	(Make a big smile and place one finger at each corner of mouth.)
But he doesn't make a sound.	(Place pointer finger in front of lips.)

Read *Where the Wild Things Are* by Maurice Sendak, New York: Harper and Row, 1963.

IN, OUT

Purpose:	To show children the meaning of the words "in" and "out."
Skill/ Concept:	To use gross and fine motor skills to move self and objects in and out.
Ages:	18 months through 5 years old.
Length of Activity:	Allow 3 to 5 minutes.
Materials:	Tent (can be made using a table covered by a large blanket) A box with a lid Small toys or objects to be placed in the box
Introduction:	Begin by asking, "Today we are going to learn about the words 'in' and 'out.' "
Procedure:	Show children the tent. Ask them, "What is this?" Help the children with the word tent if needed. "Would you like to enter the tent?" Some children may be frightened to go into the tent. You may need to go in first. After a child enters the tent say, "Now you are 'in' the tent. Can you come 'out' of the tent?" Allow the child to go "in" and "out" several more times. Encourage the child to tell you whether he or she is "in" or "out" each time. Give all children a chance to enter the tent. Show the children the box. Give a child the small toys and ask, "Can you put the toys 'in' the box?" Then ask, "Can you take the toys 'out' of the box?" Again encourage the child to tell you whether the toys are "in" the box or "out" of the box. Give all children a turn to use the box.
Closure:	Conclude by saying, "Now let's put our jackets on and go outside." (stress the "out" in the word outside)
Follow-up Activity:	Continue this game outside by defining a circle and asking a child to be "in" the circle or "out" of the circle.

APPLE-CHEESE-COCONUT SNACKS

Purpose:	To prepare an easy apple snack.
Skills/ Concepts:	To identify foods. To use fine motor skills to make a snack. To identify shapes.
Ages:	18 months through 2 years old, with help of 3 to 5-year-olds.
Length of Activity:	Allow 10 minutes.
Materials:	Apples, one-half per child Plastic knives, one per child 3 oz. of cream cheese or yellow soft cheese Napkins or paper towels Coconut
For Adult to Do Ahead:	Core apples. If younger children have trouble eating apples, peel apples. Slice apples into doughnut-shaped pieces.

Introduction: Begin by saying, "Let's make a snack with apples."

Procedure: Help the children to spread out a napkin. Children should each take an apple slice and place it on the napkin. Ask the children, "What shape is this?" and "What is this?" as each step progresses. Using your apple slice, show the children how to spread the cheese on the apple. Child may sprinkle coconut on top of the cheese.

Closure: Ask children, "Doesn't this look like a delicious snack?" Child may want to make another.

Follow-up Activity: Sing or play the song "Apples and Bananas" from *The Book of Kids Songs,* by Nancy and John Cassidy (Palo Alto, California, 1986).

ROASTED PUMPKIN SEEDS

Purpose: To make a nutritious snack using pumpkin seeds.

Skills/ Concepts: To learn that seeds can be eaten.
To use fine motor skills for pouring and stirring.

Ages: 2 through 5 years old.

Length of Activity: Allow 10 to 15 minutes.

Materials:
Pumpkin seeds (from jack-o-lantern carving)	Jelly roll pan
Butter (2 tablespoons for each cup of seeds)	Oven or electric skillet
Salt (optional)	Paper towels

For Adult to Do Ahead: Preheat oven to 350°F. Be sure to keep children away from heat source.

Introduction: Begin by asking the children, "Do you remember what these are?" Show children pumpkin seeds.
"Would you like to help make a snack with them?"

Procedure: Have children pour the seeds into the jelly roll pan and add the butter. Continue by saying, "Now we'll put the pan into the oven." Seeds can be stirred every 5 minutes and should be roasted in 15–20 minutes. Remove seeds from oven and spread on paper towels. Allow seeds to cool for 10 minutes before eating them.

Closure: Conclude by saying, "Isn't this a delicious snack!"

Follow-up Activities: Plant three or four seeds in a small pot of dirt. Remind the children to touch the soil every day and water it when it dries out.

Use pumpkin seeds to make a seed picture. Help the children spread glue or paste on a piece of construction paper. Then place seeds individually or sprinkle them on the paper. Allow the glue to dry before moving the picture.

BAKED PUMPKIN

Purpose:	To bake pumpkin for a snack or lunch.
Skills/ Concepts:	To introduce pumpkin as a food. To develop sense of taste.
Ages:	2 through 5 years old.
Length of Activity:	Allow several minutes to prepare, 30 minutes to bake.

Materials:

2 medium-sized pumpkins	2 or 3 tablespoons of honey per child
1 tablespoon of margarine per child	Aluminum foil
Cinnamon	Cookie sheet

For Adult to Do Ahead:	Preheat the oven to 350°F. Remove seeds from one pumpkin and cut it into pieces. Cut foil to hold pumpkin pieces.
Introduction:	Begin by asking, "Do you know what fruit this is?" Show children the pumpkin. "Have you ever had pumpkin to eat? We are going to bake this pumpkin."
Procedure:	Place foil in front of children. Continue by saying, "Place one of the pieces of pumpkin on your foil. Do you know what this is?" Show children margarine. "Place your margarine on top of your pumpkin. Now we are going to dribble the honey on top of the pumpkin." Show children cinnamon and have each child smell the spice. "This is a spice called cinnamon. You may sprinkle it on top of your pumpkin. Can you press your foil together?" Help children if needed. "Now let's put our pumpkin on the cookie sheet so I can put it into the oven."
Closure:	Conclude by saying, "When the pumpkin has baked long enough in the oven, I will take it out. Then we will need to let the pumpkin cool before we eat it."
Follow-up Activity:	The children will be able to eat the pumpkin from the shell. The younger child may need the pumpkin removed from shell before eating. Encourage the children to taste the pumpkin. Children may or may not like the taste or texture of the pumpkin. After the pumpkin has been eaten, give the children a damp sponge to clean the table. (The baked pumpkin could be used in a muffin, cookie, or bread recipe.)

NATURE WALK

Purpose:	To observe and discuss the out-of-doors.
Skills/ Concepts:	To identify nature objects. To develop observation skills. To discuss what is observed. To walk slowly.
Ages:	18 months through 5 years old.
Length of Activity:	Allow 10 minutes (a longer walk may be planned for older children). This walk may be taken in your back or front yard.

Materials: Signed permission slip (if leaving the school yard area)
Basket to carry "treasures" found on the walk.

Introduction: Begin by saying, "Today it is so beautiful outside. Let's go for a walk."

Procedure: Before heading outdoors, talk about some of the things you will see such as
What kinds of trees are there?
Are there any animals?
Are there any hills?
Are there any streams, ponds, lakes?
Remind the children of the procedure for taking a walk (p. 193). "Let's get our jackets and take a walk." As you walk, follow the pace set by the children. Stop and look and talk about what seems to interest the children. You may also want to point out objects to the children.

Closure: Start for home before the children start to tire.

Follow-up
Activities: Collect leaves on the walk to be used to make leaf magnets. Cut two pieces of clear contact paper, larger than a leaf. Have children place the leaf on the contact paper. Place the second piece of contact paper over the leaf. Have the children press on the contact paper. Glue a strip of magnetic tape (found in craft store) on the back of the contact paper.
Read *The Fox Went Out on a Chilly Night* by Peter Spier New York: Double-day, 1961.

CARVE A PUMPKIN

Purpose: To carve a face in a pumpkin.

Skills/
Concepts: To place eyes, nose, and mouth appropriately.
To identify parts of a pumpkin.
To learn concept of full and empty.

Ages: 3 through 5 years old.

Length of
Activity: Allow 20 minutes.

Materials:
Newspaper	Black Magic Marker
Large metal spoon	Bowl
Sharp knife, for the adult	Pumpkin

For Adult to
Do Ahead: Spread newspapers over the area to be used.

Introduction: Begin by asking, "Would you like to turn our pumpkin into a jack-o-lantern?"

Procedure: Continue with, "I am going to cut around the stem of our pumpkin. Where is the stem? When it has been cut it will look like a little hat." As you cut ask, "I wonder what will be inside of this pumpkin?" If children don't answer, suggest seeds. "Let's look inside. You were right, the pumpkin is full of seeds. Would you like to smell and touch the seeds?" Children may or may not want to smell or touch seeds. "I'm going to take the seeds out of the pumpkin and put them in this bowl. You may help if you want." Give each child a chance to help. Clean out the pumpkin using the spoon or your hand. "Is the pumpkin full or empty? Yes, the pumpkin does not have the seeds inside. It is empty." Save the seeds for roasted pumpkin seeds on page 37. "Now, our pumpkin needs eyes. Would you like to draw eyes on the pumpkin?" Pick a child to draw eyes using the marker. After the eyes are drawn, ask about the nose and mouth and pick children to draw them with the marker. "Now I am going to cut out the eyes, nose, and mouth following the pattern you drew with the marker. The knife I'm going to use is very sharp. Be sure to sit back so you won't be cut."

Closure: Conclude by saying, "This is a great looking jack-o-lantern. Let's get a candle to put in our jack-o-lantern."

Follow-up Activities: Cut a pumpkin shape from orange felt. Cut three triangular shapes from black felt for eyes and nose. Cut a grinning mouth shape from black felt. Children can make faces on the orange pumpkin shape with the black felt shapes.

Read *Mousekin's Golden House* by Edna Miller New York: Simon and Schuster, 1964.

AUTUMN TREE

Purpose: To display materials found outdoors in the fall.

Skills/ Concepts: To identify nature materials.
To develop sense of touch.
To use memory skills.

Ages: 18 months through 5 years old.

Length of Activity: Allow 5 to 10 minutes, for initial setting up of tree. Expect to spend 2 minutes a day whenever children find something new.

Materials: Tree branch, an interesting shape with many twigs
Yarn
Ornament hooks, if you want
Large pot or pan filled with sand or rocks
Variety of natural materials such as colorful leaves, pinecones, dried flower tops, dried weeds, seed pods, grasses (these items can be found on nature walk; see pp. 38–39)

For Adult to Do Ahead: Secure the branch with sand or rocks in a large pot so it won't tip. If you want, wrap pot with colorful fabric.

Introduction: Begin by saying, "Would you like to help me decorate this tree branch?"

Procedure: Continue by saying, "We're going to use these dried materials as the decorations for our 'Autumn Tree.' " Tie yarn around the materials and then help the children hang the materials from the tree branch. As the children help, ask questions about what each item is, where it was found, and how it feels (hard, soft, crunchy, etc.).

Closure: Conclude by saying, "This is a beautiful way to bring some of the outdoors inside. What is your favorite decoration hanging on the tree?"

Follow-up Activity: Add to the tree daily. Encourage the children to be on the look-out for new and interesting things to use for decorations.

MATCHING GAME

Purpose:	To match like pictures.
Skills/ Concepts:	To recognize objects in pictures. To use fine motor skill of picking up pictures. To identify like pictures.
Ages:	18 months through 3 years old.
Length of Activity:	Allow 2 to 5 minutes.
Materials:	Manufactured memory game for preschoolers sold at toy or department stores or make your own game by using posterboard and hand drawn pictures, or cutouts from magazines.
For Adult to Do Ahead:	Find two pairs of identical pictures that are easy for the child to recognize, such as two balls and two cats. Remember if using magazine pictures that the pictures have to be identical. Cut posterboard into four 2-inch by 2-inch pieces. Paste one picture in the center of each piece. Cover with clear contact paper and trim.
Introduction:	(Note: This is a good game to play individually with each child.) Begin by saying, "I have two pictures to show you." Place two different cards on the table. "Can you tell me what this is?" Point to one of the pictures. "And what picture is on this card?" Point to the other card.
Procedure:	Continue by saying, "Now let me show you two more cards." Place the other two identical cards on the table above the original two cards. Ask the child to identify the pictures. Then ask the child to pick up the two "ball" cards and place them side by side. Ask the child to do the same with the two "cat" cards. "You have just learned how to play the matching game. You matched the two balls and the two cats. Would you like to try this game again?" If the child says yes, scramble the four cards to be matched again.
Closure:	Conclude by asking, "What cards did we match today?"
Follow-up Activity:	After the child masters the first two pairs of cards add more pairs to the game one pair at a time.

COLLECTING AND SORTING

Purpose:	To offer an outdoor sorting exercise
Skills/ Concepts:	To collect objects To use fine and gross motor skills To sort or group things that are similar
Ages:	3 through 5 years old.
Length of Activity:	Allow 10 minutes.

Materials: A basket
Individual small baskets or plastic containers (one per child)

Introduction: Begin by saying, "I have a basket. Is it full or empty?" (empty) "Let's take a walk and fill it with "treasures" we find along the way."

Procedure: Adult can carry basket for large items while children can carry small container for smaller items. Pick up interesting objects such as: rocks, small sticks, acorns, pinecones, leaves or flowers. After the walk, encourage children to sort out the objects by grouping "like" things together, naming them and describing them.

Closure: Conclude by saying, "How many groups of "treasures" have you found?" (count the number of groups)

Follow-up Activity: Make a collage by gluing some of the objects found in the activity above to a sheet of posterboard or cardboard.

MEMORY GAME

Purpose: To match like pictures.

Skills/ Concepts: To use fine motor skills for picking up cards.
To recognize objects in pictures.
To identify "like" pictures.
To develop memory retention.

Ages: 3 through 5 years old.

Length of Activity: Allow 5 to 10 minutes.

Materials: Memory game sold in toy or department store or make your own using hand-drawn pictures or cutouts from magazines

For Adult to Do Ahead: Find three sets of identical pictures such as two balls, two bikes, two hats, two dogs. Cut posterboard into six 2-inch by 2-inch pieces. Paste picture in center of poster board. Cover posterboard with clear contact paper and trim.

Introduction: (Note: This is a good game to play individually with each child.) Begin by saying, "Let's play the memory game."

Procedure: Scramble the six cards and lay them out in two rows of three each. Ask the child to pick up one card. If he or she doesn't identify the picture, ask, "What is that a picture of? Can you place it picture down and choose another card?" Have the child continue until a second card identical to the first card is found. "Can you remember where the other card with that picture is?" The child may have to turn several cards over or may remember where the card is located on the first try. When the two matching cards are found, continue to turn the other cards over trying to make two more matches. The more he or she practices, the easier it will become for the child to remember where the matching cards are.

Closure: Conclude by saying, "We'll put these cards in a box or basket, and you may use them again when you want."

Follow-up Activity: When the child has mastered three sets of cards add more pairs one pair at a time. This game is also fun for two children to play together.

GROWTH CHART

Purpose:	To mark growth of children visually.
Skills/ Concepts:	To follow directions. To learn concept of tall/taller/tallest. To encourage development of attention span.
Ages:	18 months through 5 years old.
Length of Activity:	Allow 2 minutes and update in January and April.
Materials:	Length of paper 6 feet by 8 ½ inches Orange and green construction paper Yardstick Black marker
For Adult to Do Ahead:	Cut small pumpkin shape from orange paper. Print each child's name on a pumpkin. Add a stem to pumpkin cut from green paper. Tape long piece of paper to wall and mark at 6-inch intervals.
Introduction:	Begin by saying, "I am tall. Even though you are big girls and boys, you are not as tall as I am. Let's mark on this paper how tall I am and how tall you are."
Procedure:	With the help of another person mark your height on the paper. Point out to the children how you have your back against the paper and your heels against the paper. "See how tall I am standing. Here is a pumpkin with my name. I am going to print how many inches tall I am on my pumpkin." Tape pumpkin to the appropriate spot on the paper. Invite each child to stand like "I did" against the wall as you mark their height on a pumpkin and tape pumpkin to the paper.
Closure:	Conclude by saying, "Look how tall you are getting. We can check again on this chart to see how much you have grown."
Follow-up Activity:	Read *Peter's Chair* by Ezra Jack Keats (New York: Harper & Row, 1967).

LET'S GO TO THE COUNTRY

Purpose:	To "visit" and learn about the country using a flannel board.
Skills/ Concepts:	To identify objects associated with the country. To enrich vocabulary. To place flannel pieces.
Ages:	18 months (may enjoy placing objects on the flannel board); 2 through 5 years old.
Length of Activity:	Allow 5 minutes.

Materials: Flannel board
Flannel board pieces may be pictures or construction paper cutouts such as
trees,   farmhouse,
farm animals,   pond or lake
barn,

Introduction: Begin by saying, "We're going to the 'country' today. Let's use our flannel board."

Procedure: As you talk, have the children place the flannel pieces on the board. "In the country there are very few houses. There are farmhouses for the people to live in and barns for the cows and horses. There are big fields called pastures. The cows and horses eat or graze in the pastures. There are lots of trees and bushes in the country. Sometimes there might be a small pond or a lake."

Closure: Conclude by saying, "The country is a beautiful, quiet place to visit."

Follow-up Activities: Read *Let's Discover the Countryside* by Maria Ruis and J. M. Parramon (New York: Barron's Books).
Read *The Little House* by Virginia Lee Burton Boston: Houghton Mifflin, 1942.

WHO IS THAT?

Purpose: To identify self using a mirror.

Skills/ Concepts: To answer a question.
To recognize self in a mirror.
To develop attention span.

Ages: 18 months through 5 years old.

Length of Activity: Allow 2 to 5 minutes.

Materials: Mirror, any size

Introduction: Begin by saying, "I have a 'picture' of someone to show you."

Procedure: Hold mirror in front of a child. Give the child a chance to comment. If nothing is said ask, "Where is _____?" Child should respond by pointing or verbally. You may ask again, "Where is _____?" Next you may ask, "Who is that (pointing to the reflection in the mirror)?" Ask this several times. The third question you may ask is, "Can you show me _____?" Give each child a turn to look into the mirror.

Closure: Conclude by saying, "Who did you see in the mirror?"

Follow-up Activity: Purchase a small photocube or photograph album. Place pictures of the children, you, family, and friends in the cube. Talk with the child about the pictures, who is in them, what they are wearing, what they are doing.

LET'S WASH UP

Purpose:	To teach children to wash their own hands.
Skills/ Concepts:	To learn importance of keeping hands clean. To use soap and water to clean hands. To use towel to dry hands.
Ages:	18 months through 2 years old (with supervision); 3 years old through 5 years old.
Length of Activity:	Allow 1 or 2 minutes per child.
Materials:	Liquid soap, small fancy guest soaps are great for home Paper towels, small hand towel for home Sink, with sturdy step stool if needed
Introduction:	Begin by saying, "Before we eat, we should wash our hands. Would you like to wash your hands?"
Procedure:	This is an activity that should be done individually. Have the child stand facing the sink. Stand behind the child and give verbal directions to the child. "Let's push up your sleeves so they won't get wet. Can you turn on the water?" Adjust the water to a warm temperature. "After you wet your hands can you put soap on your hands and rub it between your hands?" Let the child rub hands together with and without soap. "Can you hold your hands under the warm water and rinse off the soap? Now dry your hands until all of the water and wetness is gone." The child may want to wash hands again.
Closure:	Conclude by saying, "Now that you have washed your hands let's have lunch."
Follow-up Activity:	This activity may be adapted easily for outdoors. Use a small dish pan or basin to hold the water. Talk with the children about the times they should wash their hands such as after using the toilet, before meals, or after playing in the sandbox. Read *Sam's Bath* by Barbro Lindgren New York: William Morrow and Co. 1983.

STOP, DROP, AND ROLL

Purpose:	To teach children what to do if their clothing ever caught on fire.
Skills/ Concepts:	To drop quickly to the ground. To roll over and over.
Ages:	18 months through 5 years old.
Length of Activity:	Allow 5 minutes.
Materials:	Handmade paper flames Tape

Introduction: Begin by saying, "We've learned what to do in a fire drill and we will have a visit to/from the fire department. Today we are going to learn what to do if you are ever caught in a fire and your clothes catch on fire."

Procedure: Pick an older child and say, "I will tape some make-believe flames to your clothes. Let's see if you can wrinkle those flames and put out the fire. First, you must *stop*. That means to stand still and do not run. Then, you *drop* down. Can you drop down to the floor with me? Finally we *roll*. Let's roll over and over again until we wrinkle all of our flames. *STOP, DROP, AND ROLL*—those are three important words to remember." Take the taped flames off of the child's clothing. "Look how you wrinkled these paper flames when you rolled on the ground. If these were real flames you would have put them out by rolling." Give all children a chance to stop, drop, and roll.

Closure: Conclude by saying, "Can you remember the three important words we learned today?"

Follow-up Activity: Teach the "Stop, Drop, and Roll" song. Have the children take turns wrinkling flames while the others sing the song.

Stop, Drop, and Roll

Words and music
JoAnne Calvarese

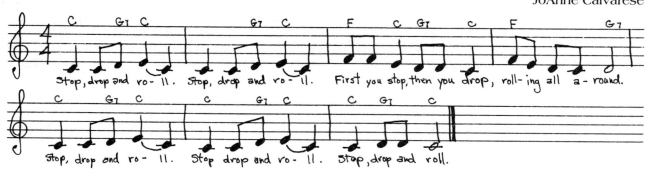

TRIP TO/OR VISIT FROM THE FIRE DEPARTMENT

Purpose: To acquaint children with the local fire department

Skills/ Concepts: To understand that the firefighter is someone who can help.
To improve listening skills.

Ages: 18 months through 5 years old. (The 18-month to 2-year-old child may not understand what is being said. Some children may be frightened of the fire truck or fire equipment. Encourage them to look with your help or in your arms. Don't force the children if they seem unwilling.)

Length of Activity: Allow 5 to 30 minutes.

Materials: Permission slip, one per child
Car seat or seat belt for each child

For Adult to Do Ahead: Contact the fire department and ask if they have a program which allows a fire truck to visit your school. If not, make arrangements for a visit to the fire station. Let the fire station know (1) how many children are coming, (2) ages of the children and their approximate attention span, and (3) what you would like to see.

Introduction: Begin by asking, "Today a fire truck is coming to visit us." Or "Today we are going to visit the fire station." "We will see the fire truck and some of the equipment."

Procedure: When you arrive at the station, make introductions. Some stations allow children to climb and explore the trucks. Check before allowing children to touch or climb on anything.

Closure: When the children become restless it is time for good-byes. Conclude with, "Thank you. We enjoyed seeing the fire truck and all of the equipment."

Follow-up Activity: Teach the fingerplay "Ten Little Firefighters."

Ten little firefighters Standing in a row.	(Hold ten fingers up straight.)
Ding goes the bell,	(Clap hands together.)
Down the pole they go.	(Motion of sliding down pole with hands.)
Jumping on the engine, Driving very fast	(Motion of driving fast with hands.)
Putting out the fire,	(Hold hose with hands.)
Driving home at last.	(Motion of driving slow with hands.)
Ten little firefighters Standing in a row.	(Hold ten fingers up straight.)

NOVEMBER ACTIVITIES

THEME: *Family*
SPECIAL DAY: *Thanksgiving*

ART:	Crayon Melt Pictures
	Cornstarch Beads
	Hand Turkeys
MUSIC:	Over the River
	Sleep, Baby, Sleep
	My Bonnie
MOVEMENT:	Toe-Heel Dance
	Walk/Run
	Reach for the Sky
LANGUAGE:	Tell Me a Story
	Mr. Turkey
	The Indians
NUTRITION:	Peanut Butter Raisin Bread Sandwiches
	Warm Apple Cider Punch
	Dairy Products
SCIENCE/ NATURE:	Loud and Soft
	Magnets
	What Would Happen If?
MATH:	More or Less
	Parquetry Shapes
	Turkey Tail Matching Game
SOCIAL STUDIES:	My Family
	Let's Go Visit the Grocery Store
	Family Party
HEALTH/ SAFETY:	Running Indoors
	Sneezing

CRAYON MELT PICTURES

Purpose:	To use crayons in a different way.
Skills/ Concepts:	To use fine motor skills. To use new vocabulary. To use tactile sense to recognize the difference between smooth and bumpy.
Ages:	3 through 5 years old. (Children should not be left alone during this activity.)
Length of Activity:	Allow 2 or 3 minutes.
Materials:	Crayons, may be broken and unwrapped Warming tray White paper Old mittens
For Adult to Do Ahead:	Place warming tray on low table or counter next to a plug. Set heat to the lowest setting.
Introduction:	Begin by saying, "Let's make some pictures by melting crayons on a piece of paper. The paper is laying on a tray that is very warm. You will wear a mitten on your hand so your hand doesn't get too hot."
Procedure:	This activity should be done with each child individually. Lay paper on warming tray. Have a child put on a mitten and, choosing crayons one at a time, draw on the paper. The heat of the tray will melt the crayon on the paper. As the melted crayon sets, the wax becomes thicker and bumpier. "Gently run your finger over your picture. Can you feel the wax from the crayons? Now feel this plain paper. How does the paper feel? The wax feels bumpy and the plain paper feels smooth."
Closure:	Conclude by saying, "Can you name the colors you see in your pictures?"
Follow-up Activities:	Place picture in art folder. Make a book of colors. Help children to make four or five crayon melt pictures using one different color per picture. Punch holes in one side of all of the pictures and bind together with yarn.

CORNSTARCH BEADS

Purpose:	To make beads.
Skills/ Concepts:	To use large and fine motor skills of arm, hands, and fingers to knead. To use sense of touch to feel textures: lumpy, smooth, hard, soft.
Ages:	2 through 5 year olds.
Length of Activity:	Allow 10 minutes to knead clay, 5–10 minutes to make beads.
Materials:	Recipe of cornstarch clay (see For Adult to Do Ahead) Picture of an Indian wearing beads Cookie sheet

For Adult to
Do Ahead:

Make clay:
 2 cups of baking soda
 1 cup of cornstarch
 1¼ cups of cold water
Mix dry ingredients and slowly add the water to prevent lumps. Cook over medium heat for 6 minutes (do not boil). Mixture is ready when it looks like mashed potatoes. Spread the dough on a cookie sheet to cool. Cover with a damp cloth to keep it moist. At this point the children will be able to help.

Introduction:

Begin by saying, "We've been talking about Indians. Some Indians wear beads in their hair or on their clothes for special occasions. We are going to make our own beads to wear." Show children pictures. Elicit their comments about the pictures.

Procedure:

Gather the dough into small portions and knead until it is smooth and pliable. While you are kneading talk about how the clay feels: cool, sticky, soft, smooth, and so on. When the kneading is finished, add a few drops of food coloring to each portion and knead the dough until the color is evenly distributed throughout the clay. Store dough in air-tight container when not in use. Children will now be able to form clay into bead shaped pieces. Holes for stringing can be formed by pressing an unsharpened pencil into the bead, or by pressing a pinky finger through the clay. Set beads on cookie sheet.

Clay will harden in 24 hours at room temperature or overnight in an oven that has been preheated to 275°F and then turned off. To bake beads, preheat oven to 200°F. Place beads on lightly greased cookie sheet and bake for 2 hours. Cool in oven for 2 hours longer, removing when the beads feel hard on the bottom side.

Closure:

Close by saying, "When these beads have hardened and cooled, we will string them."

Follow-up
Activity:

String beads on macrame string and tie with a knot to make a necklace.

HAND TURKEYS

Purpose:

To make a holiday art project.

Skills/
Concepts:

To use fine motor skills for coloring and pasting.
To trace hand (for older children).
To follow directions.

Ages:

18 months, with help; 2 through 5 years old.

Length of
Activity:

Allow 5 minutes.

Materials:

White construction paper	Paste
Pencil	Colored construction paper
Crayons	Children's scissors

For Adult to
Do Ahead:

For younger children, draw and cut out feather shapes from colored construction paper. Older children may be able to trace feather shapes and cut them out.

Introduction:

Begin by saying, "At the first Thanksgiving, the Pilgrims and Indians ate turkey and many other good foods. Let's make a picture of a turkey."

Procedure:

Help children to trace the outline of one hand, with fingers spread, onto white construction paper as shown in the accompanying drawing. This will be the turkey's

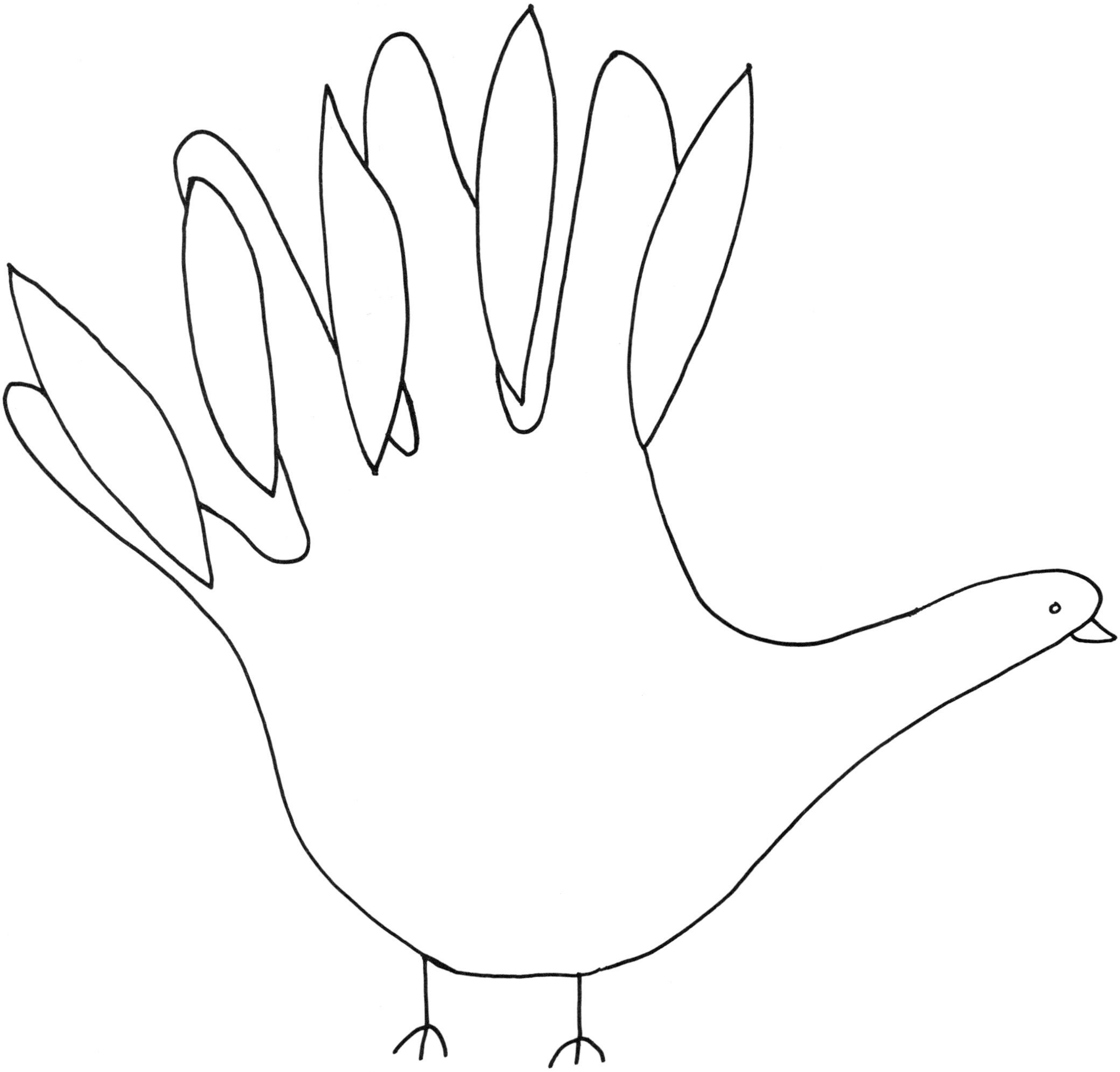

body. This may now be colored using the crayons. Don't be concerned whether the child colors "inside of the lines." It is more important that the child be happy with the completed project. Give each child three or four feathers to be pasted onto the four fingers of the body. The thumb is used for the turkey's head. Older children may like to add eyes and a beak to the turkey.

Closure: Conclude by saying, "These turkeys are really colorful! Let's decorate our room with them."

Follow-up Activity: Help the children to cut around the turkey and paste the cutout to the top of a popsicle stick. Use the stick puppet as you say the poem "Mr. Turkey" on page 57.

OVER THE RIVER

Purpose: To learn a Thanksgiving song.

Skill/ Concept: To memorize a simple song

Ages: 18 months through 5 years old.

Length of Activity: Allow 2 minutes.

Materials: Song

Introduction: Begin by saying, "Sometimes people visit their Grandma's house for Thanksgiving. This is a song that people sang before there were cars to ride. A sleigh is a large sled that is pulled by a horse. A sleigh is what the people in this song are riding through the snow."

Procedure: Sing the song through one time by yourself. Invite the older children to sing along with you a second time.

Closure: Conclude by asking, "What is a sleigh?" A large sled. "What animal pulls a sleigh?" A horse.

Follow-up Activity: Read the book *Over the River and Thro' the Woods*, illustrated by Normand Charier (A Little Simon Book, Simon & Schuster, New York).

Over the River — Traditional

SLEEP, BABY, SLEEP

Purpose:	To sing a family song.
Skill/ Concept:	To sing a lullaby about a family.
Ages:	18 months through 5 years old.
Length of Activity:	Allow 1 minute.
Materials:	Song
Introduction:	Begin by saying, "A lullaby is a song which is sung to put a person to sleep. This lullaby tells about a baby, a mother, and a father."
Procedure:	Continue with, "I am going to hum this lullaby. Can you hum?" Help children to hum if they don't know how. Hum the lullaby through once. Sing the song through a second time. Then invite the children to sing the song with you.
Closure:	Conclude by asking, "Do you listen to music before bedtime? Does someone sing to you before you go to sleep at night?"
Follow-up Activities:	Sing the song through another time while the children act out the parts of the baby, mother, and father. Read *Baby Elephant's Bedtime* by Dick McCue (A Little Simon Book, Simon & Schuster, New York). Read *Goodnight Moon* by Margaret Wise Brown (New York: Harper & Row, 1947).

Sleep, Baby, Sleep   Traditional

MY BONNIE

Purpose:	To sing a song about the ocean.
Skills/ Concepts:	To sing a simple song with a chorus To move to the song.
Ages:	18 months through 5 years old.

Length of Activity:	Allow 2 minutes
Materials:	Song
Introduction:	Begin by stating, "This is a song that tells a story about a sailor and his special friend 'Bonnie' who lives across the ocean."
Procedure:	Continue by saying, "We will sing this song slowly. If you want you may rock your body back and forth while we sing." Sing song.
Closure:	Conclude by noting, "That was a very peaceful and quiet song."
Follow-up Activities:	Find a picture book at the library of sailboats on the ocean for the children to look through. Older children may wish to draw or paint a boat on a blue ocean.

My Bonnie

Traditional

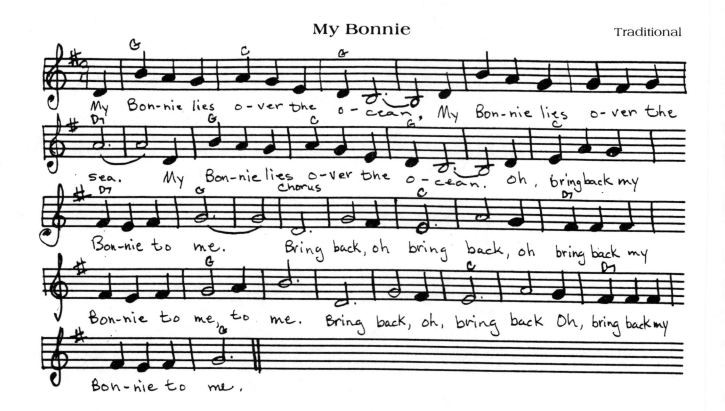

TOE-HEEL DANCE

Purpose:	To learn a simple dance.
Skills/ Concepts:	To use gross motor skills for walking. To follow a line. To move to a rhythm.
Ages:	18 months through 2 years old (will follow group around the room); 3 through 5 years old.

Length of Activity:	Allow 2 minutes.
Materials:	Colored tape or chalk if outdoors Small hand drum or wooden sticks
For Adult to Do Ahead:	Mark several patterns outside with chalk on hardtop playground or indoors with colored tape on the floor.
Introduction:	Begin by saying, "For the Indians, dancing is an important part of life. They have different dances for different feelings. They have dances for when they are happy, sad, sick, angry, praying, or telling stories. Let's learn a simple dance step used by the Taos Indians to celebrate sunset."
Procedure:	Show the children how to walk toe-heel, toe-heel, one foot directly in front of the other. When the children have mastered this ask them to try walking this way along the straight line. Once this has been mastered add the slow beat of a hand drum or wooden sticks. As they become more adept, a slight bounce from the knees with each step may be added.
Closure:	Conclude by asking, "Did you enjoy doing the dance?"
Follow-up Activity:	Mark several other patterns on the floor. Make these patterns more difficult by making them curved or winding them through and around a maze of objects.

WALK/RUN

Purpose:	To learn the difference between walking and running.
Skills/ Concepts:	To use gross motor skills for walking and running. To move to a rhythm. To differ stride on command. To listen for a different rhythm.
Age:	18 months through 5 years old.
Length of Activity:	Allow 2 to 5 minutes, depending upon attention span of children.
Materials:	Outside space to run A tambourine or small hand drum
Introduction:	Begin by saying, "Let's go outside to get some fresh air and exercise."
Procedure:	Show children the tambourine. "This is a tambourine. I can make a slow sound with it." Beat out a slow rhythm. "I can make a fast sound with it." Beat out a fast rhythm. Pick an older child to play the tambourine changing between fast and slow. As the older child plays a rhythm, clap along with it. Once the older child has the rhythm, ask the other children to walk or run around the play yard to the beat. Some children may need verbal clues from you to notice the change in the beat of the tambourine. For example, "Lauren is beating the tambourine slowly; let's walk to this beat. Lauren is beating the tambourine quickly; let's run to this beat."
Closure:	Conclude with, "Let's see if we can now walk slowly to the door and go inside. Lauren, may we please have a slow walking beat."

Follow-up
Activity:

This activity can be continued inside by having the children clap slowly, clap quickly, flap their arms slowly, flap their arms quickly, blink their eyes slowly, blink their eyes quickly, wiggle their toes slowly, wiggle their toes quickly, and so forth.

REACH FOR THE SKY

Purpose:

To learn a simple stretching exercise.

Skills/
Concepts:

To use gross motor skills for reaching.
To learn concepts of up and down.

Ages:

18 months through 5 years old.

Length of
Activity:

Allow 1 or 2 minutes, may be indoors or outdoors.

Introduction:

Begin by saying, "Stretching is a good exercise to do anytime, especially if you've been sitting still for a long time."

Procedure:

Continue with, "Let's all stand up. Now stretch your arms way up in the air and try to touch the sky (or the ceiling). Reach up as high as you can. Now let's gently bend over and touch the ground (or the rug or floor). Can your fingers touch the ground? Let's stand up straight again. Now give your body a little shake all over."

Closure:

Conclude with, "That was a very good stretch. Does that make you feel relaxed?"

Follow-up
Activity:

This activity can be expanded upon by having the children reach up and down with one arm at a time or by having the children reach up and down for the opposite foot (right hand, left toe; left hand, right toe).

TELL ME A STORY

Purpose:

To encourage children to use their imaginations.
To offer a "special" time with adult.

Skills/
Concepts:

To develop vocabulary.
To develop storytelling skills.

Ages:

3 through 5 year olds (toddlers may like to look at the the pictures and name the objects they see).

Length of
Activity:

Allow 1 to 5 minutes depending upon how long a story the child creates.

Materials:

Several bright colorful pictures
Posterboard or cardboard
Clear contact paper

For Adult to
Do Ahead:

Find interesting pictures in magazines. Cut out. Mount on posterboard or cardboard. Glue in place and cover with clear contact paper.

Introduction:

Begin by asking, "Katie, will you tell me a story about one of these pictures?"

Procedure: Child selects a picture and makes up a story. They can start by first telling about what is actually happening in the picture and then go on to tell why it is happening or what happens next. The first few times the adult often needs to ask some leading questions to encourage the child to continue the story. Once the child learns how this activity works, future stories will become more detailed, imaginative and involved.

Closure: Conclude by saying, "I really enjoyed your story!"

Follow-up Activity: Children can record their stories with a tape recorder so that other children can look at the pictures and listen to the story at another time.

MR. TURKEY

Purpose: To learn a holiday fingerplay

Skills/ Concepts: To memorize a poem.
To use hand movements to accompany poem.

Ages: 2 through 5 years old.

Length of Activity: Allow 1 minute.

Materials: Poem
Picture of a turkey with tail feathers spread

Introduction: Show children the picture of the turkey. Then ask, "Do you know what type of bird this is?" Children may or may not know it is a turkey. "Do you know what sound a turkey makes?" Gobble. "Can you make a turkey sound?"

Procedure: Continue with, "Let's learn a turkey poem."

Mr. Turkey's tail is big and wide, He swings it when he walks.	(Left hand with fingers spread is the tail. Right fist in left palm is body, thumb is head.)
His neck is long, His chin is red.	(Point to neck. Point to chin.)
He gobbles when he talks.	(Open and close fingers of one hand to talk.)
Mr. Turkey is tall and proud,	(Straighten up body very tall.)
He dances on his feet.	(Move two fingers back and forth to dance.)
And on each Thanksgiving Day,	(Fold hands in front of body.)
He's something good to eat.	(Pat stomach.)

Say, "Let's try Mr. Turkey one more time." Encourage children to recite poem with you.

Closure: Conclude with, "Can you show me how to make a turkey using your hands?"

Follow-up Activity: Cut feather shapes from construction paper. See Turkey Tail Matching Game for a pattern on page 64. Use the feather shapes to play a hide-and-seek game. While children are out of the room, hide feather shapes. Bring children into the room and allow them to find one shape per person. Older children will enjoy hiding the shapes.

THE INDIANS

Purpose:	To learn a fingerplay.
Skills/ Concepts:	To memorize a poem. To use fine motor skills. To use a quiet voice.
Ages:	2 through 5 years old.
Length of Activity:	Allow 1 minute.
Materials:	Poem Picture of an Indian
Introduction:	Begin by saying, "I have a picture to show you. Do you know who is in this picture? Indians learned how to walk so slowly and quietly that no one could hear them coming. I know a fingerplay about Indians who are very quiet."
Procedure:	Recite poem using the actions for the children.

The Indians are walking,	(Walk two fingers from right hand up left arm slowly—hand to wrist.)
Ssh, ssh.	(Place first finger upright in front of mouth.)
The Indians are walking,	(Walk two fingers from wrist to elbow.)
Ssh, ssh.	(Place first finger upright in front of mouth.)
They don't make a sound As their feet touch the ground.	(Shake first finger back and forth in front of body.)
The Indians are walking,	(Walk two fingers from elbow to shoulder.)
Ssh, ssh.	(Place first finger upright in front of mouth.)

Invite the children to join you in reciting the poem several more times.

Closure:	In a whisper say, "Let's see how quietly we can walk to the door/table on our tiptoes." Encourage the children to walk slowly and quietly to their destination.
Follow-up Activities:	Play an outdoor game. Use a hand drum or wood sticks to play rhythms that alternate between fast tiptoe walking to slower flat footed stomping. An older child will be able to tap out rhythms for the group to follow. Read *Hawk, I'm Your Brother* by Byrd Baylor, New York: Scribner, 1976.

© 1990 by The Center for Applied Research in Education

PEANUT BUTTER RAISIN BREAD SANDWICHES

Purpose:	To prepare a nutritious snack.
Skills/ Concepts:	To identify shapes. To make a sandwich. To use small muscle groups for spreading.
Ages:	18 months through 2 years old; 3 through 5 years old.

Length of Activity:	Allow 5 minutes.
Materials:	Raisin bread Plastic knives Peanut butter Plates for sandwiches Cookie cutters, very simple shapes Wax paper
For Adult to Do Ahead:	Cover table with wax paper. Tape in place.
Introduction:	Begin by saying, "Let's make some fancy sandwiches."
Procedure:	Younger children will be able to lay raisin bread out on the wax paper. Help children identify cookie cutters. "What shapes are these cookie cutters?" Older children will be able to use cookie cutters to cut raisin bread into fancy shapes. Younger children may need assistance. There should be at least two of each shape. Older children will be able to spread peanut butter onto bread shapes. The younger children can then make the sandwiches by placing two of the shapes together.
Closure:	Conclude by asking, "Can you name the different-shaped sandwiches as you place them on the plate?"
Follow-up Activities:	Serve the sandwiches for the family party. Read *Very Hungry Caterpillar* by Eric Carle, New York: Harper and Row, 1969.

WARM APPLE CIDER PUNCH

Purpose:	To make a warm nutritious drink.
Skills/ Concepts:	To differentiate between cold and warm. To identify spices. To tie a knot (for 4- or 5-year-olds).
Ages:	3 through 5 years old.
Length of Activity:	Allow 5 minutes.
Materials:	Cheesecloth Pieces of nutmeg String Cider, or apple juice if cider is not available Cinnamon sticks Pan Cloves Cups for drinking
For Adult to Do Ahead:	Cut a piece of cheesecloth 8 inches square to make a spice packet. One packet will be enough for 2 quarts of cider. Cut a piece of string 12 inches long. Place spices in small dishes.
Introduction:	Ask children, "Do you know what this is?" If children are unable to identify the cider help them. "Do you know what fruit cider comes from?" Apples. "Let's make some warm cider punch."
Procedure:	Have children lay out the piece of cheesecloth. Help children to identify spices as they place one cinnamon stick, 4 cloves, and a slice of nutmeg in the middle of the cloth. Gather cheesecloth up on all sides and tie at the top. Many 4- and 5-year-olds can tie a knot. Pour a little of the cool apple cider in a cup. Encourage the children to feel the outside of the cup of cider with their fingers to identify the temperature. "Does this

cider feel cool or warm?" Pour the rest of the cider into a pan. Place the packet of spices into the cider. "I am going to warm this cider on the stove." Warm cider gently for an hour. Do not boil. Remove spice packet before serving. Let cider cool somewhat. Pour a cup of warm cider. Encourage the children to feel the outside of the warm cup. Ask the children, "Does the cup feel warm?" Encourage the children to feel the outside of the cool cup of cider. "Does this cup feel cool? Would you like to taste the cider?"

Closure: Conclude by saying, "The cider was cool. We heated the cider and then it was warm."

Follow-up Activity: Serve the warm cider for the family party.

DAIRY PRODUCTS

Purpose: To acquaint children with nutritious foods that are dairy products.

Skills/ Concepts: To expand vocabulary.
To identify foods.
To use small muscle groups to spread with a knife.

Ages: 18 months through 5 years old.

Length of Activity: Allow 5 minutes.

Materials:

Picture of a cow	Hard cheese
Pitcher of milk	Cream cheese
Butter	Box of whole wheat crackers

Introduction: Begin by asking children, "Do you know what a dairy is? A dairy is a place where milk is put into bottles or cartons to be sold in the store. Often there is a dairy at a large farm that has lots of cows. What is this a picture of?" Show picture of the cow. "What food do we get from cows?" Children may or may not respond with milk. "Did you know that many other foods can be made from milk?"

Procedure: Continue by saying, "Let's look at some of the foods I have on this table. Would you tell me what they are?" Help children identify each food. "All of these foods are made from milk. They are called dairy products. These foods are good for your body."

Closure: Conclude by saying, "Let's make a snack from some of our dairy products. Which do you think might taste good with these crackers?" Cheese and cream cheese. "What do you think we should drink with our cheese and crackers?" Milk.

Follow-up Activities: Cut the cheese into cubes for snacking. Children should be able to spread the cream cheese using a plastic knife. Serve with a cup of milk.
Read *Mice Twice* by Joseph Low, New York: Atheneum, 1980.

LOUD AND SOFT

Purpose: To help children differentiate between loud and soft sounds.

Skills/ Concepts: To expand listening skills.
To identify sounds.

Ages: 18 months through 5 years old.

Length of Activity:	Allow 3 or 4 minutes (may be used as an indoor or outdoor activity).
Materials:	Wood blocks, two
Introduction:	Hit the wood blocks together loudly. Children should look to see what is happening. Then continue with, "That was a loud noise, wasn't it? Listen, I can make a sound with the wood blocks that is very soft."
Procedure:	Ask the children, "Can you make a loud noise with your hands?" Clap loudly. "What a great loud noise. Fold your hands and listen. Can you make a very soft noise with your hands?" Continue by asking children to identify soft and loud sounds as they are made.
Closure:	Remind the children, "The best place to use a loud voice or make a loud noise is outdoors. When we are indoors it is best to use a soft voice or make a soft noise."
Follow-up Activities:	Continue this game by asking children to identify loud or soft singing, loud or soft talking, or loud or soft music played by a tape recorder. Play the selection *Shout and Whisper* from the record/tape *Tickly Toddle: Songs for the Very Young* by Martha and Hap Palmer, Activity Records. Educational Activities, Inc. Box 390, Freeport, New York 11520. Read *Noisy Nora* by Rosemary Wells New York: Dial Books, 1973.

MAGNETS
(for 3–5 years old)

Purpose:	To use a magnet to pick up metal objects.
Skills/ Concepts:	To learn that magnets attract metal. To learn that magnets don't attract wood.
Ages:	3 through 5 years old.
Length of Activity:	Allow 3 minutes.
Materials:	Small horseshoe magnet, one for each child Several metal objects, big enough so they won't be swallowed Several wooden objects Tray or pan, to hold all objects
Introduction:	Show children the magnet and say, "This is a magnet."
Procedure:	Pick up a metal object with the magnet and say, "Look what you can do with a magnet." Place tray of metal objects on a table. Say, "Magnets attract or pick up metal. Would you like to try?" Encourage children to pick up various objects. Place wooden objects on the tray and remove the metal objects. Ask children, "I wonder if the magnet will attract or pick up any of these objects?" Encourage children to try to pick up wooden objects using the magnet. Replace the metal objects on the tray. Again encourage the children to experiment with the magnet. If the children don't offer the observation that magnets attract metal, offer a few statements such as, "The magnet will pick up the bolt. I wonder if it will pick up the pencil?"

Closure: Conclude by saying, "Magnets will pick up metal, but magnets won't pick up wood."

Follow-up Activity: Encourage children to "test" the magnet on different objects in the room or outdoors. Help children identify which objects are wooden and which are metal.

WHAT WOULD HAPPEN IF?

Purpose: To play a game of making and testing predictions.

Skills/ Concepts: To develop thinking skills.
To use memory skills.

Ages: 2 through 5 years old.

Length of Activity: Allow 1½ to 3 minutes.

Materials: A large pom-pom

Introduction: Hold the pom-pom in front of you at shoulder level, and ask, "What am I doing with this pom-pom?"

Procedure: Continue by saying, "I'm holding the pom-pom in my hand. I wonder what would happen if I let go of the pom-pom." You may receive all types of answers; you want "It will fall," or "You would drop it." If children have trouble with the response, give them some verbal help. "Do you think it would fall?" Then drop the pom-pom. Ask children, "What happened?" It fell or you dropped it. "Yes, I was holding the pom-pom, but I let go and it fell to the floor." Encourage each child to try their hand at dropping the pom-pom.

Closure: Conclude by asking, "What happened to the pom-pom when I dropped it?"

Follow-up Activity: Try this activity outdoors using a cup of water. Ask the children, "What will happen if I pour the water on the ground?" "The ground will be wet," "There will be mud," "The water will be all gone" could be some answers. Encourage each child to try their hand at pouring the water.

MORE OR LESS

Purpose: To show more and less visually.

Skills/ Concepts: To measure and pour using a 1-cup measure and a teaspoon.
To use fine motor skills.
To discriminate more and less visually.

Ages: 18 months through 2 years old (will enjoy pouring the oatmeal); 3 through 5 years old

Length of Activity: Allow 5 minutes.

Materials:
Plastic 1-cup measure
Plastic teaspoon
Large plastic basin
Dry oatmeal

Introduction: Ask, "Would you like to measure some oatmeal?"

Procedure: Pour oatmeal into the basin. Place the cup and the teaspoon in the basin. Encourage children to take turns scooping and pouring oatmeal into the cup with the teaspoon. As the children pour the oatmeal ask, "Do you know which is the teaspoon?" Point to the measuring cup and say, "This is a measuring cup. I wonder which would hold more oatmeal, the teaspoon or the cup?" The children may or may not say the cup. If there is no response, help out by saying, "The cup will hold more oatmeal. Can you fill the cup and the teaspoon?" Ask, "Do you know which will hold less?" Children again may or may not offer an answer. Help out verbally if needed. Encourage each child to take a turn.

Closure: Conclude by saying, "Would you like to do some more measuring?"

Follow-up Activity: Expand this measuring activity by providing children with water in a sink or outdoors in a plastic dish pan.

PARQUETRY SHAPES

Purpose: To use a manipulative material to investigate geometric forms.

Skill/ Concept: To sort by color.

Ages: 18 months through 2 years old (will enjoy investigating the shapes); 3 through 5 years old.

Length of Activity: Allow 1 minute for 18 months through 2 years old; allow 3 minutes for 3 through 5 years old.

Materials: Set of parquetry shapes

For Adult to Do Ahead: If needed, make the parquetry shapes following the directions on page xv.

Introduction: Begin activity by saying, "I have a set of cards. They are called parquetry shapes. We are going to play a sorting game with them."

Procedure: Lay shapes on the table. Encourage the children to investigate and touch them. "Let's see if we can name all the colors." As a child picks up a piece, help with identifying the color if needed and put each color in a separate pile.

Closure: Conclude activity by asking, "Which color do you like the best?"

Follow-up Activity: Play another sorting game using the shapes of the cards to form different piles. Encourage children to identify each shape before placing the cards into piles. Individual cards may be placed together to form bigger shapes.

TURKEY TAIL MATCHING GAME

Purpose:	To play a matching game.
Skills/ Concepts:	To identify colors. To match colors.
Ages:	18 months through 2 years old (will enjoy placing tail feathers on turkey in any random pattern); 3 through 5 years old.
Length of Activity:	Allow 1 or 2 minutes.
Materials:	Turkey game board Felt feathers
For Adult to Do Ahead:	Make turkey game board and felt feathers. Trace or copy turkey pattern (page 65) onto brown paper. Cut out and glue to heavy cardboard. Cut feather shapes out of colored construction paper. Glue feathers to cardboard at top of turkey. Cover turkey with clear contact paper. Cut another set of feathers out of colored felt to match the feathers on the turkey.
Introduction:	Begin by saying, "I have a matching game for you to play."
Procedure:	Place game board facing child. Place felt feather next to board. Say, "Here is a turkey. Can you place the red feather (hand child red feather) on top of the red feather on the turkey?" Offer verbal assistance if the child has trouble. Continue the game until all of the feathers have been placed on the game board. If child is still interested in playing ask, "Can you hand me the red feather? the blue feather?" and so on. Lay the feathers down so the child can match them again.
Closure:	At the end say, "I enjoyed playing this game with you. Let's leave the turkey matching game out on a tray to be used again."
Follow-up Activity:	Use the felt feathers to play another matching game. Ask children to place the colored felt feathers on objects of the same color in the room.

MY FAMILY

Purpose:	To talk about family members.
Skill/ Concept:	To identify relatives.
Ages:	18 months through 5 years old.
Length of Activity:	Allow 2 or 3 minutes.
Materials:	Photographs of immediate family members of each child, with proper identification on the back of each photograph Construction paper Paper photograph tabs Clear acetate sheets or clear cling sandwich wrap

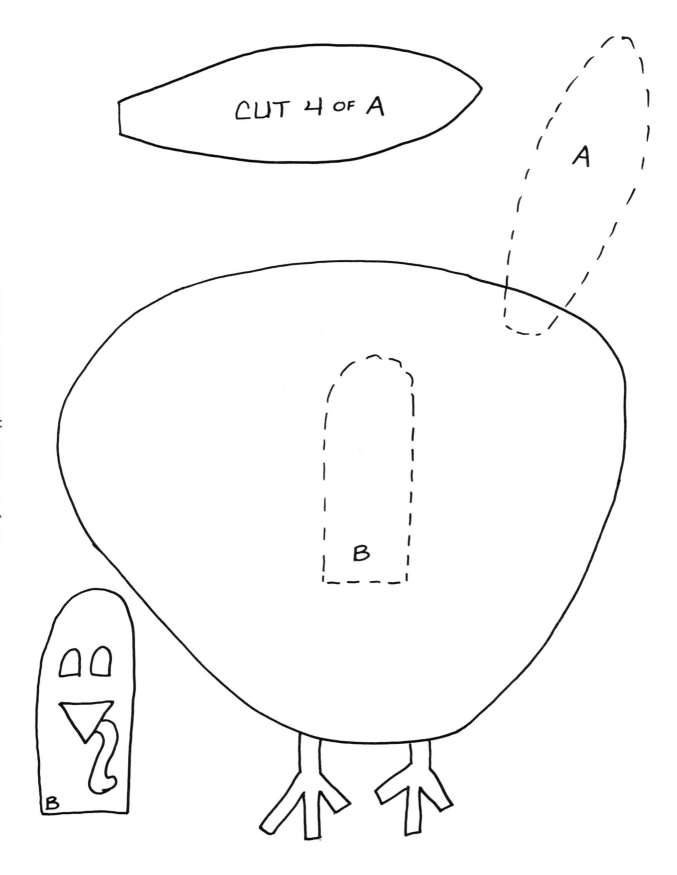

CUT 4 OF A

A

B

B

For Adult to Do Ahead:	Use the photograph tabs to mount pictures on construction paper. Cover mounted pictures with clear acetate sheets or clear cling sandwich wrap.
Introduction:	Hold up one of the photo sheets and say, "These people look familiar." "Do you know who these people are?"
Procedure:	Give verbal assistance if needed for identification of pictures. "Yes, this is *(name)*. She(He) is your *(name)*." The children may not need prompting for family names and roles. Continue until all pictures are identified.
Closure:	Conclude by saying, "Let's put these pictures where you can all look at them whenever you like." Picture sheets may be taped or tacked to the wall or a bulletin board.
Follow-up Activity:	Provide children with crayons or markers and plain white paper. Ask children to draw a picture of their mother, father, sister, a favorite person. Be sure to label who each child has drawn.

LET'S GO VISIT THE GROCERY STORE

Purpose:	To talk about what you do at the grocery store.
Skills/ Concepts:	To identify foods. To use memory to recall what you find at the grocery store. To expand vocabulary.
Ages:	18 months through 5 years old.
Length of Activity:	Allow 3 minutes.
Materials:	Pictures of foods found at a grocery store Flannel board
For Adult to Do Ahead:	Mount pictures of foods and items found at grocery store on large pieces of flannel.
Introduction:	Begin by asking, "Where do you go to buy food?" Grocery store, supermarket, health food store.
Procedure:	Continue by asking, "Do you ever go to the grocery store? What do you get at the grocery store?" Children may specify certain foods. "What other types of food might you find at the grocery store?" As the children suggest different foods, let them pick the flannel piece and place it on the flannel board. Other things to talk about might be favorite foods, foods that are good for you and your body (nutrition), and food groups.
Closure:	End the activity by saying, "It's fun to visit the grocery store. There are lots of different things to see."
Follow-up Activities:	Set up a grocery store. Provide children with empty boxes and cans to stock shelves. Brown paper bags are great to fill with groceries. A toy cash register and a toy shopping cart are fun optional items.
	Let children make collages using pictures of their favorite foods. Provide children with pictures of foods, paste, and construction paper. After children pick pictures of some of their favorite foods, help them paste the pictures on paper.

FAMILY PARTY

Purpose:	To make party invitations for family members.
Skill/ Concept:	To invite people to a party.
Ages:	18 months through 5 years old.
Length of Activity:	Allow 5 to 10 minutes.
Materials:	Colored construction paper Markers Seasonal stickers

For Adult to Do Ahead: Cut 8-inch by 12-inch pieces of construction paper in half. Fold each half in half again to form a card. Write party specifics on the inside of the card:

You are invited
to a party

Place_____
Time_____
Date_____

Introduction:	Begin by saying, "We are going to invite some people for a party. Let's ask your family. Can you tell me who is in your family?"
Procedure:	Help children to list family members. Say to them, "We are going to give each person a card that will invite him or her to our party. Could you decorate the cards for me?" Provide the children with markers and stickers to decorate the cards.
Closure:	Conclude by saying, "What beautiful party invitations. Now we will give each person on our list a card."

Follow-up Activity:	Some party suggestions:
	    Peanut butter raisin bread sandwiches, pages 58–59
	    Warm apple cider punch, page 59
	    Fingerplays, pages 57–58
	    Songs, pages 52–54

RUNNING INDOORS

Purpose:	To teach indoor safety.
Skills/ Concepts:	To learn the difference between running and walking. To learn classroom safety rule.
Ages:	18 months through 5 years old.
Length of Activity:	Allow 1 minute.
Introduction:	As you walk across the room ask, "What am I doing?" Walking. Run a few steps and ask, "What am I doing?" Running.

Procedure: Continue by asking, "What could happen if I run inside (the house/school)?" Elicit answers from children. They might include could trip/fall and hurt me, could bump into someone, could bump into something and hurt myself, could knock something over and break it. "Do you think we should run in the house/school?" An older child might offer "No, walk." "We should walk when we are inside. Running is a lot of fun, and it's good exercise too. Where do you think is a good place to run?" Outside or outdoors.

Closure: Conclude activity by saying, "Let's walk to get our coats. Then we will walk outside where we can run and play."

Follow-up Activities: Outdoors play a running game. When you say the word "RUN," the children should run, but when you say the word "WALK," the children should walk. Alternate between saying run and walk.

Play the same game with a child as the leader and you join the other children in running or walking.

SNEEZING

Purpose: To teach child what to do when they sneeze.

Skills/ Concepts: To cover your nose and mouth with a tissue or hand.
To blow your nose.
To learn that germs spread illness.

Ages: 18 months through 2 years old (the younger child will watch, listen, and learn from the adult and older children present—it's never too soon to begin good health habits); 3 through 5 years old.

Length of Activity: Allow 2 minutes.

Materials: Box of facial tissue
Spray bottle, filled with water.

Introduction: Begin by asking children, "What happens when you sneeze?" Children may not know.

Procedure: Continue by saying, "I'll show you. This spray bottle is like your nose when you sneeze. Watch what happens when I make this bottle sneeze." Have a child hold out a hand and give spray bottle a squeeze. "What happened to your hand?" It got wet. "When you sneeze if you don't cover your nose with something you will spray germs all over. Watch what happens when I use a tissue to cover this bottle." Spray the bottle while holding a tissue to catch the spray. The water should collect in the tissue. "What happened to the tissue?" It got wet. "Let's pretend to sneeze." Cover your nose and mouth with a tissue as you sneeze. "When I sneeze I collect the germs in the tissue so I do not spray them around the room. What should I do with this tissue now?" Throw it in the trash or wastebasket. "What should you do if you don't have a tissue when you sneeze?" Older children may respond with cover your nose and mouth with your hand. "Sometimes after you sneeze you need to blow your nose. What should you use to blow your nose?" A tissue or handkerchief. "When you are done blowing your nose where should the tissue go?" In the trash or wastebasket.

Closure: Conclude by saying, "The last thing you should do is wash your hands to wash off any germs that might be on them. Be sure to use soap and warm water."

Follow-up Activity: Read *Germs Make Me Sick* by Parnell Donohue. New York: Alfred A. Knopf, 1975.

DECEMBER ACTIVITIES

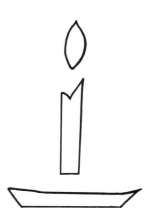

THEME: *Holiday Traditions*
SPECIAL DAYS: *Hanukkah*
Christmas

ART:	Stenciled Candle
	Christmas Trees
	Potato Print Bells
MUSIC:	We Wish You a . . .
	Christmas Bells
	The Lights
MOVEMENT:	Following the Leader
	Log Rolling
	Push/Pull Box
LANGUAGE:	Here's a Cup
	Make a Rhyme
	The Night Before Christmas
NUTRITION:	Paintbrush Cookies
	Milk Punch
	Potato Latkes
SCIENCE/ NATURE:	Sense of Touch
	Feed the Birds
	Reflections
MATH:	Building with Inch Cubes
	Advent/Hanukkah Calendar
	Sorting By Number
SOCIAL/ STUDIES:	Piñata
	Who Am I?
	Let's Have a Holiday Party
HEALTH/ SAFETY:	Let's Eat
	Cover Your Mouth
	Rub-A-Dub

STENCILED CANDLE

Purpose:	To create a holiday ornament.
Skills/ Concepts:	To use a stencil. To follow directions. To identify color.
Ages:	18 months through 2 years old (with help); 3 through 5 years old.
Length of Activity:	Allow 1 or 2 minutes, at three different sessions.
Materials:	Newspaper White felt, 3 inches square, for each child Stencil paper, available at craft and hobby stores Exacto knife Red, green, and yellow tempera paint Three pieces of sponge with a clip clothes pin at one end Masking tape
For Adult to Do Ahead:	Using the accompanying pattern for the candle, flame and holder, cut stencils out of stencil paper with the exacto knife. Cover work area with newspaper and tape in place. Cut 3-inch felt squares.
Introduction:	Show a completed stencil and ask, "Do you know what this is a picture off?" A candle. "Yes, a candle with a flame in a holder." Point to each section. "Let's make a candle."

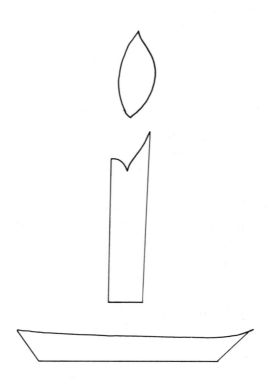

Procedure: Tape white piece of felt to covered work table. Tape holder stencil over white felt. Instruct the children, "Dip the sponge into the green paint. Fill in the stencil with the green paint. Now we need to let the paint dry." Carefully remove the stencil. Paint takes approximately 10 minutes to dry. Repeat with candle stencil lined up over the holder. Use the red paint to fill in the stencil. Repeat again by lining the flame up over the candle stencil. Use the yellow paint to fill in the stencil.

Closure: Conclude by asking, "What color did you paint the holder for your candle? What color did you paint the candle? What color did you paint the flame of your candle?"

Follow-up Activity: Turn the stenciled candle into an ornament. Cut 3-inch felt squares, one for each child. Cut 2-inch cardboard squares, one for each child. Paste or glue the cardboard square to the middle of a green square. Glue the stenciled candle to the cardboard/green felt. Ornament may be hung with a piece of heavy cotton thread or yarn.

CHRISTMAS TREES

Purpose: To create a simple holiday decoration.

Skills/ Concepts: To use fine motor skills for tearing, placement of stickers.
To identify a triangle.
To identify a rectangle.

Ages: 18 months through 5 years old.

Length of Activity: Allow 3 minutes.

Materials: Green construction paper, one-half of an 8½-inch by 11 inch sheet per child
Brown construction paper
Paste or glue
Cotton swab
Picture of an evergreen tree
Triangle cut out of construction paper
Rectangle cut out of construction paper

Introduction: Begin activity by saying, "I have a picture to show you. Can you tell me what this picture is?" Answers may range from Christmas tree or tree, to evergreen or pine tree. "What shape does this tree look like?" Older children may be able to identify the shape as that of a triangle.

Procedure: Continue with, "Today we are going to make a Christmas tree by tearing a piece of paper into the shape of a triangle. Here is what a triangle shape looks like." Hold up paper triangle. "Let's try tearing our pieces of green paper." Children may need assistance to start the tearing. Older children will be able to tear shapes that resemble trees. "Next we are going to tear a brown rectangle. A rectangle looks like this." Hold up paper rectangle. Assist children if needed. Older children can tear an extra tree and trunk for a toddler. Toddlers may enjoy tearing scraps of paper but will not be able to tear paper into a particular shape. Using the cotton swab, children can attach the trunk to the bottom of the triangular tree shape. "Let's use these colorful stickers to decorate our trees." Distribute 10 to 12 stickers to each child. Toddlers will really enjoy this part of the activity.

Closure: Conclude by asking, "Would you like to tape your tree to the wall or would you like to put your tree in your art folder?"

Follow-up
Activities: Decorate a tree outdoors for the birds. Make five or six pinecone/peanut butter bird feeders (page 82). Equipped with a blunt needle and heavy thread, older children can string chunks of fruit and vegetables to be hung from tree branches.
Read *Stregna Nona* Retold by Tomie de Paola New Jersey: Prentice-Hall, 1975.

POTATO PRINT BELLS

Purpose: To make a vegetable print.

Skills/
Concepts: To identify colors.
To use fine motor skills for dipping and pressing.

Ages: 2 through 5 years old.

Length of
Activity: Allow 5 minutes.

Materials: Raw potatoes, two
Bell-shaped cookie cutter
White construction paper, one piece per child
Red or green tempera paint, in bowls
Masking tape
Hand bell

For Adult to
Do Ahead: Cut one potato into thick slices. Press cookie cutter into slices to form bells. Fold paper in half to form a card. Cover work area with newspaper and tape in place.

Introduction: Begin by asking, "Can anyone tell me what I'm holding in my hand?" A bell. "What sound does a bell make?" It rings. "Would you like to ring the bell?" Encourage each child to take a turn to ring the bell.

Procedure: Continue with, "Let's make a holiday card with a bell on it. Do you know what kind of a vegetable this is?" Potato. "These are slices of potato. You are going to dip the slices into paint and then press the slices on paper. You may pick red or green paint. Dip your potato into paint. Now place the potato, paint side down, on your white paper and gently press. Lift the potato from the paper. What a beautiful print." If there is room on the paper, add more bell prints.

Closure: Conclude by saying, "We've used a potato to print many colorful bells today. What colors did we use? What color is your paper?"

Follow-up
Activity: Cut an apple in half crosswise, leaving the seeds in place. Use the apple half to print. The core will make a star design in the print.

WE WISH YOU A . . .

Purpose: To sing a song that can be sung for Hanukkah or Christmas.

Skill/
Concept: To sing a simple song.

Ages: 18 months through 5 years old.

Length of Activity:	Allow 1 minute.
Materials:	Song
Introduction:	Begin by saying, "At this time of year some people celebrate the holiday Christmas and some people celebrate the holiday Hanukkah. I know a song we can sing about both holidays.
Procedure:	Sing the song "We Wish You a Merry Christmas" through, and invite the children to sing with you a second time.

> 2. We wish you a happy Hanukkah,
>   We wish you a happy Hanukkah,
>   We wish you a happy Hanukkah,
>   And a happy holiday!

Closure:	Close with, "What a happy song to sing for your family and friends."
Follow-up Activities:	Have children form a circle and hold hands. As they sing the song, they should dance around the circle. Read *Nine Days to Christmas* by Marie Hall Ets and Aurora Labastida New York: Viking, 1959.

CHRISTMAS BELLS

Purpose:	To sing a holiday song.
Skill/ Concept:	To memorize a verse and a chorus.
Ages:	18 months through 5 years old.
Length of Activity:	Allow 2 or 3 minutes
Materials:	Picture of a horse pulling a sleigh Different types of bells Song
Introduction:	Introduce activity by saying, "Many years ago people traveled in sleighs pulled by horses."
Procedure:	Show picture of the sleigh. "This is a sleigh pulled by a horse. Sometimes bells were attached to the horse. At Christmas time bells are used for decorations. Bells make a jingling sound." Give each child a turn to ring bells. Comment on the sound the bells make. "Let's sing a song about Christmas bells."
Closure:	Conclude by asking, "Which bell did you like to hear ring?"
Follow-up Activities:	Give the children bells to shake while singing the song. Sing the song "Jingle Bells." Read *The Polar Express* by Chris Van Allsburg Boston: Houghton-Mifflin, 1985.

Christmas Bells

Words and music by:
JoAnne C. Calvarese

Jin-gle, jan-gle, Christ-mas bells. Jing-le, jang-le through the air. Ring-ing, sing-ing never a care, Hear those Christ-mas bells. Jing-le, jan-gle, jin-gle, jang-le hear those Christ-mas bells. Jing-le, jan-gle, jin-gle, jan-gle hear those Christ-mas bells.

THE LIGHTS

Purpose:	To sing a simple Hanukkah song.
Skill/ Concept:	To memorize a song.
Ages:	18 months through 5 years old.
Length of Activity:	Allow 1 or 2 minutes.
Materials:	Song Dreydel (available through Metropolitan Museum of Art, 255 Gracie Station, New York, NY 10028)
Introduction:	Tell children, "Hanukkah is a festival that many Jewish people celebrate. It is often called the festival of lights and many candles are used. A special toy that Jewish children play with is called a dreydel. Let's sing a song about Hanukkah."
Procedure:	Sing the song. Invite the children to sing the song with you. Show the children how to play the dreydel game.
Closure:	Ask children, "Do you have special toys you like to play with?"

Hanukkah

Words and music by:
JoAnne C. Calvarese

Softly shining in the night, Flicker on the table bright,
Lights, oh see the festive lights Flicker on the table bright.

2. What's that spinning round and round,
   Hardly seems to touch the ground.
   See my dreydel spinning round.
   Doesn't seem to touch the ground.

FOLLOWING THE LEADER

Purpose:	To follow someone.
Skills/ Concepts:	To walk on a line. To understand the concepts in front of and in back of. To follow someone.
Ages:	18 months through 2 years old (will enjoy the attempt to walk on the line); 3 through 5 years old (will be able to follow each other with verbal guidance).
Length of Activity:	Allow 5 minutes.
Materials:	White line, painted outdoors or taped to the floor inside
Introduction:	Introduce activity by saying, "Follow the leader is a fun game to play inside or outside. Let's line up on the white line to play this game."
Procedure:	Ask an older child to be the leader to start. "We are going to follow Katie as she walks on the line." You will need to give some verbal directions such as "Alison stay behind Katie" or "Thomas, Mike should be in front of you." Let different children take turns as the leader.
Closure:	Conclude by saying, "Did you enjoy walking on the line?"
Follow-up Activities:	Make the game more complex by leading the children around the playyard. As they gain skill lead the children through a maze set up indoors or outdoors. An even more complex version of the game might be to have the children change gait as they follow the leader—from walking to hopping, skipping, jumping, or running. Listen to the song "We're Following the Leader" from the movie *Peter Pan* by Walt Disney.

LOG ROLLING

Purpose:	To learn a simple tumbling exercise.
Skills/ Concepts:	To lie down in a "log position." To roll over.
Ages:	18 months through 5 years old.
Length of Activity:	Allow 5 to 10 minutes, depending on the number of children.
Materials:	Tumbling mat or exercise mat Small log
Introduction:	Hold up the log. Say, "This is a log. It is a piece of wood that is long and straight. Show me how you would make your body look like a log." Children may stand straight up with arms and hands by sides or down with arms and hands at sides.
Procedure:	Roll the log along the floor. Say, "Let's take turns being logs. We can roll over and over. We can pretend we're rolling down a hill or down a river. You will lie flat at one end of the mat. Place your arms by your sides. Now try to roll your whole body over—keeping your arms by your sides as you roll. You may keep rolling until you get to the end of the mat." Let children take turns one at a time on the mat so they do not poke or bump one another.
Closure:	Ask, "Did you have fun doing log rolls? Maybe we can do them again soon."
Follow-up Activity:	Make "bugs on a log" for snack. Slice a banana in half lengthwise. Spread peanut butter on the cut side. Place a few raisins in the peanut butter—the pretend bugs. A fun and nutritious snack.

PUSH/PULL BOX

Purpose:	To play a holiday game.
Skill/ Concept:	To develop the gross motor skills pushing and pulling.
Ages:	18 months through 5 years old.
Length of Activity:	Allow 1 to 10 minutes, depending on interest of children
Materials:	Empty cardboard box Red or green contact paper Holiday stickers
For Adult to Do Ahead:	Cover four sides of the box with contact paper to resemble a gift. Leave the bottom of the box open and uncovered. Ribbons can be glued or tied on sides. Children may add stickers for decoration.
Introduction:	Begin by asking, "What does this look like?" A present or gift. "Yes, it is wrapped like a present but it is really empty inside." Show children the box is empty. "This is a push and pull box."

Procedure: Continue with, "You are going to push this box across the floor." Show children how to push the box across the floor. "Then you are going to pull the box back." Again show the children. Encourage children to all try pushing and pulling the box.

Closure: Ask, "Did you enjoy pushing and pulling the box?"

Follow-up Activities: Use the box as a "holiday train."
Read *The Little Engine That Could* by Watty Piper, New York: Scholastic Books, 1979 for a good quiet time activity.

HERE'S A CUP

Purpose: To learn a simple fingerplay.

Skills/ Concepts: To repeat a simple poem.
To use simple finger movements to accompany a poem.

Ages: 18 months through 5 years old.

Length of Activity: Allow 1 or 2 minutes.

Materials: Poem

Introduction: Begin with, "Let's have a cup of tea."

Procedure: Recite the fingerplay for the children. Invite the children to join saying the poem a second time. The children may ask to repeat the poem a third time.

This is a cup,	(Make a circle with thumb and fingers of left hand.)
This is a cup,	(Make a circle with thumb and fingers of right hand.)
And this is a pot of tea.	(Make a fist with right hand with thumb sticking out.)
Pour one cup,	(Pour into circle in left hand.)
Pour two cups,	(Pour into circle in right hand.)
And have some tea with me.	(Offer circle cup in right hand to person sitting next to you.)

Closure: Conclude with, "It's fun to share with other people. Would you like to have a real tea party?"

Follow-up Activity: Provide children with child-sized teapot and cups. Fill teapot with juice or water to be served to each other by the children.

MAKE A RHYME

Purpose: To read a book that rhymes.

Skills/ Concepts: To learn some words rhyme (sound alike).
To expand vocabulary.

Ages: 18 months through 5 years old.

Length of Activity: Allow 3 minutes.

Materials: Book, *Hop on Pop* by Dr. Seuss New York: Random House, 1963.

Introduction: Begin by saying, "The fat cat sat. Some of those words sound alike, they rhyme. I know a rhyming story."

Procedure: Read the story to the children. The younger child, 18 months to 2 years old, may enjoy hearing just the boldface print words on each page. Older children may be able to fill in some of the rhyming words if you say the first word or phrase and leave the ending for them to add.

Closure: Conclude by saying, "Making rhymes is fun. Can you think of a word that sounds like your name?"

Follow-up Activities: Older children enjoy making rhymes anytime. Play a rhyming game and let the children take turns being the leader.
Read *The Rooster Crows* by Maud and Miska Petersham New York: Macmillan, 1945. A Collection of American Rhymes and Jingles.

THE NIGHT BEFORE CHRISTMAS

Purpose: To read a poem about Christmas.

Skills/ Concepts: To listen to a poem.
To expand attention span.
To expand vocabulary.

Ages: 18 months through 5 years old.

Length of Activity: Allow 3 minutes.

Materials: Book, *The Night Before Christmas* by Clement C. Moore Racine, Wisconsin: Western Publishing Company, 1981.

Introduction: Introduce this activity by saying, "There is a special story that is read at Christmas. It is called *The Night Before Christmas*."

Procedure: Read the story. Be sure to explain unfamiliar words to the children. A book with good pictures will help explain some words.

Closure: Conclude by asking, "Can you remember something that happened in this story?"

Follow-up Activity: Make stockings to hang on the wall. Older children can trace on red construction paper a pre-cut poster-board stocking shape. Cut one out for each child in the class. All children can help paste cotton balls to top of stocking for a trim. Adult may write name on stockings for children who cannot yet write their names.

PAINTBRUSH COOKIES

Purpose:	To make a holiday snack.
Skills/ Concepts:	To identify colors. To use small motor skills for painting.
Ages:	2 through 5 years old.
Length of Activity:	Allow 10 minutes.

Materials:

Refrigerator sugar cookies or your own recipe prepared in advance	
Butter knife	¼ teaspoon of water
Plastic butter knife	Food coloring
Cookie sheets	Small paintbrushes
Small bowls	Waxed paper
1 egg yolk	

For Adult to Do Ahead:	Mix the egg yolk and water, beat together. Divide into several small bowls. Add 2 or 3 drops of food color to each bowl and mix.
Introduction:	Introduce activity by saying, "A few days ago we made candle ornaments to decorate our classroom. Today we are going to make ornament cookies for our party."
Procedure:	Older children may take turns slicing roll of cookie dough into circles. Place cookie dough circles on wax paper. Children should paint the cookies with the egg yolk paint. Gently place cookies on cookie sheet.
For Adult to Do Ahead:	Bake cookies at 350°F. for 6 to 8 minutes.
Closure:	Close by saying, "Who can tell me what colors we used on our cookies today?"
Follow-up Activity:	Use spools of thread for a color matching game that uses the same colors used to paint the cookies.

MILK PUNCH

Purpose:	To make a drink for the holiday party.
Skills/ Concepts:	To identify foods. To measure foods. To mix foods.
Ages:	18 months through 5 years old.
Length of Activity:	Allow 2 minutes.

Materials:

Quart of milk	Vanilla ice cream, 1 to 2 tablespoons per child
Honey, 1 teaspoon per child	Paper cups, one per child
Nutmeg, a sprinkle per child	Plastic spoons, one per child

Introduction: Begin activity by saying, "We need something to drink for our party. Let's make milk punch."

Procedure: As ingredients are added, encourage children to identify them. Offer assistance to children when needed. Give each child a cup half filled with milk. Show children how to dip a spoon into the honey and stir it into their cup of milk. Help children sprinkle nutmeg onto their cups of punch. Add 1 or 2 tablespoons of ice cream to each cup. The children may want to stir their punch until the ice cream melts a little.

Closure: Conclude by saying, "Who can remember what ingredients we used to make our milk punch?"

Follow-up Activity: Older children will enjoy making a bigger bowl of punch to be served at the party.

POTATO LATKES

Purpose: To prepare a Hanukkah snack.

Skills/ Concepts:
To count to 2, 6, and 8.
To grate potatoes.
To stir.
To identify foods.

Ages: 18 months through 5 years old.

Length of Activity: Allow 15 minutes.

Materials:

FOOD	*UTENSILS*
6 medium potatoes	Plastic grater
2 T. flour	Paper towels
2 T. light cream	Bowl
2 eggs, beaten	Spoon
8 T. olive or safflower oil	Measuring spoons
	Spatula
	Frying pan

For Adult to Do Ahead:
Peel and halve the potatoes.
NOTE: This activity requires two adults.

Introduction: Begin activity by saying, "Hanukkah is a special holiday for people who are Jewish. Today we are going to make potato latkes. They look similar to pancakes and are eaten at Hanukkah."

Procedure: Help all children wash their hands. With your assistance, children should take turns rubbing halves of potatoes against the grater. Place potatoes on several layers of paper towels. Towels should then be folded around potatoes and twisted and squeezed to remove all the moisture. Children will enjoy helping with this task. As the ingredients are measured and added to the bowl, encourage children to count out loud. Put potatoes into bowl and add flour, cream, and egg. Children may take turns tossing ingredients together with a spoon until they are mixed.

For Second Adult:	Heat oil in frying pan. Put about 2 T. of the potato mixture in pan; press and shape with spatula into a flat 3½-inch pancake. Repeat until pan is full. Cook each pancake for 5 minutes at medium-low heat until bottom is crisp and brown; then turn and cook other side for 5 more minutes. Keep warm in a 300°F. oven until all are ready. Makes 18 servings.
Closure:	Close by saying, "Let's sing some songs while we wait for our treat to cook."
Follow-up Activity:	Serve potato latkes to children with apple sauce.

SENSE OF TOUCH

Purpose:	To increase the awareness of the sense of touch.
Skills/ Concepts:	To feel things with your skin. To use hands and fingers to touch. To learn the difference between smooth/rough, soft/hard, warm/cold.
Ages:	18 months through 5 years old.
Length of Activity:	Allow 3 minutes.
Materials:	Two blocks of wood 2 inches by 3 inches Piece of rough sandpaper, 2 inches by 3 inches Small foam ball, available at a toy store Golf ball Cup half filled with cold water Cup half filled with warm water
For Adult to Do Ahead:	Glue the piece of sandpaper to the top of one block of wood. Sand the other piece of wood smooth.
Introduction:	Say to the children, "Your body is covered with skin. Your skin can feel things that are hot or cold; soft or hard."
Procedure:	Continue with, "We are going to touch some objects with our hands and fingers." Place the two wood blocks on a tray. Encourage the children to pick up the blocks and feel them. Ask the children, "Which block feels rough?" and help identify the rough block. "Which block feels smooth?" Help with its identification. Do the same with the balls and use the words soft and hard. Then place the two cups on the tray. Encourage the children to feel the outside of the cups, or to feel the water with their fingers. Help identify the cold water or cup and the warm water or cup.
Closure:	Close by asking, "Can you show me something rough and something smooth? Can you show me something soft and something hard? Can you show me something cold and something warm?"
Follow-up Activities:	Make a mystery bag by placing some small objects, such as a doll's shoe, a block, a pinecone, or a shell, for example, in a small fabric bag or a lunch bag. Children should identify objects from the way they feel before removing objects from the bag.

Make several "texture boards." Glue objects with very different textures such as carpet samples, foam rubber, styrofoam peanuts, crumpled wax paper etc. to heavy cardboard. These boards may be walked on with bare feet or felt with fingers and hands. Encourage the children to talk about how the different textures feel.

Read the book "Touch" by J. M. Parramon and J. J. Puig New York: Barron's Books.

FEED THE BIRDS

Purpose:	To feed birds native to your area.
Skill/ Concept:	To observe birds "feeding."
Ages:	18 months through 5 years old.
Length of Activity:	Allow 10 minutes to set up and plan for daily check of feeder.
Materials:	These materials will make three different feeders. Bird feed (check with local pet shop or feed store for bird seed: sunflower seeds, shelled and unsalted cracked corn, millet seeds) Medium-sized pinecones, two per child ½ cup peanut butter Plastic butter knife Old natural-bristle scrub brush Thin wire Bacon fat, melted 2 or 3 mesh onion bags Plastic margarine container Bowls for seeds
For Adult to Do Ahead:	Check with library or feed store for details about what birds are native to your area and what those birds eat. Melt bacon fat and cool until it has almost hardened. Place mesh bags inside each other. Punch a hole in the bottom of the margarine container.
Introduction:	Begin activity by saying, "Sometimes animals need help finding food in the winter. Would you like to help fix a snack for the birds?"
Procedure:	1. Show the children the pinecones and help with identification if needed. Tell the children, "We're going to spread the peanut butter on the pinecone. We will spread the peanut butter between and over the scales on the pinecone. After we have spread peanut butter on the pinecone, we will roll the pinecone in a dish of seeds." Twist wire around the middle of pinecones and attach to a tree in a safe spot away from cats. 2. "Birds like to eat fat. This is bacon fat." Show children fat. "Can you dip this brush into this dish of bacon fat?" Ask another child to dip the brush into a dish of seeds. "Now we will hang this brush in a tree." Hold brush flat against the trunk of a tree with the bristles facing away from the tree. Wrap wire around the top and bottom of the brush and twist the ends of the wire tight. Attach to a tree in an area away from cats.

3. Show children mesh bags. "These are onion bags. We are going to fill the bags with two kinds of seeds for the birds. Let's put sunflower seeds in the bottom." Hold the bag while children take turns placing seeds in the bottom half of the bag. When the bag is half full, wrap a piece of wire around the bag. "Let's fill the rest of the bag with corn." Hold the bag while the children fill the bag with corn. Tie the top of the bag with wire. Pull top of the bag through hole in the margarine container. Attach the bag with wire to a tree branch in a safe spot away from cats.

Closure:
Conclude by saying, "Now that we have started to feed the birds, we must continue to feed them. The birds will depend on our food. We will check every day to see if our peanut butter pinecone, seed brush, and seed bag need to be refilled."

Follow-up
Activities:
Visit the library for a good bird identification book.
Watch for birds at feeders and keep a record of the types of birds that visit the feeders.
Read *The Big Snow* by Berta Hader and Elmer Hader New York: Macmillan, 1948. This book tells how animals cope during the long winter season.

REFLECTIONS

Purpose:
To identify objects by their reflection.

Skills/
Concepts:
To identify objects
To expand vocabulary

Ages:
18 months through 5 years old.

Length of
Activity:
Allow 2 minutes.

Materials:
Mirror, any size
Tray, for small objects
Small objects (doll, car, stuffed animal, shoe or sneaker)

Introduction:
Show the children the mirror and say, "This is a mirror."

Procedure:
Continue with, "If I look in the mirror I can see myself. If I hold something in front of the mirror what can I see?" Hold the toy car in front of the mirror. "Yes, I can see the car in the mirror. Would you like to try?" Give each child a turn at the mirror with the tray of small objects. As each child holds the objects in front of the mirror help the other children identify them.

Closure:
Conclude by saying, "Let's all look in the mirror and see who we see."

Follow-up
Activity:
After using the mirror, it will need to be cleaned. Provide children with a small dish of water, a cotton swab, and a soft rag. A younger child may need your assistance to spread water on the mirror using the cotton swab. When the mirror is wet, the mirror can be gently wiped with the rag.

BUILDING WITH INCH CUBES

Purpose: To match colored inch cubes with pattern cards.

Skills/
Concepts: To match patterns.
To match colors.

Ages: 18 months through 2 years old (will enjoy building with the cubes); 3 through 5 years old.

Length of
Activity: Allow 5 to 10 minutes.

Materials: 25 to 30 inch cubes, store bought or make your own (cut pieces of wood into inch lengths, sand, and spray paint) see page xvi.
Cards, with inch square patterns on them (can be colored or pieces of colored construction paper)

Introduction: Begin by saying, "I have a card with a pattern on it. Can you put an inch cube on each color?"

Procedure: Continue with, "Now let's see if you can make some patterns on the table." Have several cards with different patterns on the table. Offer assistance if needed.

Closure: Conclude activity with, "Let's place the cards and cubes in a basket so you may use them again if you want."

Follow-up
Activities: Use the cubes for building.
Use the cubes to play a color sorting game.

ADVENT/HANUKKAH CALENDAR

Purpose: To provide a sequencing activity.

Skills/
Concepts: To count.
To recognize numbers.
To recognize passage of time.

Ages: 18 months through 5 years old.

Length of
Activity: Allow 1 minute each day from December 1 until Hanukkah or Christmas.

Materials: Posterboard or heavy construction paper or flannel board
Holiday stickers or felt ornaments if using flannel board

For Adult to
Do Ahead: Label posterboard with the month and days of the week. Divide board as a calendar. Number the days with markers.

Introduction: Ask, "Who knows what this is? Yes, it is a calendar. Did you know that there are _____days until Hanukkah/Christmas? Let's keep track of the days."

Procedure: Continue, "Eric, would you please find number 1 on the calendar? Good. Now will you place a sticker on the number 1? Thank you."

Closure: Then ask, "Does anyone know what number comes after 1? Yes, 2 comes after 1. Tomorrow we will put a sticker on number 2."

Follow-up Activities: Make a paper chain with one link for each day before the holiday. Children can take turns pulling one link from the chain every day.

Read *Morris' Disappearing Bag* by Rosemary Wells New York: Dial Books, 1975.

SORTING BY NUMBER

Purpose: To sort sticks by number into a numbered container.

Skills/ Concepts: To recognize the number values of 1. 2. 3.
To develop the fine motor skills of picking up sticks and placing them in a container.

Ages: 3 years old through 5 years old.

Length of Activity: Allow 5 to 10 minutes.

Materials: 3 plastic bowls or boxes
Waterproof magic marker
Popsicle sticks or tongue depressors

For Adult to Do Ahead: Label the containers 1. 2. 3.
Place one stick in the container marked 1. place two sticks in the container marked 2. and place three sticks in the container marked 3.

Introduction: Note: This activity should be completed with one child at a time. Begin by saying, "I have three containers. Would you please help me count the sticks in the containers?"

Procedure: Point to the container marked 1 and continue by saying, "How many sticks are in this container?" One. "What is the number on the side of the container?" One. "Good. What about the next container? How many sticks are in it?" Two. "And what is the number on the side of the container?" Two. "Great. Finally I'd like you to count how many sticks are in this last container." Three. "And what is the number on the side of the container?" Three. "Good. So there is one stick in the container marked 1 and how many sticks are in the container marked 2?" Two. "And there are three sticks in the container marked with _____ on it?" Three. "Now let's take all of the sticks out of the containers and see if you can put the right number of sticks in each container." Allow the child to repeat this activity by herself. It may take some verbal direction from you the first few times.

Closure: Conclude by saying, "Let's put these materials away on the shelf so we can play with them another time."

Follow-up Activity: Every few weeks you can add one new container to this activity with the next number marked on it. Be sure the appropriate number of sticks are available.

PIÑATA

Purpose:	To make a piñata.
Skill/ Concept:	To follow directions.
Ages:	3 through 5 years old.
Length of Activity:	Allow 10 minutes, on two different days, and plan on 24 hours to dry.

Materials:

Picture of a piñata	Spoon
Large round balloon	Newspaper
2 cups of flour	Colored tissue paper
1 cup liquid starch	Glue
1 cup of water	String
Bowl	

For Adult to Do Ahead:
Cut or tear some of the newspaper into 1-inch strips. Children may enjoy helping with some of this. Blow up the balloon. Cover work area with newspapers. Cut or tear tissue paper into pieces.

Introduction:
Begin by saying, "In Mexico people celebrate special occasions at a party called a fiesta. At a fiesta there is an object called a piñata." Show the picture of the piñata. "Inside the pinata there are small toys, candy, raisins, and nuts. Children take turns hitting the piñata until it breaks open. We're going to make a piñata."

Procedure:
Continue the activity with, "We are going to mix flour, starch, and water together to make a mixture called papier-mâché." Stir as children add flour, starch, and then water to bowl. Show children how to dip strips of newspaper into the mixture and then press onto the balloon. Cover the balloon with papier-mâché, leaving a 2- or 3-inch opening around the knot of the balloon. After one layer of papier-mâché has been applied, wrap the string around the balloon and tie at the knot. Leave a 20-inch tail on the balloon. Apply two or three more layers of papier-mâché and then hang the balloon to dry overnight. The next day pop the balloon and remove it from the papier-mâché ball. Glue tissue paper onto the ball. Let the children decide on a design—tissue paper can be hung in strips, bunched together, or glued flat.

Closure:
Conclude activity by saying, "This is a beautiful piñata. What shall we fill it with for our party? Let's hang it up so we can look at it and enjoy the colors."

Follow-up Activity:
Use the piñata for a holiday party. Children can use a wiffle ball bat to try to break the piñata. Older children may be blindfolded before they try to break the piñata.

WHO AM I?

Purpose:	To play a game recognizing various professions.
Skills/ Concepts:	To develop the motor skills used in putting on a hat. To develop vocabulary.
Ages:	2½ through 5 year olds.

Length of Activity:	Allow 5 to 10 minutes depending upon interest of children
Materials:	A box full of hats representing various professions. For example: a tiara, a crown, a cowboy hat, a hard hat, a fancy flowered hat, a helmet, a nurse's cap, a fire hat, a police hat etc. (many of these can be found in children's sizes at department stores)
Introduction:	Begin by saying, "Who would like to play a game with these hats?"
Procedure:	Children can take turns trying on hats and asking the other children, "Who Am I?". When they guess, the adult can encourage discussion about what that person might do for work by asking follow-up questions.
Closure:	Conclude by saying, "We need to put all the hats back in the box now and put the box away. Would everyone please pick up one hat and place it in the box."
Follow-up Activity:	Invite someone from one of the professions above to visit and talk about their career.

LET'S HAVE A HOLIDAY PARTY

Purpose:	To celebrate the holidays Hanukkah and Christmas.
Skills/ Concepts:	To discuss what happens at a party. To place flannel board pieces at proper time. To use memory skills.
Ages:	18 months through 5 years old.
Length of Activity:	Allow 3 minutes.
Materials:	Flannel board Flannel board pieces, objects that might be seen at a party, pictures of people dressed up, Christmas or Hanukkah objects
For Adult to Do Ahead:	Find pictures to use for flannel board pieces.
Introduction:	Introduce this activity by saying, "Holiday time is a good time to have friends and relatives come to your house for a party. Let's have a pretend party on our flannel board."
Procedure:	Continue, "When you have a party, people sometimes dress in fancy clothes. Special foods are served. Adults like to talk with each other. Children like to play games. Parties are a lot of fun." Lay flannel pieces out and ask children questions about the pieces such as Do these people have on fancy clothes? Do the people look happy? How can you tell? What are these people doing? As you talk about each piece let a child place it on the flannel board.
Closure:	Conclude by saying, "Would you like to plan a holiday party?"
Follow-up Activity:	Leave flannel pieces out. Ask children to tell a story about one of the holiday pictures.

LET'S EAT

Purpose:	To make a book about foods people eat and foods animals eat.
Skills/ Concepts:	To use memory to answer questions. To identify foods. To learn the concept of eating good foods to stay healthy.
Ages:	18 months through 5 years old.
Length of Activity:	Allow 3 minutes.
Materials:	Construction paper Glue or paste Pictures of foods from magazines Cotton swab
Introduction:	Ask the children, "What do you like to eat?"
Procedure:	Talk about the foods that the children like to eat. Ask, "Do you know what birds like to eat?" Elicit answers from children. Other questions might be, "Do you know what puppies and kittens like to eat?" or "What animal might eat carrots?" or "Who might eat worms?" or "What animal likes to eat nuts?" Lay magazine pictures on table. Ask children to pick several of their favorite foods and some foods that animals might like to eat. Children should glue pictures to construction paper with glue and cotton swab. After pictures are in place, label each picture with "(Child's name) eats (food name)." or "(Animal name) eat (food name)." Punch holes in one side of pages and attach with yarn to form a book.
Closure:	Conclude with, "Can you 'read' your book?"
Follow-up Activity:	Make a favorite foods mural. Paste food pictures to a large piece of paper cut in the shape of a body. Print each child's name on the "body."

COVER YOUR MOUTH

Purpose:	To teach children to cover their mouths when they have to cough.
Skills/ Concepts:	To learn the concept of a "good" manner. To learn that covering mouth helps stop spread of a cold.
Ages:	18 months through 5 years old.
Length of Activity:	Allow 1 minute, with gentle reminders when needed.
Materials:	None needed.
Introduction:	Ask, "Do you know what to do when you cough?"
Procedure:	Continue, "When you cough, you should cover your mouth with your hand." Cough while covering your mouth with your hand. "If you have a cold, covering your mouth may help stop your cold from spreading to other people."
Closure:	Conclude with, "What should you do with your hand if you have to cough?"
Follow-up Activity:	When children cough, cover your mouth with your hand to remind them gently to cover their mouth.

RUB-A-DUB

Purpose:	To talk about bathing.
Skills/ Concepts:	To understand that taking a bath helps us stay healthy. To act out bath time.
Age:	18 months through 5 years old.
Length of Activity:	Allow 3 or 4 minutes.

Materials:
Baby doll   Washcloth
Sink or large basin, half filled with warm water   Towel
Mild soap, for bubbles and for doll shampoo

Introduction: Begin by saying, "You take a bath to keep your body clean. Your mother or father give you a shampoo to keep your hair clean. When you keep your body clean, it helps keep your body healthy. Let's pretend to give a baby a bath."

Procedure: Children should be supervised whenever there is water included in an activity. This can be an indoor or outdoor activity. Children will enjoy helping set up this activity. As you work, talk about the things you are doing such as filling the sink, adding soap for bubbles or laying the towel out to dry the "baby." Encourage the children to use the washcloth to wash the "baby." Encourage the children to talk about what they are doing—washing the baby's face or giving the baby a shampoo.

Closure: Conclude by saying, "This baby had a wonderful bath. I wonder what you like best about your bath?"

Follow-up Activity: Act out bath time using the selection "Rub-a-dub" from the record Tickely Toddle by Martha and Hap Palmer. Educational Activities Inc. Box 390 Freeport, NY 11520.

JANUARY ACTIVITIES

THEME: *Winter*
SPECIAL DAY: *New Year's Day*

ART:	Clay Play
	Snowflakes
	Sponge Print Snowpeople
MUSIC:	Marching Band
	The North Wind Doth Blow
	Snowflakes
MOVEMENT:	Toss
	Let's Pretend to Skate
	Mitten Scramble
LANGUAGE:	Mittens, Hats, and Boots
	The Chimney
	A Winter Poem
NUTRITION:	Popcorn
	Bread and Cereal Group
	Peanut Butter Crackers
SCIENCE/	Me and My Shadow
NATURE:	Winter
	What Should I Wear in the Winter?
	Pine Bough Potpourri
MATH:	Counting Raisins
	Shapes
	Block Building
SOCIAL	Growth Chart
STUDIES:	A Trip to Kindergarten
	Let's Go to the Mountains
HEALTH/	The Police Officer
SAFETY:	I Have a Healthy Body

CLAY PLAY

Purpose: To create a three-dimensional object with clay.

Skills/
Concepts: To use gross motor skills of rolling and pressing clay.
To learn hard, soft.

Ages: 18 months through 5 years old.

Length of
Activity: Allow 5 to 15 minutes depending upon interest of children.

Materials
Needed: Commercial clay softened or make your own (see pp. 49–50 cornstarch beads)
Small rolling pins
Cookie cutters
Small butter knives, spoons

Introduction: Begin activity by saying, "What are some of the ways we can play with clay?" (build with it, roll it, make designs on it, cut it out into shapes) "Let's have some fun with clay."

Procedure: Show children 18 months to 2½ years old how to roll balls and snakes. For older children, let them experiment using the utensils provided to create their own works of art. Let them feel hardened clay and the softened clay they work with. Ask them to describe what they feel.

Closure: Compare results by saying, "Let's look at what we made." Encourage children to look at each other's creations and talk about them if they wish. "Now let's roll our clay back up in a ball and put it away for another day."

Follow-up
Activity: Three- and 4-year-olds can wash and dry the utensils they used in their clay play.

SNOWFLAKES

Purpose: To create snowflakes for decoration.

Skills/
Concepts: To fold paper.
To cut paper with scissors.

Length of
Activity: Allow 5 minutes.

Ages: 4 through 5 years old.

Materials
Needed: Squares of white paper 5 inches by 5 inches
Scissors

Introduction: Introduce activity by saying, "Let's make some snowflakes to hang from our ceiling."

Procedure: Have children fold paper in one-half, then in one-half again, in one-half once again, and finally in one-half again. (Adult supervision for the folding process is necessary, at least for the first few times until the child has mastered the process.) Next demonstrate how to make little V-shaped snips into the four edges of the paper, making sure to leave a space between each snip.

Closure: When cutting step is completed say, "Let's unfold our papers and see what we have made. These are beautiful snowflakes, and each one is different."

Follow-up Activities: Hang snowflakes by thread from the ceiling or tape to windows to create a winter decoration.
Sing the song "Snowflakes" on page 95.
Read *First Snow* by Emily McCully. New York: Harper and Row, 1985.

SPONGE PRINT SNOWPEOPLE

Purpose: To create snowpeople by using sponge art.

Skills/ Concepts: To learn dipping, pressing.
To name colors.

Length of Activity: Allow 5 minutes.

Ages: 2 through 5 years old.

Materials:

Blue and red construction paper	Glue or paste
Sponges	Raisins
White poster paint	Scissors

For Adult to Do Ahead: Cut sponges in circle shapes. Add a few drops of liquid soap to paint (it facilitates washing paint off bodies and clothing). Cut hat shapes from red construction paper. Place glue or paste on a paper plate. Fill shallow pan with white poster paint. Find or draw a picture of a snowperson made from three snowballs.

Introduction: Show children the picture of a snowperson. "Who knows what this is? How many round snowballs were used to make this person? (three) Let's paint our own snowpeople."

Procedure: Have children dip one side of a round sponge into paint and then press it paint side down onto blue paper. Repeat two more times so there are three circles one on top of the other. Let paint dry. Later children can paste red hats onto paper above head and raisins for eyes and buttons.

Closure: Ask, "How many raisins did you use on your snowperson? What color is the hat?" (You may have many different answers for the number of raisins depending on how many buttons each child put on his or her snowperson and whether or not a nose and mouth were added.)

Follow-up Activities: Sing "Frosty the Snowman."
In snowy climates, build a snowperson outside. In warmer climates use shaved ice such as that in slush drinks or sno-cones to build a small snowperson in a sink or shallow pan.
Read *The Snowman* by Raymond Briggs, New York: Random House, 1978.

MARCHING BAND

Purpose:	To play rhythm instruments while marching.
Skills/ Concepts:	To develop gross motor skill of marching on a masking tape line. To play rhythm instruments. To follow directions.
Ages:	18 months through 5 years old
Length of Activity:	Allow 3 minutes
Materials:	Simple rhythm instruments Masking tape Record or cassette with marching music, optional
For Adult to Do Ahead:	Using masking tape or chalk, mark a large circle on the floor or hardtop play area outdoors. (This can be an indoor or outdoor activity.)
Introduction:	Ask the children, "Do you remember how to play the rhythm instruments?"
Procedure:	Show the children the instruments and let them select what they would like to play. "Can you show me how to play that instrument? Let's bring our instruments to the circle." Indicate the tape on the floor. "I wonder if we can march around the circle and play our instrument while we march." March around the circle. "Can you turn around and march around the circle in the other direction?"
Closure:	Continue by asking, "Would you like to pick another instrument or would you like to put the instruments away?"
Follow-up Activity:	Play a record or cassette of marching music while marching around the circle. Let one child be "the leader" and have class follow him or her while marching and playing instruments. Read *Ben's Trumpet* by Rachel Isadora. New York: Greenwillow, 1979.

THE NORTH WIND DOTH BLOW

Purpose:	To sing a winter song.
Skill/ Concept:	To sing a simple song.
Ages:	18 months through 5 years old.
Length of Activity:	Allow 1 minute.
Materials:	Song
Introduction:	Begin this activity by saying, "I know a song about a poor little robin who was cold all winter."
Procedure:	Sing the song. Invite the child to sing the song with you a second time.

Closure: At the end, ask, "Where did the little robin go when it was cold?"

Follow-up
Activity: Read *The Snowy Day* by Ezra Jack Keats New York: Viking 1962.

The North Wind Doth Blow

Mother Goose
Traditional

The north wind doth bl-ow and we shall have snow, And what will the rob-in do then? Poor thing! He'll

sit in the ba-rn to keep him-self warm, And hide his head under his wing, poor thing!

SNOWFLAKES

Purpose: To sing a song about snowflakes.

Skills/
Concepts: To memorize a simple song.
To expand vocabulary.

Ages: 18 months through 5 years old.

Length of
Activity: Allow 1 minute.

Materials: Song

Introduction: Begin the activity by saying, "In the winter where it is very cold, snowflakes fall from the sky. I know a snowflake song. Listen while I sing it for you."

Procedure: Sing song. Then ask, "Can you tell me how the snowflakes fall to the ground?" (softly, gently, quietly) "Would you sing with me?"

Closure: Conclude by saying, "The snowflake song is a very peaceful, quiet song." Then ask, "Would you like to paint some snowflakes?"

Follow-up
Activity: Let children experiment with white tempera paint on black construction paper by using a paint brush or a small piece of sponge attached to a spring clothespin. Or let children use white chalk on black construction paper.
Read *White Snow, Bright Snow* by Alvin Tresselt (Wm. Morrow Co., 1988) and (N.Y.: Lothrop, Lee and Shepard, 1947).

Snowflakes

Words and music by:
JoAnne C. Calvarese

Pret-ty snow-flakes fall-ing down, Fall-ing soft-ly to the ground. Cold and white, day or night; fall-ing all a- round. See the snow-flakes fall-ing 'round, Soft-ly, soft-ly touch the ground. Float-ing through the cold clear air, Melt-ing in my hair.

TOSS

Purpose:	To toss an object into a basket.
Skills/ Concepts:	To learn to toss (gross motor skill development), to aim. To take turns.
Length of Activity:	Allow 2 to 10 minutes depending upon age and number of children playing.
Ages:	2 through 5 years old.
Materials:	Pom-poms or Ping Pong balls Basket or box Masking tape
For Adult to Do Ahead:	Set the basket or box up on the floor and then place a line of masking tape 3 to 4 feet away from the box (the box can be moved further and further away from the line as the children master each challenge).
Introduction:	Begin by saying, "Let's try a new game of toss."
Procedure:	Have children stand behind masking tape line and try to toss the ball into the basket. They may have three tries each time. After their turn they should go to the end of the line if they want to try again. Once the children repeatedly get two to three balls in the basket each time, move the basket 6 inches further away.
Closure:	Conclude by saying, "This is a great game to practice at home. You can use a clothespin and a box if you don't have a small soft ball and a basket."
Follow-up Activity:	A quiet activity is a good follow-up to this game which often gets the children quite excited. Have the children sit or lay on the floor and slowly breathe in and out to relax. Playing relaxing music to breathe by also helps to calm things down.

LET'S PRETEND TO SKATE

Purpose:	To move body in time to waltz music.
Skills/ Concepts:	To develop gross motor skills of moving arms and legs in a skating motion. To improve listening skills. To move to a rhythm.
Ages:	18 months through 5 years old.
Length of Activity:	Allow 2 to 3 minutes.
Materials:	Record player or cassette tape player Record or cassette tape of waltz music such as the "Skater's Waltz" or *Fiedler's Favorites for Children* (Fiedler/Boston Pops, RCA, 1971)
Introduction:	Begin by saying, "Have you ever gone ice skating or seen an ice skater glide across the ice? Let's pretend this rug (or floor) is a big ice pond and we are skating."
Procedure:	Encourage children to pretend to put on their skates by doing so yourself. Glide around the room rhythmically. (Note: If you rest your hands behind you on your back as skaters sometimes do, the children will probably copy you. This way there will be fewer flailing arms, which is especially helpful in a smaller room.) Next add some waltz music. Listen to the rhythm for a moment and then begin to glide to the music.
Closure:	Conclude by saying, "I had a great time pretending to ice skate today. What about you? Let's take our pretend skates off before we leave the pond."
Follow-up Activity:	Distribute paper and crayons. Play the music again and encourage the children to draw to the music.

MITTEN SCRAMBLE

Purpose:	To play a matching game with mittens.
Skills/ Concepts:	To develop gross motor skills of moving arms and legs. To match two of the same items. To discern color. To put on mittens by oneself.
Ages:	3 through 5 years old (though some toddlers can put on their own mittens). If toddlers do play, separate children into groups with the younger children together so that they do not have to scramble with the older 3-, 4-, and 5-year-olds.
Length of Activity:	Allow 2 or 3 minutes.
Materials:	A matching pair of mittens or gloves for each child (Mittens are easier to put on, especially for younger children) Box

Introduction: Instruct the children, "Everyone get your two mittens and put them in the box. Now I'm going to mix them up." Stir them around to separate the pairs and then toss them out on the floor.

Procedure: Have children look for their own mittens and put them on their hands. By the process of elimination and with some help from their friends, everyone will find his or her two mittens or gloves. (Note: Check before the scramble to be sure no two children have the same mittens. If they do, put them in separate groups. Also, suggest to the parents they sew name tags in to avoid confusion.)

Closure: Conclude with, "Do you each have a matching pair of mittens on? Tell me what color mittens you are wearing."

Follow-up Activity: Read the nursery rhyme "The Three Little Kittens."

MITTENS, HATS, AND BOOTS

Purpose: To match "like" objects by color and shape.

Skills/ Concepts: To sort objects.
To identify color.
To identify shape.

Ages: 18 months through 2 years old.

Length of Activity: Allow 3 minutes.

Materials: Colored construction paper
Heavy posterboard, 8 inches by 12 inches
Clear contact paper

For Adult to Do Ahead: Make pattern for mittens, hats, and boots.
Cut three pink hats, three blue mittens, and three brown boots.
Divide posterboard into three sections.
Place a cutout hat in the first section, a mitten in the second section, and a boot in the third section. Cover with clear contact paper.
Cover remaining mittens, hats, and boots with contact paper and trim.

Introduction: Begin activity with, "When it is very cold outdoors, we cover our hands, head, and feet (point to each part of the body as you name it). Do you remember what we put on our hands to keep them warm?" (mittens or gloves) "Yes. What do we wear to keep our head warm?" (hat or hood) "Yes, we wear a hat. And what do we wear to keep our feet warm?" (boots) "I have a mitten, hat, and boot game to play."

Procedure: Show the children the game board. They will probably identify the shapes. If they don't, help them name each shape as they point to it. Lay remaining shapes next to the game board. Encourage children to name these shapes. The object of this game is to place the loose hats, mittens, and boots on top of their matching pictures on the game board.

Closure: Conclude activity by asking, "Would you like to match the shapes again?"

Follow-up Activity: Give children verbal directions to place shapes in different parts of the room. For example, "Can you put the mitten on the table?" or "Can you put the boot under the chair?"

THE CHIMNEY

Purpose:	To learn a simple fingerplay about a chimney.
Skills/ Concepts:	To memorize words to a fingerplay. To repeat words to a fingerplay. To use fine motor skills to complete hand actions.
Ages:	18 months through 5 years old.
Length of Activity:	Allow 1 minute.
Materials:	Poem Picture of a house with a chimney
Introduction:	Begin by asking, "Do you know what this is?" Show picture and point to chimney. "Yes, it's a chimney. A chimney lets smoke out of a fireplace or furnace. I know a poem about a chimney."
Procedure:	Recite the poem for the children while you accompany it with the hand motions described.

Here is the chimney	(Left hand in fist with thumb inside.)
This is the top	(Place palm of right hand on fist with fingers extended.)
Take off the lid	(Remove right hand.)
And out the smoke pops.	(Pop left thumb out of fist.)

Closure:	Conclude by asking, "Would you like to try the poem with me?"
Follow-up Activity:	On a cold day take a short walk around the neighborhood. Encourage the children to look for chimneys on the buildings and tell you whether or not there is smoke coming out of them.

© 1990 by The Center for Applied Research in Education

A WINTER POEM

Purpose:	To learn a poem about winter.
Skills/ Concepts:	To memorize a poem. To learn about clothing worn in winter. To learn that spring follows winter.
Ages:	3 through 5 years old.
Length of Activity:	Allow 2 minutes.
Materials:	Poem
Introduction:	Begin by asking, "What kinds of clothing do we wear outdoors in winter?" (Answers to this will vary depending upon your climate.)

Procedure: Say poem for children. Then say it line by line having children repeat each line after you. After only a few repetitions children will be able to fill in the last word in every sentence for you.

> Winter can be very cold
> We bundle up head to toe.
> We wear a hat, mittens and boots,
> To play out in the snow.
>
> Winter can be very cool,
> Sometimes rainy too.
> Boots and raincoats keep us dry,
> As we walk to school.
>
> Winter days can be sunny,
> Bright and crystal clear.
> We keep our warm clothes handy though,
> Until springtime days are here.

Closure: Ask children, "Does it snow where we live? Does it rain where we live?"

Follow-up Activities: Make a flannel board child with outdoor clothing appropriate for your winter climate. Children can add felt rain coat, hat, and boots or hat, coat, scarf, mittens, and boots. Read *Owl Moon* by Jane Yolen. New York: Philomel Books, 1987.

POPCORN

Purpose: To make a nutritious snack.

Skills/ Concepts: To learn how to make popcorn.

Ages: 18 months through 5 years old.

Length of Activity: Allow 5 minutes.

Materials: An ear of corn or a picture of one
Popcorn kernels
A popcorn machine

Introduction: Begin by saying, "Look at this vegetable. What is it called?" Corn. "Can you see the tiny kernels inside?" (point to the kernels) "I have some corn kernels here in a cup." (show the children) "Let's pour them in this machine and see what happens."

Procedure: Encourage children to pour premeasured kernels into machine. Explain that machine is hot while it is working and that children must stand away from it while corn pops. "What did these kernels turn into?"

Closure: Ask the children, "Who would like to help me eat this delicious treat?"

Follow-up Activity: Draw the outline of a snowperson on a piece of paper. Show child how to glue pieces of popcorn to fill in snowperson.

BREAD AND CEREAL GROUP

Purpose:	To introduce the bread and cereal food group.
Skills/ Concepts:	To view bread and cereal as nutritious foods. To recognize the difference between sugar-sweetened cereal and low-sugar or no-sugar cereals.
Ages:	18 months through 5 years old. (Three- to 5-year-olds will take part in the discussion, all children will enjoy eating the breakfast.)
Length of Activity:	Allow 10 minutes.
Materials:	Homemade bread Soft margarine, peanut butter or cream cheese Butter knives Paper plates, bowls, cups and napkins A nutritious cereal such as Cheerios Spoons Milk and juice
For Adult to Do Ahead:	Set up a breakfast buffet so children can spread their own choice of topping on bread and pour their own cereal.
Introduction:	Begin by saying, "Breakfast is a very important meal. The food we eat at breakfast gives us energy to work and play."
Procedure:	Have children take turns at buffet spreading a topping on their bread, placing it on a plate, and taking it to their seat, then returning to pour a bowl of cereal. Juice and milk can be offered as a pouring exercise to 4- and 5-year-olds who have practiced pouring liquids or can already be placed at each child's place by an adult. Remember: Accidents are bound to happen. Respond by calmly stating that a spill has occurred and asking the child who made it to please clean it up (have sponges, mops, broom, and dustpan available).
Closure:	After the activity, say, "That was a very healthy breakfast. Not all cereals are as good for you as _____" (whatever they ate). "Some cereals contain lots of sugar. What does sugar do to your teeth? Can you name some cereals that contain lots of sugar? Do you know what cereals have less sugar and are better for you?" Name some leading brands with low or no sugar "I hope you'll try eating cereals with low sugar or no sugar for breakfast at your home."
Follow-up Activities:	Reserve bread and cereal crumbs to take outside to birds and small animals. Have children clear their places and wash off tables with small wet sponge squares. Cut regular sponges into smaller squares to make it easier for little hands to hold and squeeze.

PEANUT BUTTER CRACKERS

Purpose:	To learn to prepare a simple snack.
Skills/ Concepts:	To improve muscle development through spreading activity. To learn independence through preparing snack on own.
Ages:	18 months through 5 years old. (The older children can spread while the younger children serve crackers.)
Length of Activity:	Allow 5 minutes.
Materials:	Whole wheat or cracked wheat crackers Smooth peanut butter Several small butter knives (rounded edges) Napkins and cups
Introduction:	Begin activity by saying, "Let's prepare our own snack today. Who would like to help me?"
Procedure:	Toddlers place a napkin at each child's place. Then hand crackers one at a time to older children. Older children spread peanut butter on crackers. Younger children serve by placing one or two crackers on each napkin.
Closure:	Conclude by saying, "Here is a glass of milk to go with your peanut butter and crackers. This is a nutritious snack."
Follow-up Activity:	Have children spread peanut butter on crackers or pieces of bread and place them outside to feed birds and small animals. (Note: If placed outside a window, the children can watch to see who eats the food.)

ME AND MY SHADOW

Purpose:	To play with shadows.
Skills/ Concepts:	To experiment with light.
Ages:	3 through 5 years old.
Length of Activity:	Allow 2 to 10 minutes.
Materials:	Stick puppets (see To Do Ahead) Table lamp (children using an electrical appliance should be supervised by an adult)
For Adult to Do Ahead:	Cut free hand shapes from construction paper (older children will enjoy doing this) or shapes may be traced from cookie cutters and cut out Eyes can be punched out using a paper punch Tape or paste each shape to a popsicle stick
Introduction:	Begin by saying, "Let's have a puppet show using shadows."

Procedure: Sit with wall on one side and the table lamp behind you. Puppets will reflect their shadows on the wall. Children can make up their own stories or choose a nursery rhyme or fairy tale to act out. "When we block the light, we make a shadow on the wall." (hold the puppet between the light and the wall)

Closure: Conclude by asking, "Would you like to play with the puppets some more?"

Follow-up Activities: On a sunny day, introduce older children to shadow tag. One child is "it" and must step on another person's shadow for them to become "it."
   Children can use their hands (using table lamp) to make animal shapes against the wall.

WINTER

Purpose: To talk about the season of winter.

Skills/ Concepts: To expand vocabulary.
   To view winter as a time of change.

Ages: 18 months through 2 years old (use pictures for simple word identification); 3 through 5 years old (use pictures for discussion).

Length of Activity: For children 18 months to 2 years old, allow 2 or 3 minutes; for 3- to 5-year-olds, allow 5 to 10 minutes.

Materials: Pictures of winter
   Holding the discussion by a window may be helpful

Introduction: Show children a picture of a winter scene. Ask, "Do you know what season this picture shows?"

Procedure: Use some statements and questions to start the children talking about the picture and then about winter in general. For example,
   "What is happening in this picture?"
   "What colors do you see?"
   "Is it warm or cold in winter?"
   "In some places there are snow and ice on the ground during winter. Does it snow where we live?"
   "What kind of clothes do we wear in the winter?"
   "Do flowers and plants grow in the winter where we live?"
   "Tell me what you see outside our window."

Closure: Note that "Winter is the season that follows fall. The weather is cooler. Some places have snow in the winter."

Follow-up Activities: Older children can look through magazines to find winter pictures, cut them out, and paste them on construction paper to make a book about winter.
   Younger children can paste precut pictures onto colored paper to be hung on the wall.
   Read *Happy Winter* by Karen Gundersheimer. New York: Harper and Row, 1982.

WHAT SHOULD I WEAR IN THE WINTER?

Purpose:	To talk about what to wear in the winter.
Skills/ Concepts:	To identify clothing worn outdoors in winter. To put on warm clothing when cold. To expand vocabulary.
Ages:	18 months through 5 years old.
Length of Activity:	Allow 2 minutes.
Materials:	Pictures of winter clothing such as hats, mittens, boots, coats, sweaters, snowsuits
For Adult to Do Ahead:	Paste the pictures of winter clothing to flannel pieces for use on the flannel board
Introduction For Areas That Receive Snow:	Say to children, "In the fall when the weather gets cooler, we wear sweaters and jackets outdoors to keep warm. What do we wear in the winter to keep warm?"
Introduction For Areas That Do Not Receive Snow:	Say to children, "Winter has arrived. Some days it is cool outdoors. What do we wear in the winter to keep warm?"
Procedure:	Continue with, "Let's look at some pictures of clothing we wear to keep warm in winter. We'll also look at what people wear to keep warm in places where the weather is warmer/colder." Lay pictures of clothing out in front of children. Ask for volunteers to name a picture and place it on the flannel board. Ask follow-up questions of the other children. For example, "Do you know on what part of your body you would wear mittens?" or "Do you know where the hat is worn? (Head.) "Yes, a hat will keep your head warm," or "What covers your feet and keeps them warm and dry?" Boots.
Closure:	Say to children, "These are pictures of clothing that will keep you warm. (point to flannel board) Will you tell me what they are again?" (point to them one at a time and have children name them)
Follow-up Activity:	Play "the winter clothing game." JACK FROST SAYS TO PUT YOUR HAT ON. (Everyone pretends to put a hat on his or her head.) JACK FROST SAYS TO PUT YOUR BOOTS ON. This continues using all the clothing from the exercise. The game reinforces naming the pieces of clothing as well as where on your body you wear it. With the pictures for a guide, older children can lead younger ones in this game by themselves.

PINE BOUGH POTPOURRI

Purpose:	To use leftover pine needles from the holidays to make potpourri.
Skills/ Concepts:	To develop the sense of smell. To expand vocabulary. To develop the sense of touch.

Ages:	3 through 5 years old.
Length of Activity:	Allow 5 to 10 minutes.
Materials:	Large decorative bowl or jar 1 cup oak moss 25 small pinecones (available from a florist) 1 cup red rosebuds (from a florist) 5 to 10 drops of balsam oil or pine needle oil (from florist or drugstore) 3 or 4 cups of pine needles (may be branches from a Christmas tree or pine boughs used for decoration) Spoon and measuring cup
For Adult to Do Ahead:	Remove pine needles or have children help to remove needles from branches. Cut up oak moss.
Introduction:	Say to children, "We are going to make a special mixture today called potpourri. Can you say the word 'potpourri'?" Let the children practice the word. "We won't be able to eat the potpourri, but we will be able to smell it."
Procedure:	Place the ingredients on the table one at a time. Encourage the children to name as many of the ingredients as they can. Name each ingredient the children do not know and encourage them to repeat the word. Many children will enjoy touching and smelling the ingredients. Ask the children about each ingredient: "How does this smell?" or "What does that feel like?" Children can measure the pine needles and place them in the bowl. Then add the moss and rosebuds. Children can count aloud as they place the pinecones in the bowl. Let everyone have a turn gently stirring the dried materials with their hands. Supervise the addition of the pine or balsam oil.
Closure:	Say to the children, "Our potpourri has a very fragrant smell. Do you like the smell? (Remember: Any answer to this question is correct, everyone is entitled to his or her opinion.) Let's leave our potpourri on a shelf (or table) so we can enjoy its fragrance. We can take turns giving it a stir every day or so."
Follow-up Activity:	Extra pine branches can be stuck in pots (use sand and rocks for stability) and decorated with bits of dried fruit, apple cores, stale bread, peanut butter, and bird seed balls. Set this "tree" outside a window so children can watch the birds and small animals who come to feast on it.

COUNTING RAISINS

Purpose:	To reinforce counting.
Skills/ Concepts:	To count from 1 to 5 or from 1 to 10. To use fine motor skill of picking up raisins.
Ages:	3 through 5-year-olds.
Length of Activity:	Allow 2 to 3 minutes.
Materials:	Small cup of raisins Napkins

Introduction: Say to the children, "I've heard you count to five. Let's see if you can count out five raisins."

Procedure: Encourage children to take raisins out of the cup and place them on the napkin one at a time while they count aloud to 5. For children who can count to 5 easily, encourage them to count to 10.

Closure: Conclude with, "Let's eat those 5 (or 10) raisins for a little snack."

Follow-up Activity: For an added challenge, place five small cups numbered 1 to 5 on a tray. Ask children to place one raisin in the cup numbered 1, two in the cup numbered 2, and so on up to 5.

Read *Bunches and Bunches of Bunnies* by Louise Matthews. New York: Scholastic Inc., 1978.

SHAPES

Purpose: To recognize different shapes.

Skills/ Concepts: To recognize a circle, square, and triangle.
To use gross motor skills to move body from shape to shape.
To develop listening skills.

Ages: 18 months through 2 years old (will enjoy following the older children from shape to shape); 3 through 5 years old (will recognize the different shapes).

Length of Activity: Allow 2 or 3 minutes.

Materials: Masking tape or chalk

For Adult to Do Ahead: For an indoor game, use masking tape to make the shapes of a circle, square, and triangle. Make them large enough for all the children playing to fit inside the shape at the same time. For an outside game, use chalk on pavement to draw shapes as described.

Introduction: Ask to children, "What shapes have I drawn on the floor (ground)?" If children can name the shapes, have them point to each shape as it is named. If the adult names the shape, indicate the shape you are naming and ask the children to repeat the name of the shape. "Now let's play a game with these shapes."

Procedure: Call out the name of the shapes one at a time and ask the children to stand inside each shape as it is named. Younger children who do not yet know the shapes will follow the lead of older children who do until through repetition they too learn to recognize the shapes.

Closure: Conclude activity by saying, "Let's sit on the circle now so that I can play a song for you about shapes."

Follow-up Activity: Play the song *Triangles, Circles, and Squares* in *Learning Basic Skills Through Music—vol 2* by Hap Palmer, Educational Activities, Inc. Freeport, NY 11520

BLOCK BUILDING

Purpose:	To create three-dimensional structures.
Skills/ Concepts:	To develop fine and gross motor skills. To balance blocks on top of each other. To create geometrical shapes.
Ages:	18 months through 5 years old.
Length of Activity:	Allow 5 to 10 minutes, depending upon interest of child.
Materials:	Sturdy set of blocks
Introduction:	Ask the children, "What is in this bucket? (blocks) Playing with blocks can be lots of fun. What are some things you can make with blocks?"
Procedure:	Block building is a wonderful activity for all ages. Toddlers can simply line several blocks up in a row or stack them till they fall. Three-year-olds may build roads, towers, or rooms (houses) with four walls and no roof. Four- and five-year-olds can use their creativity to build elaborate houses, bridges, castles, even cities out of blocks and then imagine what is happening in each.
Closure:	Ask the children, "What did you build with blocks today?"
Follow-up Activity:	Children can make a path lined on both sides with blocks and ask others to follow their path, or they can build low walls to hop over.

GROWTH CHART

Purpose:	To update growth chart started in October.
Skills/ Concepts:	To follow directions. To learn the concept of tall/taller/tallest. To encourage development of attention span.
Ages:	18 months through 5 years old.
Length of Activity:	Allow 2 minutes, updated again in April.
Materials:	Growth chart started in October (see page 43) White construction paper Yardstick Black marker
For Adult to Do Ahead:	Cut snowperson shapes from white construction paper. Print children's names on snowpersons.
Introduction:	Begin by saying, "It's time to check our growth chart to see if you have grown any taller."
Procedure:	Remind children that they must stand with their backs and heels flat against the paper. Measure each child's height with the yardstick. Put child's height on the snowperson. Tape it to the chart. "You were this tall at Halloween time." Point to the pumpkin. "Now you are *taller*, you have grown." Point to the snowperson.

Closure: "How tall were you at Halloween?" Encourage each child to point to his or her pumpkin. "Yes, the pumpkin shows how tall you were. The snowperson shows you are taller, it shows you are growing."

Follow-up Activity: Play the selection "Growing" from the record *Learning Basic Skills Through Music,* Vol. 1, by Hap Palmer. Educational Activities Inc. Freeport, N.Y. 11520

A TRIP TO KINDERGARTEN

Purpose: To visit a kindergarten classroom.

Skills/ Concepts: To observe a kindergarten room.
To become familiar with the local school and kindergarten teacher.

Ages: 4 through 5 years old.

Length of Activity: This is a morning activity to do when the children are rested and not hungry. Twenty minutes will probably be a long enough visit.

Materials: Permission slip, one for each child (see page xviii)
Car seats, one for each child

For Adult to Do Ahead: Contact the local public school several weeks in advance. Talk to the kindergarten teacher and set up a time for visiting.

Introduction: Explain to the children, "We are going to visit Ms./Mr._____. She/he is the kindergarten teacher at _____school. When you are older, you may have Ms./Mr. for a teacher. When we get to school there may be older children there working and playing. We will get to see the things they do every day."

Procedure: Take the field trip.

Closure: Close the activity by saying, "Thank you Ms./Mr._____ for letting us visit your room. We've had a wonderful time."

Follow-up Activity: Talk with the children about what you saw during your visit. Encourage them to recall objects as well as activities. Send a thank you note to teacher. Older children can copy a few simple words. All visiting children can help color it.

LET'S GO TO THE MOUNTAINS

Purpose: To visit the mountains using pictures.

Skills/ Concepts: To identify objects in pictures.
To expand vocabulary skills.

Ages: 18 months through 2 years old (will enjoy looking at pictures); 3 through 5 years old (will also take part in discussion).

Length of Activity: Allow 2 or 3 minutes.

Materials: Pictures of mountains (may be mounted on pieces of flannel)
Flannel board (see p. xv) if needed

Introduction: Show children a mountain picture. Ask them, "Do you know what this picture is?"

Procedure: Help children with the word mountain. "Mountains are very tall. They are very rocky and rugged. There are rocks on mountains. There are trees on some mountains. Sometimes there is snow on mountains." Encourage children to look at the pictures. Ask them to tell you about each picture as they place it on the flannel board.

Closure: Point out, "Mountains are higher than hills. There are rocks and trees on many mountains. Sometimes there is snow on mountains."

Follow-up Activity: Provide the children with brown clay. Help them form big mountains, bigger mountains, and the biggest mountain. Small rocks and twigs could be added to indicate forestation.

THE POLICE OFFICER

Purpose: To introduce children to their local police department.

Skills/ Concepts: To improve listening skills.
To encourage the idea that a police officer is someone who can help you.

Ages: 3 through 5 years old. (Some children are frightened of a person in a uniform. Don't force them to take part in this activity if they are uncomfortable or afraid.)

Length of Activity: Allow 15 minutes.

For Adult to Do Ahead: Contact local police department and ask to have a police officer who enjoys working with children come speak to the children for 5 minutes. Emphasize brevity and simplicity in talk. Topics to be covered might include dialing 911 in an emergency, looking for a police officer if you are lost, and, how to cross the street safely.

Introduction: Begin by saying, "We have a special visitor today. Does anyone know by looking at his/her uniform who our visitor is?"

Procedure: Introduce the police officer to the children and encourage them to listen to what he/she has to say. Older children may ask questions if encouraged to by the speaker.

Closure: Conclude the activity by saying, "Thank you Officer _____ for coming to visit us today."

Follow-up Activities: Participate in the national fingerprinting program sponsored by local police departments. Check first with parents of children.
Send thank you note decorated by children to police officer.

I HAVE A HEALTHY BODY

Purpose: To help children understand it is important to care for their bodies.

Skills/ Concepts: To use good health habits for a healthy body.

Ages: 2 through 5 years old.

Length of Activity:	Allow 2 to 3 minutes.
Materials:	Picture of a child eating a nutritious snack or meal Picture of a child sleeping Picture of a child bathing
For Adult to Do Ahead:	Collect pictures and cover with clear contact paper Attach a small piece of felt to the back of each picture for flannel board use
Introduction:	Begin by asking, "Will you help me tell a story on the flannel board?"
Procedure:	Show children the picture of the child eating. Children may respond immediately to picture; if not, ask, "What is this child doing? Eating good foods will help you stay healthy. What type of snack do you like?" Show picture of child sleeping. "Will you place this on the flannel board for me? What is happening in this picture? It is important to get plenty of rest. Do you take something special to bed with you?" Show picture of a child bathing. "Can you put this picture on the flannel board? Do you take a bath or a shower? When we bathe we are keeping our body clean which helps us to stay healthy. Do you play with toys in the bathtub?"
Closure:	Conclude by asking, "What are the children doing in these pictures?"
Follow-up Activities:	Set a basin up so that children can give their dolls a bath and then get them ready for naps. Play a guessing game. Children pantomime eating, sleeping or bathing and the others guess what they are doing.

FEBRUARY ACTIVITIES

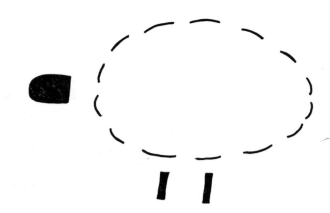

THEME: *Nursery Rhymes*
SPECIAL DAY: *Valentine's Day*

ART:	Lambs
	Heart Collage
	Spiders
MUSIC:	Baa, Baa Black Sheep
	Mary Had a Little Lamb
	Tiddley Winky
	Twinkle, Twinkle Little Star
MOVEMENT:	London Bridge
	Pat-a-Cake
	Ring Around the Roses
LANGUAGE:	Feelings
	Little Miss Muffet
	Goldilocks and the Three Bears
NUTRITION:	Meat, Fish, and Chicken
	Valentine's Party Drink
	Gingerbread Cookies
SCIENCE/ NATURE:	Melting
	Sense of Smell
	A Nest for the Birds
MATH:	Matching Hearts
	Counting and Clapping
	One, Two Buckle My Shoe
SOCIAL STUDIES:	Learning Names
	Having a Puppet Show
	A Trip to the Library
HEALTH/ SAFETY:	Scissors
	Rest Time
	Walking Up and Down Stairs

LAMBS

Purpose:	To construct a figure using paste.
Skills/ Concepts:	To use fine motor skills for pasting. To place parts of lamb's body.
Ages:	2½ through 5 years old.
Length of Activity:	Allow 5 minutes.
Materials:	Blue construction paper Polyester fiberfill Wooden match sticks (without heads), two per child Black construction paper Paste Cotton swabs Small bowl (paper is preferable)
For Adult to Do Ahead:	Break the flammable tip off each match stick. Cut 8-inch by 12-inch sheets of blue paper in half. Cut black paper into one head shape per child. Cut fiberfill into 3-inch by 5-inch pieces with rounded corners. Place paste or glue in a small bowl.
Introduction:	Begin by saying, "I have a piece of material that is very soft." Show the children the fiberfill. Encourage them to touch it. "Let's use this soft material to make a lamb."
Procedure:	Children should each have a piece of blue paper for the background. Using the cotton swabs they can paste the fiberfill piece in the center of the paper. (Note: It is easier to spread the glue or paste on the paper and then press the fiberfill onto it.) "This is the body of your lamb. Now your lamb needs a _____." (point to your head) "That's right. The head is the little black shape." Show them how to paste the head at the side of the body. "Next we will use these sticks for legs." Children can dip sticks in glue and then press in place under body. Older children can help younger ones.

© 1990 by The Center for Applied Research in Education

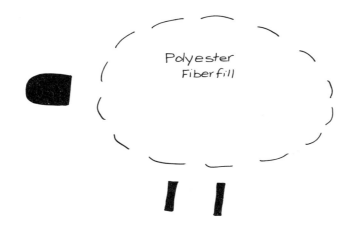

Closure: Conclude by saying, "Let's sing the song, 'Mary Had a Little Lamb' while we clean up." See page 114.

Follow-up Activity: Read *Lambs* by Martin and Virginia Weaver (New York: Alfred A. Knopf) or *Little Lamb's Curl* by Polly Miller McMillian (New York: Lothrup, Lee and Shepard).

HEART COLLAGE

Purpose: To create a collage using heart shapes.

Skills/ Concepts: To develop fine motor skills used in pasting.
To identify shapes.
To recognize color.

Ages: 18 months through 5 years old.

Length of Activity: Allow 5 to 10 minutes.

Materials: Red, pink, and white construction paper
Small white lacy paper doilies (optional)
Paste or glue
Cotton swab (to spread glue or paste)
Small bowl (paper is easiest)

For Adult to Do Ahead: Cut different size heart shapes from the red and pink construction paper. Place paste in small bowl.

Introduction: Begin by saying, "I have a shape to show you." Show children a heart. "Do you know what shape this is?" "Do you know what color this heart is?" "We're going to paste a picture using hearts."

Procedure: Children should each have a piece of white construction paper. They can choose the number, size, and color of hearts they wish to paste on this construction paper. Lace doilies add another texture to the collage. As the children select hearts, the adult can ask them questions such as, "Which heart is bigger, this one or that one? What color heart did you just choose?"

Closure: Conclude by saying, "You've made some colorful pictures. What is this shape?" (point to one of the hearts) "Yes, it's a heart."

Follow-up Activities: The heart collage may be folded and used as a Valentine's Day Card.
Read *Who Said Red?* by Mary Serfozo. New York: Macmillan, 1988.

SPIDERS

Purpose: To create a spiderlike picture.

Skills/ Concepts: To develop listening skills.
To follow directions.
To blow through a straw.

Ages: 3 through 5 years old.

Length of Activity:	Allow 2 minutes.

Materials: White construction paper (one piece per child)   Straw (one per child)
Black tempera paint in a small bowl   A picture of a spider
Spoon

Introduction: Begin by saying, "Do you know what this is?" Show children picture of spider. "Yes, it is a picture of a spider. It has eight legs. How many legs do you have?" (two) "Let's paint a picture of a spider."

Procedure: Continue with, "We aren't going to use a paintbrush for this picture. Instead we are going to use a straw. Can you blow air through your straw? Now we will drop some black paint on your paper and then you can blow air at the paint through your straw like this." (demonstrate) As the air is blown through the straw, the paint will spread out to look like spider legs. If there is room on the paper the children may wish to add more than one spider.

Closure: Conclude by saying, "While your paintings dry, let's sing a song about a spider." Sing "The Itsy, Bitsy Spider."

Follow-up Activity: Recite the nursery rhyme "Little Miss Muffet." Children may like to take turns acting as the spider and as Miss Muffet. (see page 119)

BAA, BAA BLACK SHEEP

Purpose: To sing a nursery rhyme.

Skills/ Concepts: To memorize words.
To memorize a melody.

Ages: 18 months through 5 years old.

Length of Activity: Allow 2 minutes.

Materials: Song

Introduction: Begin by saying, "I know a song about a sheep that I think you've heard before. Listen and then join me if you know the song."

Procedure: Sing song together as many times as the children are interested. Repetition helps the younger children learn the words.

Closure: Continue with, "Let's add some new verses to this song."

Follow-up Activity: Change the color of the lamb as you sing the verse. Ask the children what color they would like the sheep to be each time. They'll have fun imagining a pink, green, or purple sheep as they sing.

Baa, Baa, Black Sheep

Mother Goose

MARY HAD A LITTLE LAMB

Purpose:	To sing a nursery rhyme.
Skills/ Concepts:	To memorize verses. To sing a simple tune.
Ages:	18 months through 5 years old.
Length of Activity:	Allow 2 minutes.
Materials:	Song
Introduction:	Begin by saying, "Sometimes children have pets. I know a song about a little girl named Mary who has a pet."
Procedure:	Sing song. Children already familiar with the song will join in. After singing it once, encourage the others to join in as well.
Closure:	Ask children, "What kind of animal did Mary have?"
Follow-up Activity:	Using the tune to "Mary Had a Little Lamb," add your own verses, such as Jennifer had a little cat, little cat, little cat. Jennifer had a little cat its fur was very soft.

Mary Had a Little Lamb

Mother Goose

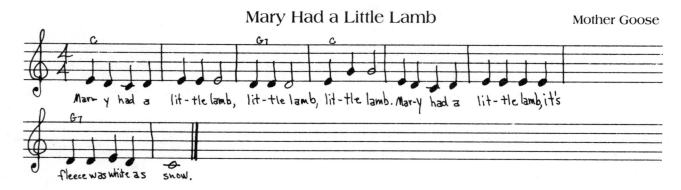

TIDDLEY WINKY

Purpose: To learn a simple song for Valentine's Day.

Skill/
Concept: To memorize words to a song.

Ages: 18 months through 5 years old.

Length of
Activity: Allow 1 to 2 minutes.

Materials: Song

Procedure: Begin by saying, "Let's learn a song we can sing to someone we love."

Procedure: Sing song through for children. Invite them to join you. The words are learned through repetition, so sing it together every day or so for several weeks before Valentine's Day.

Closure: Conclude by saying, "On Valentine's Day people often give cards or presents to people they like. This song could be a singing Valentine's Day present for someone you like."

Follow-up
Activity: Children may wish to make Valentine's cards to go with their song. Use half a sheet of construction paper. Have available heart stickers, cutout hearts, paste, crayons, and markers so the children can decorate their cards individually.

Tiddley Winky

Traditional

TWINKLE, TWINKLE LITTLE STAR

Purpose:	To learn a simple song.
Skills/ Concepts:	To memorize words of a song. To hum a tune.
Ages:	18 months through 5 years old.
Length of Activity:	Allow 2 minutes.
Materials:	Song
Introduction:	Ask the children, "Would you help me sing 'Twinkle, Twinkle Little Star'?"
Procedure:	Sing the song together with children. Then say, "Now let's hum the song. Do you remember how to hum? That's right, you don't sing the words, you keep your lips together and "hum" the tune like this." Demonstrate. Encourage the children to join you.
Closure:	Conclude by asking, "Did you like singing the song or humming the song?"
Follow-up Activities:	Teach the children the nursery rhyme "Star Light, Star Bright":

Star light, star bright,
First star I see tonight.
I wish I may,
I wish I might,
Have the wish I wish tonight.

Read *Many Moons* by James Thurber. New York: Harcourt Brace, 1942 and 1971.

LONDON BRIDGE

Purpose:	To use a familiar nursery rhyme in a movement exercise. To have a game that may be played indoors or outdoors.
Skills/ Concepts:	To join hands to form a bridge. To stand in a line. To memorize words to a song.
Ages:	2 through 5 years old.
Length of Activity:	Allow 1 to 5 minutes, depending upon age and interest.
Materials:	Song
Introduction:	Ask the children, "Have you ever heard this song before?" (sing 'London Bridge') "Do you know how to play the game?"

Procedure: First, sing the song a few times until the children are familiar with it. Then have two older children form the London Bridge by facing each other, joining hands and raising their arms up in the air to form an arch. Everyone sings the song while the rest of the children form a line and walk under the bridge one at a time then return to the end of the line to walk through again. While singing the second verse, the "bridge" comes down gently and traps whoever is passing under it at the time. At the end of the song, the trapped person replaces one of the children pretending to be the bridge.

Closure: Ask the children, "What did you think about that game? Did you like it?" (Note: Feeling free to express one's opinion is very important for young children. Accepting both positive and negative answers to this question shows the child that the adult respects his or her opinion.)

Follow-up Activity: Tell children, "London Bridge is a real bridge. It was originally built in London, England and has been moved to the state of Arizona in The United States." Show children a picture of the bridge if possible—libraries are a great place to start looking. "Let's use our blocks to build some bridges."

PAT-A-CAKE

Purpose: To learn a nursery rhyme.

Skills/ Concepts: To develop gross motor skills.
To develop hand-eye coordination by clapping hands together.
To learn how to mime.
To memorize words to the nursery rhyme.

Ages: 18 months through 5 years old.

Length of Activity: Allow 2 minutes.

Materials: The nursery rhyme

Introduction: Begin by saying, "I know a nursery rhyme about baking a cake. Does anyone else know it?"

Procedure: Recite the nursery rhyme and encourage children to join you with words and motions.

Pat-a-cake, pat-a-cake, baker's man,	(Children clap hands.)
Bake me a cake as fast as you can.	(Continue clapping.)
Roll it and pat it and prick it with B,	(Pretend to roll, pat and draw a letter "B".)
And put it in the oven for baby and me	(Pretend to put cake in oven.)

Closure: Conclude activity by saying, "Now that we've pretended to bake a cake, how would you like to eat a real piece of cake?"

Follow-up Activity: Serve small slices of carrot cake. Children can carry paper plates to the table themselves as well as clean up the crumbs afterward.

RING AROUND THE ROSES

Purpose:	To introduce a game using a familiar nursery song. (This game may be played indoors or outdoors.)
Skills/ Concepts:	To form a circle. To hold hands with another child while in motion. To memorize the words to a song. To move as a group.
Ages:	2 through 5 years old.
Length of Activity:	Allow 1 to five minutes, depending upon age and interest.
Materials:	Song A circle on the ground drawn with chalk outdoors or made with masking tape on floor indoors
For Adult to Do Ahead:	Draw the circle on the floor or ground.
Introduction:	Say to the children, "Let's play a game together. Stand on the circle and hold hands with the child on each side of you."
Procedure:	Have children walk around the circle holding hands and singing this famous old song. When singing the words, "We all fall down," everyone sinks gently to the floor.
Closure:	Conclude by saying, "When we sing 'a pocket full of posies,' does anyone know what posies are?" (flowers) "Let's make a picture of a pocket full of posies."
Follow-up Activity:	Precut flower shapes out of many colors. Cut a pocket shape ⛉ for each child. Children can paste a pocket shape on a piece of paper and then choose some flowers to paste at the top spilling out of the pocket.

FEELINGS

Purpose:	To introduce a variety of everyday emotions through the use of facial expressions.
Skills/ Concepts:	To recognize the feelings happy, sad, angry and surprised. To mime.
Ages:	18 months through 5 years old (though toddlers may not always duplicate the facial expressions with the the group, they will enjoy watching others)
Length of Activity:	Allow 5 to 10 minutes (depending on number of children and their degree of verbal participation)
Introduction:	Begin by saying, "Everyone has feelings. Sometimes we are happy, sometimes we are sad, sometimes we are angry and sometimes we are surprised. Let's talk about these feelings."

Procedure: Ask the children if they can tell you about something that made them happy. (mime a happy face) After they each have a turn to speak, encourage them to show you a happy face. Repeat with sad, angry and surprised. Then ask if the children would like to take turns making a face and letting the others guess how they are feeling.

Closure: Conclude by saying, "We've talked about some special feelings today and had some fun making faces to go with those feelings."

Follow-up Activities: Leave flannel board out. Have a blank face with various eyes, nose, and mouths available to make different facial expressions.

Read *Sing Pierrot, Sing* by Tomie de Paola. New York: Harcourt Brace, 1983. This is a book about mime.

LITTLE MISS MUFFET

Purpose: To act out a nursery rhyme.

Skills/ Concepts: To use hand and body motions to tell a story.
To memorize a poem.

Ages: 18 months through 5 years old (the younger children may enjoy trying to mime the poem, but may not say the words).

Length of Activity: Allow 10 minutes.

Introduction: Ask the children, "Who knows the nursery rhyme 'Little Miss Muffet'? Let's say it together."

Procedure: Continue by saying, "Now let's try to act out the nursery rhyme."

Little Miss Muffet	(Stand with smile on face.)
Sat on her tuffet	(Pretend to sit.)
Eating her curds and whey	(Pretend to eat.)
Along came a spider	(Hold one hand above head and, wiggling the fingers, have it descend to side.)
Who sat down beside her	(Wiggling hand comes to a rest beside thigh.)
And frightened Miss Muffet away.	(Look shocked and throw hands up in fright.)

Closure: Exclaim, "That was very good! Would you like to try it again?"

Follow-up Activity: Older children may like to make up their own motions to other familiar nursery rhymes such as "Hickory, Dickory, Dock" and "Humpty Dumpty."

GOLDILOCKS AND THE THREE BEARS

Purpose: To use hand puppets to tell a story.

Skills/ Concepts: To use a hand puppet.
To listen for verbal clues.
To follow a story.

Ages:	3 through 5 years old.
Length of Activity:	Allow 5 to 10 minutes.

Materials:

Felt	Glue (glue gun helpful)
Yarn	Paper or posterboard
Fake fur	Markers or crayons
Needle and thread	The story of Goldilocks and the Three Bears

For Adult to Do Ahead: Make four simple hand puppets (Goldilocks and three bears) using felt, fake fur, and the pattern on the following page. Draw three chairs, three beds, and a table with three bowls (each in baby size, mother size, and father size) on paper or posterboard and hang them low enough on a wall for a child to reach.
Practice story and use of puppets with four children.

Introduction: Begin activity by saying, "Today Mike, Katie, Thomas, and Alison are going to put on a puppet show for us. Let's sit and watch."

Procedure: Have adult read the story or tell it in his or her own words, while puppeteers enact story using the puppets. The Goldlilocks puppet can be held up to each size chair, bed or bowl as the narrator indicates. *The Three Bears* by Robin Spowart. (New York: Knopf, 1987)

Closure: Ask the children, "Do you remember the name of this puppet?" (Goldilocks) "How about this one?" (Baby Bear) See if children can identify Papa Bear and Mama Bear as well.

Follow-up Activities: Other children may wish to try on hand puppets and play with them after the puppet show.

Make some "porridge" with the children by using instant or quick cooking oatmeal. Add milk and sweeten with honey or brown sugar.

Puppet Pattern: Cut eight pieces using the accompanying pattern (two from felt for Goldilocks and two each in fake fur for baby bear, mother bear, and father bear). Hand or machine sew along dashed line on pattern leaving bottom edge open for hand to be inserted. Using scraps of felt, colored pens and glue, decorate each puppet. See samples for suggestions.

MEAT, FISH, AND CHICKEN

Purpose:	To introduce the child to the meat, fish, and poultry food group.
Skills/ Concepts:	To taste. To feel texture. To smell. To sense color.
Ages:	18 months through 5 years old.
Length of Activity:	Allow 5 to 10 minutes.
Materials:	Bite sized portions of cooked beef, chicken, and fish 3 plates 1 napkin per child

Papa
Bear

Mama
Bear

Baby
Bear

Goldilocks

—yellow
yarn

For Adult to Do Ahead: Check with parents to determine whether any child is a vegetarian, does not eat red meat, or has a food allergy to any foods served. Cook the food and place each type on a different plate.

Introduction: Ask the children, "How many plates do you see?" (three) "Does anyone know what is on each plate?"

Procedure: Continue: "There are three plates on the table. One has pieces of meat, one has pieces of fish, and one has pieces of chicken. Can you tell which is the meat? the chicken? the fish?" Encourage children to talk about the colors of each. Children can serve themselves. Encourage older children to describe taste and smell if they can.

Closure: Conclude with, "Now we need to clean up and wash our hands."

Follow-up Activity: If there is a vegetarian in the class, talk about what he or she eats in place of meat, fish, and poultry. Encourage children to sample nuts and cheeses which replace this group for them.

VALENTINE'S PARTY DRINK

Purpose: To provide a nutritious drink for a Valentine's Day party.

Skills/ Concepts: To identify the color red.
To identify apples and cranberries.

Ages: 18 months through 5 years old.

Length of Activity: Allow 1 to 2 minutes.

Materials:
A cranberry	A bottle of cranapple juice
An apple	Cups

Introduction: Begin activity by saying, "I always enjoy drinking fruit juices. They taste great and are good for you. Today let's have a special fruit drink for our Valentine's Day party."

Procedure: Continue by asking, "What color is this juice?" (red) "It is called cranapple juice because it is made from cranberries and apples." Show children cranberry and apple. "Which fruit is an apple and which fruit is a cranberry?"

Closure: Conclude activity by saying, "Let's pour some of this cranapple juice into our cups and have a drink." (Note: If juice is in a plastic pitcher, 4- and 5-year-olds can do the pouring.)

Follow-up Activity: Continue discussion on pieces of fruit. Talk about color and size. Slice fruit open so children can examine the insides.

GINGERBREAD COOKIES

Purpose: To make a snack to eat while listening to the story of the little gingerbread boy.

Skills/ Concepts: To stir.
To roll.
To use a cookie cutter.
To place raisin eyes and buttons.

Ages: 18 months through 5 years old (younger children may need help from older children).

Length of Activity: Allow 15 minutes.

Materials:

A box of gingerbread mix	Cookie cutter in gingerbread man shape
Raisins	Rolling pin
Measuring cup	Cookie baking sheet
Mixing bowl	Spatula
Spoon for mixing	

For Adult to Do Ahead: Preheat oven. If no oven is available, make cookies with children, bring them home to be baked and return them the next day to be eaten.

Introduction: Tell the children, "I am going to make some gingerbread boy cookies. Who would like to help me?"

Procedure: Follow directions on gingerbread mix box for making cookies. Older children can measure the ingredients, younger children can pour ingredients into the bowl. Everyone can take a turn stirring, rolling dough, and cutting out a gingerbread man. Older children will tend to be more involved while toddlers will come and go periodically to watch activity and then go off to play. Everyone can place raisins on their gingerbread man for eyes and buttons, though children under three will probably need some assistance or verbal guidance from an older child.

Closure: Conclude by saying, "Now we need to bake our cookies. Let's count how many we made." (count together out loud)

Follow-up Activity: Read the story "The Little Gingerbread Boy" while eating the baked cookies served with juice or milk.
The Gingerbread Boy illustrated by Karen Schmidt New York: Scholastic, 1967.

MELTING

Purpose: To watch snow or ice melt at room temperature.

Skills/ Concepts: To observe snow turning from a solid to a liquid.
To observe color change.

Ages: 18 months through 5 years old.

Length of Activity: Allow 5 minutes total, including periodic observations while the ice or snow is melting.

Materials: Snow or a ball of crushed ice
Glass pan

Introduction: Ask the children, "What do I have in this pan? What color is it? (white) Touch the snow/ice. Does it feel warm or cold? Snow/ice must be kept cold to keep this shape."

Procedure: Continue with, "Let's see what happens if we leave this snow/ice here in our room." Check on it periodically with the children. Ask them to describe the changes they see as it slowly melts. (Note: If time is at a premium, place the pan of snow in a sunny window to speed up the melting process.)

Closure: Then ask, "What has happened to the snow/ice?" It melted. "What did it turn into?" Water. "What color is it now?" Clear.

Follow-up Activity: Try watching other solids melt, for example, a dish of ice cream or a chocolate candy bar set in a warm sunny place.

SENSE OF SMELL

Purpose: To stimulate the sense of smell.

Skills/ Concepts: To identify smells.
To enjoy different smells.

Ages: 18 months through 5 years old.

Length of Activity: Allow 5 minutes.

Materials: A variety of objects with distinctive smells such as

Rose water or perfume	Cinnamon
Peppermint extract	Butter
Orange extract	Coffee
Onion	Cotton balls

Small plastic margarine containers with opaque lids

For Adult to Do Ahead: Punch holes in tops of containers and fill each container with one substance. If you are using extracts, heavily soak a cottonball with the extract and place cottonball in container.

Introduction: Ask, "What part of your body lets you smell things?" (nose) "Let's use our noses to guess what's in these containers."

Procedure: As children smell each container, ask them to identify the smell. "What does this smell like?" Not every child will recognize every smell. Encourage them to ask another child to help them identify the smell. Children may wish to open containers to investigate what is inside. Supervise so that children do not eat the substance, but they may look, smell, and touch the substance.

Closure: Ask, "Which smell did you like the most? Was there a smell that you did not like?" (Answers will vary.)

Follow-up Activity: Older children may enjoy using a mortar and pestle to release scents from objects such as flower petals, cloves, or cinnamon sticks.

A NEST FOR THE BIRDS

Purpose: To teach a fingerplay about habitats.

Skills/ Concepts: To memorize a poem.
To develop fine motor skills.
To discover where some animals/insects live.

Ages: 3 through 5 years old.

Length of
Activity: Allow 5 minutes.

Materials: Poem

Introduction: Ask the children, "Where do you live?" (answers may include a house, apartment, condo, trailer) "Does anyone know where birds live?" (nest, tree, bush, sky, birdhouse) "What about a bee?" (beehive, on the side of my house, in a hole in the ground, under my roof) "Where do bunnies live?" (hole in the ground, bunny hutch, cage) (Note: Be prepared for a variety of answers such as those suggested.)

Procedure: Tell the children, "I know a fingerplay about where birds, bees, and bunnies live." Recite poem with hand motions.

A nest is where the bird lives	(Cup hands together with palms up to form nest.)
A hive is for the bee	(Make a fist with one hand.)
A hole is for the bunny	(Loosen fist so that thumb and first finger form a hole.)
But a house is for me	(Put hands together palms facing each other with fingers touching.)

Closure: Ask the children, "Do you remember where the bird lives in the poem? What about the bee? And where does the bunny live?"

Follow-up
Activity: Make a matching game to go with the fingerplay. Draw a house, a nest, a hive and a hole on a piece of posterboard. Cover with clear contact paper. Draw, color and cut out a bird, bee, bunny, and a child. Children can place these figures on top of the appropriate house.

Read the book *Who Lives Here?* (Changing Picture Books) Los Angeles, California: Price, Stern, Sloan, 1986.

MATCHING HEARTS

Purpose: To match large, medium, and small hearts.

Skills/
Concepts: To classify hearts—large, medium, and small.
To identify shapes.

Ages: 18 months through 5 years old.

Length of
Activity: Allow 3 minutes.

Materials:
Heavy posterboard | Glue or paste
Red construction paper | Clear contact paper

For Adult to
Do Ahead: Cut three large hearts, three medium-sized hearts, and three small hearts from red paper. Divide posterboard into three sections. Paste a large heart in the first section, a medium-sized heart in the second section, and a small heart in the third section. Cover front and back with clear contact paper. Cover remaining hearts with clear contact paper on the front and back and trim edges.

Introduction: Ask the children, "Do you know what shape this is?" Show children one of the hearts. "Yes, it is a heart shape."

Procedure: Show children the game board. "Can you show me the biggest heart? Can you show me the smallest heart? Which heart is the medium sized heart?" Lay the loose hearts next to the game board. "Can you place the large heart on top of the large heart on the game board? Great! Now find the smallest heart and place that on the smallest heart on the game board." Continue with the medium sized heart.

Closure: Conclude by saying, "We played a game with three sizes of hearts today. (point to the biggest heart) What size heart is this?" Repeat with other two. If children do not know the answer, offer them a choice. For example, "Is this the biggest or the smallest heart?" Be sure all three sizes are in view when they are answering.

Follow-up Activity: Ask older children to place the largest heart on the smallest heart, the medium on the largest, and the smallest on the medium. This is a more challenging game for children who have mastered matching hearts which are the same and can identify the different sizes on their own. Then remove the hearts from the game board and let the children take turns giving instructions as to where to place the hearts.

COUNTING AND CLAPPING

Purpose: To reinforce counting from 1 to 10.

Skills/ Concepts: To memorize numbers from 1 to 10. To use gross motor skill of clapping.

Ages: 18 months through 5 years old.

Length of Activity: Allow 2 minutes

Introduction: Begin by saying, "Let's all sit down and clap and count together."

Procedure: This is a very simple game, but preschoolers love it. Start counting to 2 or 3 then add another number each week. "Let's clap our hands together 1,2,3 . . .(clap and count at the same time). Now on our knees 1,2,3 . . . Now on our shoulders 1,2,3 . . . Now tiny little baby claps 1,2,3 . . .(clap two fingers together and use a tiny little voice). A tiny little baby cheer for a good job of counting. Yeah!"

Closure: Conclude by saying, "Do you remember what number we counted to today? We counted to number _____ today."

Follow-up Activity: Draw 10 squares in a row on the pavement or sidewalk. Number the boxes 1 to 10. Ask the children to take turns jumping from box to box. Count the boxes as each child jumps. Toddlers can jump two feet together. Older children may try hopping on one foot.

ONE, TWO BUCKLE MY SHOE

Purpose: To teach a counting rhyme.

Skills/ Concepts: To memorize a rhyme. To recite the rhyme with a group.

Ages: 2 through 5 years old.

Length of Activity: Allow 1 minute.

Materials: Nursery rhyme

Introduction: Say to the children, "Let's learn a counting rhyme."

Procedure: Invite the children to say the rhyme with you. As you say the rhyme, hold up a finger for every number. Start by raising the thumb and pointer finger on one hand. Continue with poem as if counting on your fingers.

> One, two buckle my shoe.
> Three, four shut the door.
> Five, six pick up sticks.
> Seven, eight lay them straight.
> Nine, ten start again.

Closure: Ask, "How many fingers did we count with?" (ten)

Follow-up Activity: Encourage the child to act out each phrase of the nursery rhyme.
Read *Anno's Counting Book* by Mitsumasa Anno. New York: Crowell, 1975.

LEARNING NAMES

Purpose: To help children remember the names of other children in their group.

Skills/ Concepts: To memorize other children's names.
To sing a familiar tune (use the tune of "Mary Had a Little Lamb").
To identify self by name (for toddlers).

Ages: 18 months through 5 years old.

Length of Activity: Allow 2 or 3 minutes.

Materials: The tune to "Mary Had a Little Lamb" (see p. 114)

Introduction: Say to the children, "Let's sing a song about the children here today."

Procedure: Substitute your own words to the song for each child. For example,

> Lauren had a blue dress on,
> Blue dress on, blue dress on,
> Lauren had a blue dress on,
> She put it on today.

Each child may stand as the verse is sung about him or her.

Closure: Look at a toddler and ask, "What is your name?" For an older child you could ask, "Who is sitting beside you?" or "Who is sitting across from you?"

Follow-up Activity: Have children sort themselves into groups by the color of their hair (blonds, brown, black, red) or by clothes they are wearing (anyone with a blue dress or shirt, etc.).
Read *Jessica* by Kevin Henkes. New York: Greenwillow Books, 1989.

HAVING A PUPPET SHOW

Purpose:	To perform a puppet show.
Skills/ Concepts:	To develop language. To follow directions.
Ages:	2 through 5 years old.
Length of Activity:	Allow 2 to 5 minutes
Materials:	Purchased or handmade hand puppets, stick puppets, or finger puppets A rope and blanket or sheet to hide behind
For Adult to Do Ahead:	String rope up about 2 feet from ground. Hang crib sheet or blanket over it.
Introduction:	Ask, "Have you ever talked to a puppet?"
Procedure:	Let children choose a puppet. Place puppet on hand and say, "Hi, how are you?" The puppet can respond by saying, "Hi, what's your name?" or "I'm great—how about you?" Encourage children to talk back and forth with their puppets. Then say, "Sometimes puppets are used by people to act out a story or poem. The person who has the puppet stands or sits behind something like this blanket so he or she is hidden. Then the person lifts his or her hand and the puppet over the blanket and lets the puppet 'talk.' Why don't you take turns letting your puppet talk or sing or say a nursery rhyme? The rest of us will sit on the other side of the blanket and watch."
Closure:	Tell the children, "You all put on a wonderful show. Would you like to try using one of the other puppets?"
Follow-up Activities:	Turn to page 119 for the instructions for doing the puppet show of "Goldilocks and the Three Bears." Leave the puppets and blanket up so children may experiment with different puppets on their own.

A TRIP TO THE LIBRARY

Purpose:	To visit the library. To listen to a fairy tale.
Skills/ Concepts:	To learn what is found at a library. To learn that you can borrow books. To develop listening skills.
Ages:	18 months through 5 years old.
Length of Activity:	Allow 20 to 30 minutes.
Materials:	Permission slip for each child (see p. xviii) A car seat and seat belt for each child if being transported by car

For Adult to Do Ahead:	Contact the library at least a week ahead of visit. Set a time for the visit (mornings are preferable). Tell librarian number and age of children. Ask to have a fairy tale or special story read to children (many libraries have a children's section or special story hours). Hand out permission slips. Arrange for transportation if necessary.
Introduction:	Say to the children, "This morning we are going to the library. The library is a place to read and look at books. We need to speak softly while we are in the library so that other people can read."
Procedure:	At the library follow the directions of the librarian. "This is Ms./Mr. _____. She/he is going to show us where the children's books are and then read us a story."
Closure:	Conclude by saying, "Thank you for the story. May we look around?"
Follow-up Activities:	If the children are not too tired or restless, they can look at books for a few minutes. For example, *Cinderella* translated by Marcia Brown (New York: Scribner's Sons, 1954. or *Sylvester and the Magic Pebble* by William Steig. New York: Simon & Schuster, 1969. or *One Fine Day* by Nonny Hogrogian. New York: Macmillan 1971.
	Have children decorate and send a thank you note to the librarian.

SCISSORS

Purpose:	To teach children how to carry scissors safely.
Skills/ Concepts:	To use fine motor skills for carrying scissors. To use listening skills. To use comprehension skills.
Ages:	3 through 5 years old.
Length of Activity:	Allow 2 minutes.
Materials:	A pair of blunt-tip scissors
Introduction:	Say to the children, "Watch how I am carrying these scissors." Hold scissors with your palm wrapped around the blunt tips and walk across room with handle up and the end that cuts down.
Procedure:	"How was I holding the scissors? Which part was I holding in my hand?" (the part that cuts) "Can you hold the scissors in your hand as I did? Good. Now take the scissors over to the table and put them down."
Closure:	"You did a wonderful job carrying the scissors."
Follow-up Activity:	Provide colored paper or magazines to cut. Cut pieces may be used for a pasting exercise.

REST TIME

Purpose: To teach the child that resting is good for your body.

Skills/ Concepts: To develop awareness of self.
To use listening skills.
To use fine motor skills.
To invite repetition of a fingerplay.

Ages: 18 months through 5 years old.

Length of Activity: Allow 2 minutes.

Materials: Poem

Introduction: Ask children, "Do you know why we sometimes take a nap and go to sleep each night? We sleep to give our bodies a rest. Resting your body helps you stay healthy."

Procedure: Tell the children, "I know a fingerplay about a little girl." (show children fingerplay) "Will you try to put the little girl to bed with me?"

This little girl is going to bed	(Hold up pointer finger of right hand.)
Down on the pillow she lays her head	(Lay pointer finger in palm of left hand, left thumb is pillow.)
She wraps herself in the covers so tight	(Close fingers of left hand around right pointer finger.)
And there she stays all the night.	
Morning comes and she opens her eyes	
Back with a toss the covers fly	(Open left fingers.)
Up she jumps, she's off and away	(Right pointer finger flies off left hand.)
Ready for work and ready for play.	

Closure: Ask the children, "Do you jump into bed like this little girl?"

Follow-up Activity: Teach the nursery rhyme "Wee Willie Winkie."

Wee Willie Winkie runs through the town,
Upstairs and downstairs in his nightgown,
Tapping at the window, crying at the lock,
Are the babes in their beds, for now it's ten o'clock.

Play lullabies from the record "Childhood's Greatest Hits with Wright and Reiman," from Rooster Records RFD 2, Bethel, Vermont 05032.
Read *Geraldine's Blanket* by Holly Keller, New York: Mulberry Books, 1984.

WALKING UP AND DOWN STAIRS

Purpose: To practice walking up and down stairs.

Skills/ Concepts: To control (gross motor) leg movements for walking.
To understand the terms "up" and "down."

© 1990 by The Center for Applied Research in Education

Ages: 18 months through 5 years old.

Length of Activity: Allow 2 minutes.

Materials: One or two stairs with a handrail

Introduction: Say to the children, "When you walk up and down stairs you should be very careful."

Procedure: Continue with, "Let's walk up and down these stairs. We must walk very slowly and hold on the hand rail. Let's go *up.* Now let's go *down.*"

Closure: Remind the children, "When we use stairs we must walk very slowly and hold on to the hand rail."

Follow-up Activities: Whenever stairs are used, give children a quick reminder to walk slowly and hold on to the handrail.

Play up/down games such as stand up, sit down; or throw a balloon up and watch it drift down; or walk up a hill and then walk back down; or "I see something up in the sky, I see something down on the ground."

MARCH ACTIVITIES

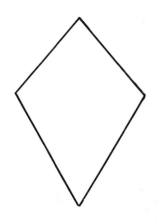

THEME: *Weather*
SPECIAL DAY: *St. Patrick's Day*

ART:	Shamrock Potato Prints
	Paper Bag Windsocks
	Kites
MUSIC:	The Weather Song
	Rain, Rain Go Away
	Mr. Sun
MOVEMENT:	Obstacle Course
	Lion Hunt
	Hop Across the Stream
LANGUAGE:	My Hat
	The Weather
	The Robin
NUTRITION:	Food Groups—Fruits
	Measuring
	Fruit and Vegetable Salad
SCIENCE/ NATURE:	Weather Calendar
	Seasons
	Sense of Taste
MATH:	Sequencing
	Some, None
	Halves and Wholes
SOCIAL STUDIES:	What Would You Wear?
	Tea Party
	The Veterinarian
HEALTH/ SAFETY:	Washing Your Hands
	Combing Your Hair

SHAMROCK POTATO PRINTS

Purpose:	To make a design using a potato.
Skills/ Concepts:	To develop fine motor skills used for dipping and pressing. To identify a shape.
Ages:	2 years old through 5 years old.
Length of Activity:	Allow 3 minutes.

Materials:	White construction paper	Potato
	Green tempera paint	Picture of a shamrock
	Paring knife or shamrock shaped cookie cutter	

For Adult to Do Ahead:	Cut the potato in half. If using a cookie cutter, cut into a 2-inch slice. Cut out shamrock shape with cookie cutter or use paring knife to carve the shape of a shamrock into the flat section of potato half. Pour paint into a bowl or plate.
Introduction:	Tell the children, "Today is St. Patrick's Day. It is a holiday celebrated by the Irish and many people in the United States. This is a shamrock." Show the picture of the shamrock. "The shamrock is a sign of good luck. We can make a picture of a shamrock."
Procedure:	Continue with, "To make this picture you will dip the shamrock shape into the green paint and then press the shape onto the white paper. You press the shamrock into the paint and fill your paper with shamrocks."
Closure:	Ask the children, "What is this called?" Shamrock. "Do you remember what today is?"
Follow-up Activities:	Picture may be hung or put in art folder. Play potato toss. Make a brown potato-shaped bean bag. Have children take turns attempting to toss the "potato" into a basket.

PAPER BAG WINDSOCKS

Purpose:	To make a windsock.
Skills/ Concepts:	To develop fine motor skills used for pasting and coloring. To see how the wind moves objects.
Ages:	18 months through 2 years old (with help); 3 through 5 years old.
Length of Activity:	Allow 10 minutes.

Materials:	Crayons	Scissors
	Lunch-sized paper bags, one per child	Paper punch
	Crepe paper streamers, six per child	String or yarn
	Self-sticking stickers	

For Adult to Do Ahead:	Cut off the bottom of each paper bag so that the bag is open at both ends. Cut streamers.

Introduction: Ask the children, "Does anyone know what this is called?" Show a real windsock or one you have made. "It is called a windsock. If we hang this windsock outside, it will tell us which way the wind is blowing. The wind will make the windsock move. Let's each make a windsock."

Procedure: Let children decorate their bags with crayons and stickers. Older children may be able to staple streamers to the bottom of their bags. Punch two holes, one on either side of the top of the bag, and tie a piece of yarn to each hole. Join the yarn above the bag and tie together in a knot.

Closure: Conclude by saying, "Let's take our windsocks outside and see if the wind is blowing today." Have children hold windsocks away from their bodies by the knotted yarn at the top.

Follow-up Activity: Talk about what else could make a breeze that would move the windsock: try blowing on the windsock, try holding the windsock in front of a fan (be sure there is adult supervision by the fan at all times), or try turning in a circle.

KITES

Purpose: To make kites.

Skills/ Concepts: To identify colors.
To use fine motor skills for painting and pasting.
To follow directions.

Ages: 18 months through 5 years old.

Length of Activity: Allow 2 minutes for painting and 3 minutes for pasting.

Materials:
Tempera paint	Paste or glue
Paint brushes	Cotton swab
White construction paper	Scissors
Black construction paper	Stapler
Yarn	A kite

For Adult to Do Ahead: Set up paint easel with several colors of paint. Cut bow tie shapes from black paper, four or five per child. Cut yarn into 12-inch lengths, one per child.

Introduction: Ask the children, "Has anyone ever seen something like this before?" Show the kite. "What is it called? Do you play with a kite inside or outside? Let's make some little kites to decorate our classroom."

Procedure: Each child should paint a colorful design on a piece of white construction paper. After the paint dries, 4- and 5-year olds may be able to lay a posterboard kite shape like that on the following page down on their painting, trace the shape, and then cut it out. Older children or an adult can do the same for younger children. Staple the yarn to the bottom of the kite. Using the cotton swab, have children paste the black bow tie shapes to the yarn. When everything has dried, tape or tack the kites to a bulletin board or wall or hang them with string from the ceiling.

Closure: Conclude by asking, "What did we make today? What kind of weather do you need to fly a kite?" Windy.

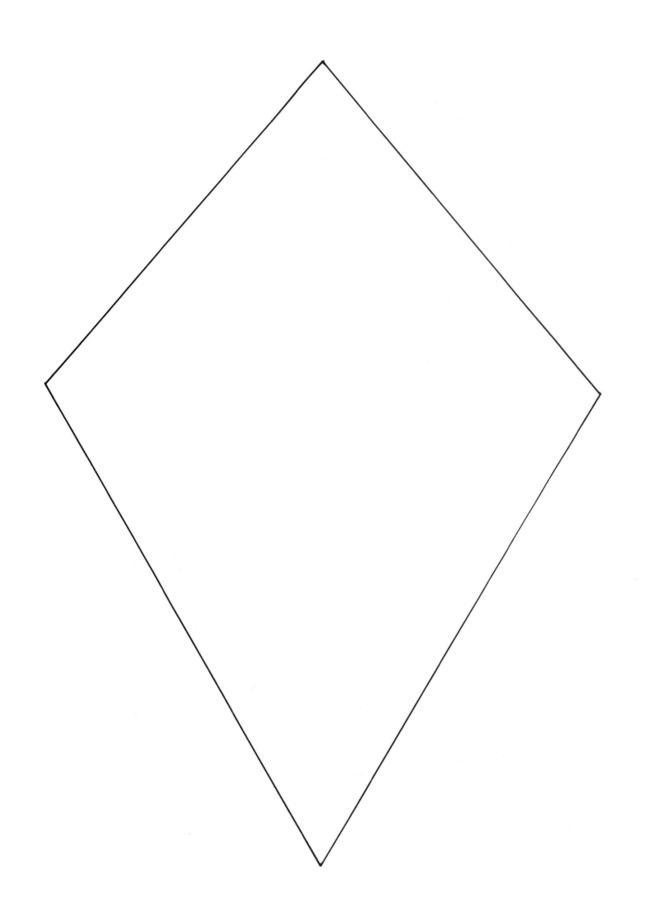

Follow-up
Activities: Using one real kite per adult, take children outside on a windy day and take turns flying a kite.

Listen to the selection "Let's Go Fly a Kite" from the sound track of *Mary Poppins*.

THE WEATHER SONG

Purpose: To sing a song about the weather.

Skill/
Concept: To repeat a song with verses.

Ages: 18 months through 5 years old.

Length of
Activity: Allow 2 minutes.

Materials: Song

Introduction: Begin by saying, "Let's sing a song about three different types of weather: rainy, sunny and warm, and snowy."

Procedure: Sing the song.

Closure: Ask the children, "Can you remember what three types of weather we sang about?"

The Weather Song

Words by:
JoAnne C. Calvarese

2. Summer sunshine shining 'round,
    Warming flowers in the ground.
    Out to swim or ride a bike,
    Throw a ball or take a hike.
    Summer sunshine shining 'round,
    Warming flowers in the ground.

3. Snowflakes falling softly down,
    Only whiteness on the ground.
    Out we go to cold and ice,
    Making snowballs very nice.
    Snowflakes falling softly down,
    Only whiteness on the ground.

Follow-up
Activity: Read *The Storm Book* by Charlotte Zolotow. New York: Harper and Row, 1952.

RAIN, RAIN GO AWAY

Purpose:	To sing a song about rain.
Skills/ Concepts:	To sing a song. To repeat a song. To insert a name at the proper time.
Ages:	18 months through 5 years old.
Length of Activity:	Allow 1 to 3 minutes.
Materials:	Song
Introduction:	Introduce this activity by saying, "Sometimes when it rains we can't go outside to play. This is a song asking the rain to go away so we can go outside to play."
Procedure:	Sing the song. Each time the song is repeated, fill in the blank with a child's name.
Closure:	Close with, "Did you like this song? We can't make the rain go away by singing a song."
Follow-up Activity:	Read *Rain* by Peter Spier. (New York: Zephyr.—Double-day, 1987).

Rain, Rain
Traditional

MR. SUN

Purpose:	To sing a traditional folk song.
Skill/ Concept:	To memorize a song.
Ages:	18 months through 5 years old.
Length of Activity:	Allow 2 minutes
Materials:	Song

Introduction: Introduce this activity by saying, "When the sun shines we can go outside and play. It is warm when the sun shines. Let's sing a song about the sun."

Procedure: Sing the song. Invite the children to sing with you.

Closure: Conclude by saying, "Can we go outside to play when the sun is shining?"

Follow-up Activity: Make a tissue paper collage. Provide the children with different shades of yellow tissue paper. Tear the tissue paper into pieces. Spread thinned-down white glue on a piece of white construction paper. Press the tissue paper pieces onto the construction paper in a random pattern.

Read *Arrow to the Sun* by Gerald McDermott. New York: Viking, 1974.

Mr. Sun

Words and music by:
JoAnne C. Calvarese

When Mis-ter Sun came out to-day, All the child-ren laughed and played. Hap-py in the warm spring air,

Ran and played with-out a care.

OBSTACLE COURSE

Purpose: To use an obstacle course.

Skills/ Concepts: To develop gross motor skills through use of arms and legs.
To use the terms "over," "under," "around," and "through."

Ages: 18 months through 2 years old (will pick one part of the course to repeat over and over); 3 through 5 years old.

Length of Activity: Allow 2 to 10 minutes, depending on how many times the children would like to repeat the course.

Materials: Any objects you have available such as chair, table, cardboard box, blocks
Note: This game may be played indoors or outdoors.

For Adult to Do Ahead: Cut the ends off of the box. Set up the obstacle course.

Introduction: Begin by saying, "Let's play 'Follow the Leader.' "

Procedure: Lead the children under a table, over a bridge of blocks, through a cardboard box, and around a chair. Describe out loud what you are doing as you approach each obstacle in the course. "First, I am going to crawl under the table; next, I will carefully step over the blocks; then, I will crawl through the box; finally, I will walk around the chair." You may add or subtract objects to the course to make it longer or shorter. Give all children an opportunity to be the leader.

Closure: Conclude by saying, "What was your favorite part of the obstacle course?"

Follow-up Activities: Older children might like to set up their own obstacle course.
        Cut holes in the sides of the cardboard box and use it for play.

LION HUNT

Purpose: To play a game that will help develop motor skills in hands and arms.

Skills/ Concepts: To develop the ideas of "over," "under," "through," "across," "up," and "down."
To develop motor skills in hands and arms.

Ages: 2 through 5 years old.

Length of Activity: Allow 2 to 3 minutes.

Materials: Words to lion hunt

Introduction: Begin by saying, "I feel like traveling to our make believe jungle today and going on a lion hunt. Who would like to join me?"

Procedure: In a seated position begin by gently, rhythmically slapping hands (palms down) on thighs. Children should follow your lead. "I want you to repeat what I say. Here we go!"

We're going on a lion hunt.	
We're searching everywhere. We're looking for the lion.	(Place side of hand to brow and turn head side to side as if searching.)
First we come to a great river. Can't get over it. Can't get under it. Guess we'll have to swim across it.	(Hold one hand over other arm.) (Hold one hand under other arm.) (Use arms to pretend to swim.)
Shake off that water.	(Shake shoulders, head, and arms.)
Back on the trail. Searching for the lion. Looking everywhere.	(Slap thighs.) (Hold hand to brow.)
I see a swamp! Can't go over it. Can't go under it. Guess we'll have to go through it.	(Hold one hand over other arm.) (Hold one hand under other arm.) (Hands palms down, fingers spread, say plop, plop, plop, etc.)
Still on the lion hunt. Looking everywhere. Searching for the lion.	(Slap thighs.) (Hold hand to brow.)
I see a tree. Let's climb up. I see the lion's cave.	(Pretend to climb up a tree.) (Hold hand to brow and point.)
Climb down the tree Shh, let's quickly tip toe to the cave.	(Pretend to climb down tree.) (Hold finger to lips.)
Peek inside the cave.	(Frame eyes with both hands.)

© 1990 by The Center for Applied Research in Education

Quietly tip toe in.	(Slowly move body up and down like you are on tip toe.)
Help! Here comes the lion!	(Shout and hold both hands up.)
Quickly tip toe out.	(Quickly move body up and down like you are on tip toe.)
Here comes the lion!	(Slap thighs quickly.)
Back up the tree.	(Climb tree.)
Looking everywhere.	(Pretend to look for lion.)
Here he comes!	(Point.)
Climb down the tree.	(Pretend to climb down the tree.)
~~Back through the swamp.~~	(Plop through the swamp.)
~~On the trail again.~~	(Slap thighs quickly.)
Back across the river.	(Pretend to swim.)
He's still after us!	(Slap thighs quickly.)
Home at last!	(Use motions to open and shut door and lock door. Brush brow with hand for "safe at last.")
Open the door, shut the door.	
~~Throw the lock, safe at last!~~	

TURN

Closure: At the end say, "That was a pretty exciting hunt!"

Follow-up Activities: Make a lion hunt mural using magazine cut outs.

Make flannel board pieces so the children can go on a lion hunt by themselves.

Read *Jumanji* by Chris Van Allsburg. Boston: Houghton Mifflin, 1981.

HOP ACROSS THE STREAM

Purpose: To play a hopping game.

Skills/ Concepts: To develop gross motor skills through use of legs and feet.
To hop or jump.

Ages: 2 through 5 years old.

Length of Activity: Allow 5 minutes.

Materials: Light blue posterboard
Tape

For Adult to Do Ahead: Draw a winding streamlike shape, narrow in some areas and wide in others, on the posterboard. Tape the "stream" to the floor.
Note: This game may be played indoors or outdoors.

Introduction: Say to the children, "Look at the shape on the floor. Let's pretend it's a little stream. Let's see if we can hop or jump across the stream."

Procedure: Spread children out along the stream and show them how to hop across the stream. Some may "fall in," but they'll improve with practice.

Closure: Ask, "How many of you fell in the stream? Let's shake the water off of our feet before we go inside." (With a smile lift feet one at a time and shake from the ankle.)

Follow-up Activity:

Do a cut- and-paste activity with children. Cut a blue tissue paper stream for each child (4- and 5-year-olds can cut their own, younger children will need adult help). Paste the stream to white construction paper. Cut several fish shapes out of colored construction paper. Paste fish in stream. Use crayons or markers to draw grass and flowers along the edge of the stream.

MY HAT

Purpose:

To sing a song with hand and body movements.

Skills/ Concepts:

To use hand and body movements.
To sing a simple song.

Ages:

18 months through 5 years old.

Length of Activity:

Allow 2 minutes.

Materials:

Song
A hat

Introduction:

Put on the hat and ask, "What is on my head?"

Procedure:

Continue with, "I know a song that will keep our heads warm and our hands busy." Sing the song for the children. Invite the children to sing the song with you again.

Closure:

"What was this song about? Where do you wear a hat?"

Follow-up Activities:

Make paper plate hats. Decorate plates with crayons, cutouts, flowers, crepe paper, and so on. Attach two 12-inch pieces of heavy yarn to paper plate with staples. These pieces of yarn can then be tied under the chin in a bow.
Have children bring a favorite hat from home to wear for Hat Day.

My Hat   German

My hat it has three corn-ers ; Three corn-ers has my hat ; And had it not three corn-ers ; It would not be my hat.

THE WEATHER

Purpose:	To learn a poem about the weather.
Skills/ Concepts:	To memorize a poem. To use hand and arm actions.
Ages:	18 months through 5 years old.
Length of Activity:	Allow 1 or 2 minutes.
Materials:	Poem
Introduction:	Begin by saying, "We've sung some weather songs. Let's learn a weather poem."
Procedure:	Recite the poem, using the hand and arm movements. Encourage the children to join you in repeating the poem.

I wish I was a sunbeam.   (Hands in circle above head.)
Sunbeam, sunbeam.
I wish I was a sunbeam,
Shining in the sky.   (Point to the sky or ceiling.)

I wish I was a raindrop   (Wiggle fingers down from head to toes.)
Raindrop, raindrop.
I wish I was a raindrop,
Falling from up high.

I wish I was a snowflake.   (Slowly drift hands down from head to toes.)
Snowflake, snowflake.
I wish I was a snowflake,
Drifting slowly by.

But, if the wind was blowing,   (Brush hands quickly in front of body left to
Blowing, blowing.   right.)
If the wind was blowing,
I'd shiver, my oh my.   (Wrap arms around body and shiver.)

Closure:	Conclude by asking, "If you were a sunbeam, would you be warm? If you were a rain drop, would you be wet? If you were a snowflake, would you be cold? If you were the wind, would you blow very fast?"
Follow-up Activity:	Provide paper and crayons, paints or markers. Encourage the children to illustrate the poem to make a mural for the wall.

THE ROBIN

Purpose:	To read a nursery rhyme about the weather.
Skills/ Concepts:	To repeat a poem. To dramatize a poem.
Ages:	18 months through 2 years old (for listening and repeating the poem); 3 through 5 years old (for dramatic interpretation).

Length of Activity:	Allow 2 minutes.
Materials:	Poem
Introduction:	Tell the children, "I know a poem about the weather I'd like to teach you."
Procedure:	Recite the poem. Pick five children (the wind, the snow, the robin, and two for the barn) to act out the poem as it is recited again. Children may want to switch roles and repeat the poem.

The north wind doth blow.
And we shall have snow.
And what will robin do then, poor thing?

He'll sit in a barn.
And keep himself warm.
And hide his head under his wing, poor thing!

Closure:	Ask the children, "Do you think the robin was cold? What did the robin do to help keep warm?"
Follow-up Activities:	Flannel board pieces could be made to illustrate the poem. Older children might like to make costumes to help dramatize the poem. The snow child might be dressed in all white and sprinkle confetti, the wind child might be dressed in all gray, and the robin child could be dressed in brown with paper wings. Use a table for the barn.

FOOD GROUPS—FRUITS

Purpose:	To introduce children to different fruits.
Skills/ Concepts:	To identify fruits. To develop sense of taste. To develop sense of touch.
Ages:	18 months through 5 years old.
Length of Activity:	Allow 5 to 10 minutes.
Materials:	A variety of fruits such as apples, oranges, pears, grapes, bananas Butter knife
Introduction:	Say to the children, "Fruits are very good to eat. They help your body grow big and strong. Let's look at some of the fruits I have here today."
Procedure:	Encourage the children to identify each fruit. Slice fruits one by one. Talk about the color inside and outside. Let everyone taste each fruit. Use descriptive words like hard, soft, crunchy, juicy, sweet, and sour.
Closure:	You may conclude by saying, "That was a delicious and nutritious snack!"

grapes

apple

pear

banana

© 1990 by The Center for Applied Research in Education

Follow-up Activities: Play a fruit matching game. Draw two sets of pictures on posterboard and cover with clear contact paper.
Ask children to match the fruits that are alike. Encourage the children to name each fruit.

Using a processor, process fruits such as orange, apple, grapes, and strawberries to obtain their natural juices. Serve in 3-oz. paper cups and encourage children to sample a variety of fruit juices.

MEASURING

Purpose: To measure specific amounts using a recipe.

Skills/ Concepts: To identify utensils.
To use fine motor skills through use of pouring, measuring, and stirring.

Ages: 3 years old through 5 years old.

Length of Activity: Allow 10 to 15 minutes.

Materials:

FOOD	*UTENSILS*
1 c. powdered milk	Measuring cups
¾ c. peanut butter	Measuring spoons
3 or 4 Tablespoons of honey	Mixing bowl
	Cookie sheet

Introduction: Begin by saying, "Measuring can be lots of fun. We can use a ruler to measure how long or tall something is. We can also use these two utensils to measure when we are cooking." Show cups and spoons. "Does anyone know what these are? Let's use them now to measure some ingredients and make a special snack today."

Procedure: Encourage the children to do the measuring of ingredients. Older children usually will automatically monitor younger ones and let them know when they've measured out too much or too little. Show children how to add or subtract ingredients from a cup to get the proper amount. Recipe:

Put powdered milk, peanut butter, and honey in bowl and mix well. With clean hands roll small portions of mixture into balls. Refrigerate until served.

Closure: Conclude by saying, "Now we've finished making cookies. Does anyone remember what we used to measure our ingredients?" Help children identify the different utensils used.

Follow-up Activity: Provide plastic cups to use with sand outdoors or dry oatmeal or water indoors. Children will enjoy filling and emptying measuring cups.

FRUIT AND VEGETABLE SALAD

Purpose: To prepare a nutritious lunch or snack using fruits and vegetables.

Skills/ Concepts: To identify fruits and vegetables.
To use fine motor skills through pouring, stirring, measuring, and grating.

Ages: 18 months through 2 years old (can help with the pouring and stirring); 3 through 5 years old (can help with the measuring and grating).

Length of Activity: Allow 10 to 15 minutes

Materials:

FOOD	*UTENSILS*
1 cup shredded carrots	Bowl
¼ cup crushed pineapple	Spoon
¼ cup raisins	Measuring cup
¼ cup chopped walnuts	Measuring spoons
2 tablespoons pineapple juice	Plastic grater
lettuce leaves	Plates
	Plastic spoons

For Adult to Do Ahead: Open can of crushed pineapple. Drain pineapple, saving juice. Place pineapple in a bowl. Chop nuts. Older children will be able to use a nut chopper.

Introduction: Tell the children, "This month we've talked about fruits and vegetables. Today I have a recipe for us to make that uses fruits and vegetables. Let's look at some of the ingredients and decide whether they are a fruit or a vegetable." Show carrots, lettuce, raisins, and pineapple.

Procedure: With adult supervision, older children can take turns grating the carrots. Be sure to supply a new carrot frequently so hands will not come too close to the grater. Next measure pineapple and carrots and encourage younger children to pour them into the bowl. Give each child a turn to mix the salad. Add pineapple juice, nuts, and raisins. Mix again.

Closure: Conclude by saying, "Now let's each place a lettuce leaf on a plate and put a spoonful of salad on top of it. We're ready to enjoy our salads!"

Follow-up Activities: Wash and dry utensils. Clean up preparation area with a damp sponge.
Keep some of each ingredient separate. Offer children who do not want the foods mixed a serving of individual fruits and vegetables.

WEATHER CALENDAR

Purpose:	To make a visual recording of the weather.
Skills/ Concepts:	To identify weather. To develop sense of sight. To develop skills used for sequencing.
Ages:	2 through 5 years old.
Length of Activity:	Allow 1 to 2 minutes each day weather board is to be used.
Materials:	Weather board (directions below) Weather symbols: sunny, rainy, cloudy, snowy
For Adult to Do Ahead:	Cut heavy piece of cardboard 9 inches by 24 inches. Divide into five equal portions and mark. Place lines 3 inches and 2 inches from the top and mark following illustration. Purchase Velcro heavy-duty self-gripping fasteners from fabric store or sewing section. Apply one-half of fastener under each day of the week. Draw small pictures (five each) of sunshine, clouds, clouds with rain, and snow. Apply other half of fastener to back of pictures.

WEATHER				
M	T	W	Th	F

Introduction:	Begin by saying, "It is *(sunny)* outside today. I can see the *(sun)*. I have a weather board." Show board. "You can mark the board with these special stickers." Show stickers. "Can you find the sticker for the sunny day?"
Procedure:	Continue with, "Yes, let's use the sticker with the sun. Can you press the sticker here?" Indicate in which space the child should place the sticker. "Today is *(Monday)*. It is *(sunny)*."
Closure:	Then say, "Today it is *(sunny)*. I wonder what the weather will be tomorrow? We will look at the weather tomorrow and put up another sticker."
Follow-up Activity:	Sing "The Weather Song" on page 136.

SEASONS

Purpose:	To identify the seasons.
Skills/ Concepts:	To identify spring, summer, winter, and fall. To expand vocabulary.
Ages:	18 months through 2 years old (will enjoy looking at pictures and placing pictures on flannel board); 3 through 5 years old.
Length of Activity:	Allow 2 or 3 minutes.
Materials:	Flannel board Two or more pictures of each season
For Adult to Do Ahead:	Glue a large piece of flannel to the back of each picture. Cover pictures with clear contact paper.
Introduction:	Say to children, "I have some pictures. Will you help me put them on the flannel board?"
Procedure:	Lay the pictures in front of the children. Ask a child, "Can you find a picture that looks like summer?" Give children verbal hints if necessary: "Can you see children swimming or at the beach? Are there people dressed in shorts?" After the correct picture is located, have child place the picture on the flannel board. Continue asking children to find winter pictures, fall pictures, and spring pictures.
Closure:	Conclude by saying, "Which of these pictures is a favorite of yours?"
Follow-up Activity:	Collect more seasonal pictures for children to paste onto construction paper. Print the name of the season on each page and attach all pages together to make a seasons book.

SENSE OF TASTE

Purpose:	To increase awareness of sense of taste.
Skills/ Concepts:	To identify familiar tastes. To identify objects. To develop idea of tasting with your tongue. To expand vocabulary.
Ages:	2 through 5 years old.
Length of Activity:	Allow 3 minutes.
Materials:	Soda crackers Plate, one for each child Orange Small cup of water, one for each child Sour pickle
Introduction:	Say, "We are going to taste some foods."

Procedure: Place a small piece of each food on each plate. "Let's taste the cracker. How does it taste?" If no one offers "salty" say, "The cracker tastes salty. What other food tastes salty?" Potato chips, nuts, pretzels. "Let's sip some water and then taste the pickle. How does it taste?" If "sour" isn't offered say, "The pickle tastes sour. Do you know another food that tastes sour?" Lemon, some grapefruit, vinegar. "Let's sip some more water and taste the orange. How does the orange taste?" Sweet. "What other foods taste sweet?" Cake, sugar, honey, apples.

Closure: Conclude by saying, "Which food tasted better to you: salty, sour, or sweet?"

Follow-up Activity: Offer children a plate of citrus fruit and crackers for a snack.

SEQUENCING

Purpose: To help children learn to order objects in sequence.

Skill/ Concept: To identify place: 1st, 2nd, 3rd.

Ages: 3 through 5 years old.

Length of Activity: Allow 2 minutes.

Materials: Three toys
Three children

Introduction: Say, "Let's play a game called "First, Second, Third."

Procedure: Place a toy in front of you and say, "This is first." Give the second toy to a child and say, "This is second. Can you put this behind the first toy?" Give the third toy to another child and say, "This will be third. Can you put this behind the second toy?" Help children place the toys in order. Point out that the toys are in a line first, second, and third, with the first closest to you and the third furthest away. "Can we form a line? Thomas can be first, Katie can be second, and Mike can be third."

Closure: As you touch each child on the head say, "Thomas is first, Katie is second and Mike is third."

Follow-up Activities: Form a line behind the three children and march around the room. Use rhythm instruments, a record, or tape to add some music.
   To further the concept of sequencing, use pictures that can be put in first, second, and third place order, for example, a child, a child with coat on, a child outdoors.

SOME, NONE

Purpose: To teach the opposites some and none.

Skills/ Concepts: To learn the meaning of the opposites some and none.
To use fine motor skills of thumb and first finger for picking up.

Ages: 18 months through 5 years old.

Length of
Activity: Allow 2 or 3 minutes.

Materials: Box of raisins
Plates or bowls

Introduction: Pour a few raisins out of the box onto your plate. "I have *some* raisins on a plate. Would you like to help me eat them?"

Procedure: Let the children eat all of the raisins. Then say, "Now there are *none*." Point to the plate. "Before we had *some* raisins and now we have *none*. Can you show me *some* raisins?" Give each child the box of raisins and let them pour a few onto their plates. Ask, "Are there *some* on your plate?" Offer help if needed. "How can you show me *none*?" Children should eat the raisins. Children may want to repeat the exercise.

Closure: Conclude by saying, "When there were raisins on the plates, we had *some*. Now the plates are empty, and we have *none*."

Follow-up
Activity: Hold several crayons in your hand. Say to the children, "I have *some* crayons in my hand." Hand the crayons to a child and say, "Now I have *none* (show your empty hands), but you have *some* (point to the child's hands)." Encourage the children to repeat the exercise by handing the crayons to another child.

HALVES AND WHOLES

Purpose: To play a math game with halves and wholes.

Skill/
Concept: To understand the idea of half of something.

Ages: 3 through 5 years old.

Length of
Activity: Allow 2 minutes.

Materials: Knife
An orange, apple, and pear
Plate

Introduction: Begin by saying, "I have something round and orange on my plate. What is it?" An orange. "Do you think it is a fruit or a vegetable?" Fruit. "Watch as I cut this orange in half."

Procedure: Cut orange in half. Point out that you have two halves and that each is the same size. Then hold the halves back together to show that two halves make a whole. Repeat with the apple and the pear. Encourage the children to identify each piece as a half and that the two placed together equal a whole. Cut enough fruit so each child may have a half.

Closure: Conclude by saying, "I've placed all the halves on this plate. You may each choose a half for a snack."

Follow-up
Activity: Provide a basket of felt circles in several different colors. Cut some of the circles in half. The children can experiment with putting the halves together to form a whole. Be sure the wholes and halves are all exactly the same size.

WHAT WOULD YOU WEAR?

Purpose:	To talk about what to wear for different types of weather.
Skills/ Concepts:	To identify types of clothing visually. To identify seasons.
Ages:	18 months through 2 years old (can identify some clothing); 3 through 5 years old.
Length of Activity:	Allow 2 to 3 minutes.
Materials:	Pictures or drawings of clothing to wear in rain (rain coat, boots, umbrella), snow (snow suit, hat, mittens, boots), the sun (shorts, bathing suit) Flannel board
For Adult to Do Ahead:	Glue a large piece of flannel to the back of each picture.
Introduction:	Tell the children, "We wear different types of clothing for different types of weather. Some special clothes are worn when it rains or snows."
Procedure:	Lay pictures in front of children. "What would you wear if it were raining?" Encourage children to pick rain clothing and then place the pictures on the flannel board. Help children to identify rain coat, umbrella, and boots. Continue with other pictures giving verbal encouragement when necessary.
Closure:	Ask the children, "What type of clothes are we wearing today?"
Follow-up Activities:	Provide a rain, snow, or warm weather outfit for children in dress-up center. Sing "The Weather Song" on page 136. Talk about the clothes you might wear for each verse. Read *Jesse Bear, What Will You Wear?* by Nancy Carlstrom. New York: Macmillan, 1986.

TEA PARTY

Purpose:	To practice manners.
Skills/ Concepts:	To use manners.
Ages:	18 months through 5 years old.
Length of Activity:	Allow 5 to 10 minutes or until children tire.
Materials:	Child-size dishes Juice or water Small crackers and pieces of cheese or small pieces of fruit

Note: This is a great rainy day activity, but it may also be used outside.

Introduction:	Say to the children, "I think we should have a tea party. Will you help me get the dishes?"

Procedure: Help children to set up places, putting one of everything at each place. Help children fill teapot and place food on plate. Start by asking a child if they would please pour some juice. Don't forget to say thank you after you have been served. Encourage children to ask for juice or food by saying please and thank you. Give each child an opportunity to pour and serve.

Closure: Say, "What a wonderful tea party. We'll have another one soon."

Follow-up Activities: Provide children with dish water and sponges for cleaning up.

Practice table setting. Trace the pattern of a child's plastic plate, cup, spoon, fork, and knife onto construction paper the same color as the dishes. Cut out the dish shapes and glue onto posterboard. Cover with clear contact paper. Children can practice placing the dishes in the correct spot on the board.

Read *May I Bring A Friend?* by Beatrice Schenk de Regniers. New York: Atheneum, 1964.

THE VETERINARIAN

Purpose: To visit with a veterinarian and learn about caring for a pet.

Skill/ Concept: To learn that a veterinarian is a doctor who cares for animals.

Ages: 3 through 5 years old.

Length of Activity: Allow 5 to 10 minutes.

Materials: Pictures of pets, dogs, cats, birds, fish

For Adult to Do Ahead: Contact a local veterinarian several weeks before the planned visit. Specify what the ages of children are and their approximate attention span. Request that the veterinarian talk about caring for pets—dogs, cats, birds, fish—their diet needs, where they sleep, how to play with pets, how to help pets stay well.

Introduction: Begin by saying, "This is Dr. _____. She/He is a veterinarian. A veterianrian is a doctor for animals. Dr. _____ will tell us how to care for animals."

Procedure: As the veterinarian talks about pets and animals, help elicit answers from the children if needed.

Closure: At the end of the talk help children thank the doctor for coming. "Thank you Dr. _____. We enjoyed your talk."

Follow-up Activities: Make thank you cards for the veterinarian. Children can draw their own illustrations or paste cut out magazine pictures to construction paper. Help children sign the cards, and then mail them to the veterinarian.

Older children might like to draw a picture of their pet or favorite animal. Drawings may be hung or placed in child's art folder.

WASHING YOUR HANDS

Purpose:	To teach children to wash their own hands.
Skills/ Concepts:	To learn the importance of keeping hands clean. To learn to use soap and water to clean. To learn to use a towel to dry hands.
Ages:	18 months through 2 years old (with help); 3 through 5 years old.
Length of Activity:	Allow 1 minute.
Materials:	Poem
Introduction:	Begin by saying, "Let's learn a poem to say while we wash our hands."
Procedure:	Say the poem and use the hand movements. Invite the children to join repeating the poem a second time.

TWO DIRTY HANDS
By JoAnne C. Calvarese

Two dirty hands, as dirty as can be;	(Hold up both hands.)
Watch how we wash them 1, 2, 3.	(Rub hands together and hold up fingers 1, 2, 3.)
Push up my sleeves,	(Pretend to push up sleeves.)
And turn the water on;	(Pretend to turn water on.)
Soap is for bubbles,	(Rub hands together.)
Then the dirt is gone.	(Hold hands in front of body with palms up.)
Two dirty hands, as dirty as can be,	(Hold up both hands.)
Washed with soap and water	(Rub hands together.)
Clean as clean can be.	(Hold hands in front of body with palms up and then turn hands.)

Closure:	Conclude by saying, "This is a good poem to say when you want to wash your hands."

COMBING YOUR HAIR

Purpose:	To encourage children to comb their hair each day.
Skills/ Concepts:	To develop gross motor skills used in combing. To develop grooming skills.
Ages:	2½ through 5 years old.
Length of Activity:	Allow 1 to 2 minutes.
Materials:	None needed.

Introduction: Begin by saying, "Combing your hair everyday helps keep you looking neat and helps your hair stay healthy."

Procedure: Continue with, "Let's pretend we are holding a comb in our hand. What color is your comb? Now let's sing a song while we pretend to comb our hair." Sing:

This is the way we comb our hair,
Comb our hair, Comb our hair,
This is the way we comb our hair,
So early in the morning.

"Make sure you did a good job and combed the top, the sides, the back and your bangs if you have them." (point to each part of the head as you name it)

Closure: Conclude with, "When you go home today, try practicing with your own comb."

Follow-up Activity: Try this same activity pretending to do other grooming skills such as brushing your hair, brushing your teeth, washing your hands, washing your face, or shining your shoes.

APRIL
ACTIVITIES

THEME: *Spring*
SPECIAL DAYS: *Easter*
Passover

ART:	Easter Bunny Finger Puppet
	Eggshell Mosaics
	Watercolor Painting
MUSIC:	Ham and Eggs
	Spring Time Is Here!
	It Rained a Mist
MOVEMENT:	Egg Toss
	Egg Hop Game
	Hide the Egg
LANGUAGE:	The Rain
	I Saw a Little Bunny
	Spring
NUTRITION:	Egg Salad Sandwiches
	Spring Bunny Salad
	Charoset, a Passover Snack
SCIENCE/ NATURE:	Spring Tree
	Sense of Hearing
	Natural Egg Dyes
MATH:	Box Building
	Eggs in a Basket
	Matching Shapes
SOCIAL STUDIES:	Field Trip to the Greenhouse/Florist
	Baby Face
	Growth Chart
HEALTH/ SAFETY:	Cleaning Up Spills
	Brush Your Teeth

EASTER BUNNY FINGER PUPPET

Purpose:	To make a finger puppet.
Skills/ Concepts:	To identify and place the various parts of a bunny's body. To recognize color. To paste.
Ages:	18 months through 2 years old (toddlers can use these puppets if made for them by an older child or adult); 3 through 5 years old.
Length of Activity:	Allow 15 minutes.
Materials:	One empty toilet paper roll per child Scissors Construction paper (white, pink, blue) Paste, glue Pink yarn Cotton swab One cotton ball per child
For Adult to Do Ahead:	From the pink construction paper cut the number of shapes per bunny as shown here. Cut white construction paper into pieces with the same measurements as the toilet paper roll. Cover one side of construction paper with glue and wrap it around the toilet paper roll with the seam where the two ends meet in the back. Cut short pieces of yarn for whiskers. Put paste or glue on a small paper plate.
Introduction:	Begin by saying, "Puppets are a fun way to act out a song or a story. Let's make our own bunny puppet today."
Procedure:	Talk about where to place the eyes, ears, nose, paws, and tail on the puppet. Show the children how the pasted side of each bunny part is placed against the bunny's body (toilet paper roll). Help children paste features on to the roll using the cotton swab.
Closure:	Conclude by saying, "Let's all put our bunny puppets on our fingers and take them for a little hop."
Follow-up Activity:	Use these finger puppets for a bunny parade. Have the children sing the song "Here Comes Peter Cottontail" as they march around the room or yard.

EGGSHELL MOSAICS

Purpose:	To use leftover colored eggshells from egg dyeing activity (see page 168).
Skills/ Concepts:	To use new vocabulary—"sprinkle." To recognize color. To use fine motor skills—sprinkling egg shells.
Ages:	18 months through 5 years old.
Length of Activity:	Allow 5 minutes.
Materials:	Crushed colored egg shells Cotton swab White construction paper, one sheet per child Glue

cut
2 ears

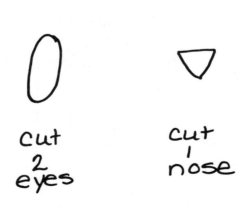

cut
2
eyes

cut
1
nose

cut
2
paws

For Adult to Do Ahead:	Place egg shells in plastic bag and crush them with wooden mallet or spoon. Pour white glue in a small container or paper cup for each child.
Introduction:	Begin by saying, "Today we are going to work with the shells leftover from the Easter eggs we dyed several days ago. We used the inside of the egg to make egg salad sandwiches. Today we are going to use the pretty colored outside shell.
Procedure:	Help children to spread glue on paper with cotton swab and sprinkle crushed egg shells onto the paper. Shake off pieces of egg shell that did not stick to the glue.
Closure:	Conclude with, "Let's look at and enjoy our colorful pictures. What colors do you see in these pictures?"
Follow-up Activity:	Hang pictures mounted on colored construction paper.

WATERCOLOR PAINTING

Purpose:	To experiment with colors that blend easily.
Skills/ Concepts:	To develop fine motor skill of holding a paintbrush. To develop large motor skill of arm sweeps while stroking paint on paper. To mix colors.
Ages:	18 months through 5 years old.
Length of Activity:	Allow 5 to 15 minutes depending on interest of child.
Materials:	Watercolor paper Large paintbrushes Watercolors Easel
Introduction:	Tell the children, "In springtime, plants and trees burst forth with beautiful colors. Many of these colors can be found in a paintbox. Let's do some painting."
Procedure:	Encourage the children to paint on their own. Sometimes a gentle reminder that too many colors placed on top of each other "muddy" the colors. Suggest a fresh sheet of paper for a child who wishes to continue painting.
Closure:	Conclude by saying, "Today we'll let our paintings dry, and later (tomorrow) we will turn them into colorful umbrellas."
Follow-up Activity:	Cut each dried painting into a large umbrella shape. Cut a handle shape from a piece of construction paper. Talk about where the children should spread the paste and help press the handle onto the back of the umbrella shape. Decorate walls or windows with these or hang them by a string from the ceiling.

HAM AND EGGS

Purpose:	To sing a song.
Skill/ Concept:	To learn how a song uses repetition.
Ages:	18 months through 5 years old.

Length of Activity:	Allow 1 minute.
Materials:	Song
Introduction:	Begin by saying, "We've colored eggs and we've eaten eggs. Let's learn a song about ham and eggs."
Procedure:	Sing song for the children. Invite the children to sing the song again.
Closure:	Ask, "Did you like singing about ham and eggs?"
Follow-up Activity:	Help children to make up hand actions for the song "Ham and Eggs."

Ham and Eggs

Traditional

Ham and eggs, ham and eggs, I like mine fried nice and brown, I like mine fried up-side down. Ham and eggs,

Ham and eggs, Flip 'em, flop 'em, flop 'em, flip 'em, Ham and eggs.

SPRING TIME IS HERE!

Purpose:	To sing a simple song.
Skill/ Concept:	To memorize a song.
Ages:	18 months through 5 years old.
Length of Activity:	Allow 1 minute.
Materials:	Song
Introduction:	Say to the children, "I have a spring time song to sing for you."
Procedure:	Sing the song for children. Invite the children to sing the song with you a second time.

Spring Time Is Here

Words and music by:
JoAnne C. Calvarese

Flow-ers are bloom-ing, Birds fly-ing, sing-ing; Spring time is here!

2. Warm breezes blowing,
Green grass is growing.
Spring time is here!

Closure: Ask, "What things did we sing about that tell us spring has arrived?"

Follow-up
Activity: Draw or paint a spring scene that illustrates the song. Provide children with markers, crayons, paints, paper, and brushes. Sing the song as the children hold up their pictures.

IT RAINED A MIST

Purpose: To learn a song to sing on rainy days.

Skills/
Concepts: To memorize words.
To think of objects that rain falls upon.

Ages: 18 months through 5 years old (children 2½ to 5 will offer suggestions; younger children will enjoy the music).

Length of
Activity: Allow 1 to 3 minutes, depending on how many verses you sing.

Materials: Song

Introduction: Begin by saying, "Look at the rain falling outside our windows. Let's look for some things outside that are getting wet in the rain." Ask the children to name some wet objects in sight. "Now I'll teach you a little song about rain."

Procedure: Sing the song asking the children to fill in the blanks. For example, ". . . it rained all over the grass, the grass, it rained all over the grass." Repeat the tune over and over choosing a different word for each verse. Some ideas are road, flowers, cars, houses, school, garden, children.

Closure: Conclude by saying, "Can you remember any of the things we named that are getting wet outside?"

Follow-up
Activity: Give children sponges and a bowl of water. Talk about dry and wet as they squeeze the water out of the sponges.

© 1990 by The Center for Applied Research in Education

It Rained a Mist   Folk Song—Virginia

EGG TOSS

Purpose:	To practice the gross motor skill of throwing.
Skill/ Concept:	To throw at a target.
Ages:	18 months through 2 years old (may like to walk over to the box and push the egg through the mouth hole); 2½ through 5 years old.
Length of Activity:	Allow 5 to 15 minutes depending on the number of children involved and their attention spans.
Materials:	Large box Three plastic or rubber eggs Masking tape
For Adult to Do Ahead:	Paint a bunny face on the side of the box. Draw a large round mouth for the bunny and cut it out. Set the box on a table so the bunny's face is at the children's chest level. Place a strip of masking tape on the floor about 2 feet away from the box to indicate where the children should stand.
Introduction:	Ask, "Can someone tell me whose picture is painted on the side of this box? Can someone show me the bunny's mouth? Let's play a game using our bunny."
Procedure:	Have the children stand one at a time behind the masking tape line on the floor. Ask the children to try to toss the eggs one at a time into the bunny's mouth. When a child is getting two out of every three eggs through the mouth, increase the level of difficulty by having the children stand 3 feet away from the box. Remember to move the masking tape marker.
Closure:	Conclude by saying, "Let's place the eggs in a bowl beside the bunny. Then you may play with the game again later."
Follow-up Activity:	Read *The Easter Bunny That Overslept* by Priscilla and Otto Friedrich. New York: Lothrop, Lee and Shepard Co.

EGG HOP GAME

Purpose:	To teach a game using the gross motor skills walking, jumping and hopping.
Skills/ Concepts:	To jump forward with both feet. To balance oneself upon landing. To follow a pattern.
Ages:	18 months through 3 years old—jumping or walking; 3 through 5 years old—jumping or hopping.
Length of Activity:	Allow 3 to 5 minutes.
Materials:	Ten large egg-shaped pieces cut from colored posterboard

For Adult to Do Ahead: Cut ten large egg-shapes from cardboard or colored posterboard. Decorate them with paint or magic markers to resemble Easter eggs. Cover with clear plastic contact paper to protect the side with the decorations. Place the ten Easter eggs about 1 foot apart in a straight line on the floor. (A loop of masking tape may be placed under the eggs to hold them in place on the floor.)

Introduction: Begin by saying, "Let's count the paper Easter eggs I have placed on the floor. There are ten eggs. Can you jump from egg to egg?"

Procedure: Show the children, if needed, how to follow the pattern from start to finish, landing on two feet each time. "Who would like to follow the egg trail?" Give each child a turn to follow the trail by jumping or walking. The children should jump one at a time onto the first egg, if possible landing on both feet. Continue on in the same manner until the last egg is reached. Once the children have mastered jumping on the eggs in a straight line, vary the line by having it curve back and forth around chairs and tables.

Closure: Say to the children, "Watch what I am doing." Hop on one foot. "Can anyone tell me what I am doing? Let's try to hop together. Can you hop from egg to egg along our egg trail?"

Follow-up Activities: After jumping about on colored eggs, the child might like to relax with a quiet activity. Read *The Remarkable Egg* by Adelaide Holl (New York: Lothrup, Lee and Shepard Co.).

    Another great song that can be used to help develop large motor skills is that old favorite "The Bunny Hop." Have the children make their hands into loose fists and hold them up against their chests as they hop around the room to the tune.

HIDE THE EGG

Purpose: To play a game that uses fine and gross motor skills.

Skills/ Concepts: To make a simple hypothesis (where is something hidden?).
To test the hypothesis.
To make a new hypothesis if necessary.
To use fine and gross motor skills.

Ages: 18 months through 5 years old.

Length of Activity: This game is limited only by the attention span of the children.

Materials: Plastic or rubber eggs, one for each child
Basket

Introduction: Begin by asking, "What do I have in my hand?" Plastic or rubber egg. "Look at my basket. What do I have?" More eggs. "What colors are the eggs? Now I am going to hide the eggs." Children should either leave the room or cover their eyes. When the eggs have been hidden, call the children back into the room. "Now let's all find an egg."

Procedure: Encourage children to look for eggs. Give verbal hints if needed. After everyone has found an egg, place the eggs back in the basket to be hidden again.

Closure: Ask the children, "Did you enjoy finding the eggs? Would someone like to hide the eggs so we may look for them again?"

Follow-up
Activity: Provide a basket filled with plastic eggs of different colors. Separate the eggs in half. Ask the children to match the colors by putting two egg halves of the same color back together.
　　　　Read *The Egg Tree* by Katherine Milhous. New York: Charles Scribner's Sons, 1950.

THE RAIN

Purpose: To teach a simple poem using hand and arm motions.

Skills/
Concepts: To use fine and gross motor skills through actions of arms, hands, and fingers.
To expand vocabulary.
To learn where rain comes from.

Ages: 18 months through 5 years old (the younger child may try only a few of the hand motions, while the older child will repeat the poem and finger motions).

Length of
Activity: Allow 1 to 2 minutes.

Materials: Poem

Introduction: Say to the children, "Rain is important. It gives us water to drink. It also provides water for plants and animals. Today we are going to learn a poem about rain."

Procedure: Repeat poem several times while doing the actions.

THE RAIN

by JoAnne C. Calvarese

Thirsty flowers
Standing high,
Wait for raindrops
From the sky.

(Hold ten fingers in front of body in an upright position.)

(Point towards sky.)

Pitter, patter
Hit the ground.
Tumble down
Without a sound.

(Wiggle fingers down in front of body like rain falling.)

(Wiggle fingers all around the body to quietly touch floor.)

I SAW A LITTLE BUNNY

Purpose: To participate in repetition of a simple fingerplay.

Skills/
Concepts: To develop fine and gross motor skills through arm, hand, and finger motions.
To memorize a poem.

Ages: 18 months through 5 years old.

Length of
Activity: Allow 1 minute.

Materials: Poem
Fresh head of cabbage

Introduction: Ask, "Does anyone know what I am holding in my hands?" A cabbage. "What color is it? What shape is it? Let's try to make a pretend bunny with our hands. Make a fist with one hand like this. Then with your other hand make a bunny's head like this (see directions below). This is his head (point to fist) and these are his ears (point to upright fingers). I'm going to teach you a poem about a bunny and a cabbage."

Procedure: Repeat poem and finger motions two or three times:

I saw a little bunny sitting,	(Make bunny head by making a fist with right hand and holding first two fingers up for ears.)
By a cabbage head.	(Left hand in a fist for a cabbage.)
"I think I'll eat some cabbage,"	
The little bunny said.	(Pretend bunny is nibbling cabbage.)
So he nibbled at the cabbage,	
Then he pricked his ears and said,	(Wiggle fingers that are bunny ears.)
"Now I should be hopping,	(Hop bunny head away.)
Hopping on ahead."	

Closure: "Now that we have learned the poem, does anyone know what we do with a cabbage?" Eat it. "Let's take this cabbage and make a special snack out of it."

Follow-up Activity: Make cole slaw. Using a food processor, finely shred the cabbage. The children can add a prepared salad dressing and toss to mix well.
Read *Seven Little Rabbits* by John Becker. New York: Scholastic Inc. 1973.

SPRING

Purpose: To discuss the spring season.

Skills/ Concepts: To learn new vocabulary.
To learn that spring is a time of change (growth).

Ages: 18 months through 2 years old (simple word identification); 3 through 5 years old (discussion of pictures).

Length of Activity: Allow 2 to 5 minutes, younger children; 5 to 10 minutes, 3 to 5 year olds.

Materials: Pictures of spring (having the discussion outside or by a window is helpful)

Introduction: Hold up a picture showing a spring scene. Ask, "Does anyone know what season this picture shows?"

Procedure: The adult will have to lead the discussion. Some thoughts or questions to use:
Spring is the season that follows winter.
In some places the weather becomes warmer.
Do we wear heavy coats and boots in spring?
What happens to the trees in spring?
What happens to the flowers?
Is the grass green or brown?

Closure: Ask, "What do you see outside our window?"

Follow-up Activity: Collect spring pictures to be pasted on construction paper.

Closure: "Today we learned some new words. What does 'tumble' mean?" (When raindrops tumble from the sky, they fall from the sky.) "Does anyone know what happens when raindrops patter?" (They splash lightly and bounce as they touch the ground.) "Let's make our fingers be the raindrops again as they fall from the sky and patter on the ground."

Follow-up Activity: Sing "Rain, Rain Go Away" on page 137.

EGG SALAD SANDWICHES

Purpose: To make a nutritious lunch or snack.

Skills/ Concepts: To use fine motor skills—stirring and spooning.
To make a sandwich.

Ages: 18 months through 2 years old (the younger child will need help from an older child or adult); 3 through 5 years old.

Length of Activity: Allow 10 minutes.

Materials:

FOOD	*UTENSILS*
see natural egg dyes page 168	Bowl
Hardboiled eggs, one per sandwich	Spoon for stirring
Mayonnaise	Plates (paper/plastic)
Whole wheat bread	Egg slicer
	Plastic knife
	Pastry blender

Introduction: Say to the children, "Inside these pretty colored eggs we'll find a surprise. Watch what happens when I crack this egg." Crack and peel egg. Put shells in one bowl and hold up egg for children to see. "This is called a hard boiled egg. We are going to use these eggs to make a delicious and nutritious sandwich."

Procedure: After washing hands, encourage older children to help crack and peel eggs. Remember to check eggs when the children are done to make sure all shell pieces have been removed. Older children (younger children with help) can use the egg slicer to slice the eggs. After the eggs have been sliced give each child a turn to chop the eggs with the pastry blender. Place chopped egg in bowl. Add mayonnaise and give each child a turn stirring the egg mixture. Give each child a slice of bread on a plate and place one or two large spoonfuls of egg mixture on bread. Children who eat less can fold their piece of bread in half. Children who eat more can add another slice of bread on top. Sandwiches may be cut into halves or quarters to make them more manageable for small hands and mouths.

Closure: Conclude activity by saying, "Let's carefully take our plates to our tables and eat our sandwiches."

Follow-up Activities: Clear the table and give children a damp sponge to wipe their places.
Use hard boiled eggs to make egg boats. Cut eggs in half. Save the egg white and chop up the yolk. Add a little mayonnaise and a little mustard to the yolk. Place the egg mixture into the egg white and serve.

SPRING BUNNY SALAD

Purpose: To present fruits and vegetables in a novel way.

Skills/ Concepts: To place bunny facial features.
To recognize the various fruits and vegetables.
To identify colors.
To develop sense of smell.
To develop sense of taste.

Ages: 18 months through 2 years old (with guidance); 3 through 5 years old.

Length of Activity: Allow 20 minutes.

Materials:

FOOD (per child)	*UTENSILS*
Washed lettuce leaf	Pot
1 pear half	Small bowls to hold raisins, grapes, and eggs
2 raisins	Medium bowl for celery
Half a red grape	Knife
4 celery sticks	Plates for each salad
2 slices of hardboiled egg	
Ice cubes	

For Adult to Do Ahead: Hard boil eggs (you will need half an egg per child). Drain and cool in refrigerator. Slice each egg in quarters lengthwise. Cut celery into 2-inch strips. Then slice in half lengthwise. Place in ice water to curl. Wash and dry lettuce leaves (you will need one or two leaves per salad depending on their size). Wash and drain grapes, then slice in half. Arrange raisins, grapes, and eggs in separate bowls. Drain celery.

Introduction: Begin by saying, "We have a real surprise for lunch today. You will each put together a bunny salad to eat!"

Procedure: Have each child arrange a lettuce leaf on a plate. Ask the children to find the hollowed side of the pear and place the pear hollowed side down on the lettuce. Talk about where to place the raisin eyes, grape nose, celery whiskers, and egg ears. Ask the children to point to their own eyes, nose, and ears. Remember to have extra ingredients available as some may be popped into a child's mouth before they reach the plate.

Closure: Say, "Now let's enjoy eating our bunny salads."

Follow-up Activity: Pretend to be bunnies. Ask children how a bunny moves. Children will enjoy hopping around the room or outdoors. Older children will be able to hop on one foot or in a squat position, while younger children may hop around the room on both feet.

CHAROSET, A PASSOVER SNACK

Purpose: To introduce a food prepared during the Jewish holiday of Passover.

Skills/ Concepts: To identify food.
To use fine motor skills, stirring and spreading.

Ages: 18 months through 5 years old.

Length of Activity: Allow 5 to 10 minutes.

Materials:

FOOD	UTENSILS
1 apple	Sharp knife and butter knife
1 teaspoon cinnamon	Measuring spoons
1 tablespoon honey	Bowl
1 tablespoon nuts	Wooden board for chopping
$\frac{1}{8}$ teaspoon lemon juice	Napkins or plates
Matzos bread	Plastic knife

For Adult to Do Ahead: Finely chop apples and nuts. Sprinkle apples with lemon juice to keep them from browning. Older children may be able to use a nut chopper to help chop the nuts.

Introduction: Introduce activity by saying, "Passover is a Jewish holiday celebrated each spring. The Jewish people eat many special foods during this celebration. Today we are going to make one of them. Charoset (pronounced ha-ro-ses) is a tasty snack of apples, nuts, and honey."

Procedure: Ask the children to add the honey and nuts to the chopped apples. Give each child a chance to stir ingredients. Have each child place a large spoonful of the mixture in the center of a piece of matzos bread and spread it to the edges with a plastic knife.

Closure: Say, "This smells delicious! Let's try our new snack."

Follow-up Activity: Play "Hide the Nut," a Passover game. One person hides a few nuts in his or her hand, and everyone else tries to guess how many nuts are hidden. Use one, two, or three small nuts.

SPRING TREE

Purpose: To display materials found outdoors in the spring.

Skills/ Concepts: To identify nature materials.
To develop senses of touch and sight.
To use memory skills.

Ages: 18 months through 5 years old.

Length of Activity: Allow 5 to 10 minutes for initial set up of tree and 2 minutes a day to add additional items found.

Materials: Tree branch, an interesting shape with many twigs
Yarn or curling ribbon
Large pot or pan filled with sand or rocks
Variety of spring materials such as
new leaves
silk flowers
small spring pictures
small colorful bows

For Adult to Do Ahead: Secure the branch with sand or rocks in a large pot so it won't tip. Pot may be wrapped in colorful fabric. Cut out spring pictures. Punch hole in top and tie a bow. An older child will be able to help cut out pictures.

Introduction: Ask children, "Do you remember our autumn tree? Would you like to help me decorate this tree branch for spring?"

Procedure: Continue by saying, "It is spring. We are going to have a spring tree. We're going to use these things for our decorations. Can you tell me what these things are?" Help children to identify spring materials if needed. Children will enjoy hanging the decorations from the branch. As they hang the materials, ask questions about what each item is, where it might be found, and how it feels (hard, soft, crunchy, etc.).

Closure: When finished, ask, "Doesn't our tree look beautiful? This is a wonderful way to bring some outdoors inside."

Follow-up Activity: Add to the tree daily. Encourage the children to be on the lookout for new and interesting things to use for decorations.

SENSE OF HEARING

Purpose: To play a listening game.

Skills/ Concepts: To identify sounds.
To develop sense of hearing.

Ages: 18 months through 5 years old.

Length of Activity: Allow 1 minute, for younger child and 5 minutes, for those 3 through 5 years old.

Materials: None needed.

Introduction: Put your finger to your lips and say, "Sh-h-h, what do you hear? Listen very carefully with your ears." Encourage children to listen for any noises.

Procedure: As children hear sounds, help them to identify what they hear. Continue listening and sharing what is heard.

Closure: At the end of the activity, ask, "Can you remember what sounds we heard today?"

Follow-up Activities: Standing out of sight of the children, make various sounds using items such as a bell, rattle, closing door, whistle, and running water. Ask the children to guess and identify each sound.
Read the *Country Noisy Book* by Margaret Wise Brown. New York: Harper & Row, 1940.

NATURAL EGG DYES

Purpose:	To color eggs using all-natural dyes.
Skills/ Concepts:	To enhance color recognition. To identify fruits and vegetables.
Ages:	18 months through 5 years old.
Length of Activity:	Allow 2 to 3 minutes.

Materials:

FOOD	*UTENSILS*
Boiling water	Stove or hot plate
Vinegar	Pot for boiling water
Spinach	Measuring spoons
Curry	Measuring cups
Carrot tops	Paper towels to drain eggs and for any spills
Beet juice	Deep cups or mugs to hold dyes
Blueberries	Blender
Hardboiled eggs (white)	Large serving spoon
	Strainer

For Adult to Do Ahead:	Make dyes. Read and follow recipes given here. Transfer cooled dyes to a cup or mug before children dip eggs.
Recipes:	Yellow Eggs: Mix 1 cup boiling water with 1 tablespoon of vinegar and 1 tablespoon of curry. Dip the egg in the dye solution until it turns yellow. Rinse off any curry powder still sticking to the egg while it is still wet. Olive or Light Green Eggs: Cut off several carrot tops and place in a pan of water. Bring this to a boil. Remove pan from heat. Cool and dip egg in dye until it is green. For Green Eggs: Place several spinach leaves in a pan of water. Bring this to a boil. Remove pan from heat. Cool and dip egg in dye. For Pink Eggs: Dip egg in ⅓ cup of beet juice. Rotate egg with a spoon to make sure all sides of the egg are colored with the juice. For Lavendar Eggs: Mash one cup of blueberries in a blender or with a fork. Strain the blueberries. Dip egg in blueberry juice.
Introduction:	Say to children, "Before dyes and artificial colorings were invented, people depended upon fruits, vegetables, and roots to produce colors. Today we're going to color eggs using berries, vegetables, and juices."
Procedure:	Talk about the different colors of dye. Show the children which fruits and vegetables were used to make the dyes. Help the children to identify the foods. Ask each child: "Which color do you want to use to dye or color your egg?" Help children individually to balance an egg in a large serving spoon. Gently lower the egg into the dye bath. When the egg is the desired color, remove from dye. Drain the egg and let it dry.

Closure: Conclude by saying, "Let's name the colors that we see." Point to each egg as the children identify the color. When the lesson is completed, remember to refrigerate eggs.

Follow-up Activity: Read *The Runaway Bunny* by Margaret Wise Brown. New York: Harper & Row.

BOX BUILDING

Purpose: To extend block building.

Skills/ Concepts: To improve hand-eye coordination.
To develop gross motor skills by lifting and placing boxes.
To improve spatial relations by working with large 3-dimensional objects.
To encourage use of imagination.

Ages: 18 months through 5 years old.

Length of Activity: Allow 5 to 30 minutes depending upon interest of children.

Materials: Cardboard shipping and packing boxes in a variety of shapes and sizes (check with supermarkets, department stores, and appliance stores for leftover boxes)

For Adult to Do Ahead: Set up cardboard boxes on playground.

Introduction: Say to the children, "Look at what is out on the playground. (children see boxes) Let's go out and play with them."

Procedure: Children can build with boxes just as they would with blocks—creating bridges, towers, and cities. Large appliance boxes with doors and windows (precut by adult) can become imaginary forts, houses, castles, spaceships.

Closure: Ask the children, "What did you make with the boxes? Did you enjoy playing with the boxes?"

Follow-up Activities: Older children can paint the boxes turning them into buildings or spaceships.
Children can play hide and seek hiding inside of or under boxes. Adult supervision is always a good idea when children are playing with such large objects.

EGGS IN A BASKET

Purpose: To count objects.

Skills/ Concepts: To count one to ten objects.
To understand "in" and "out."

Ages: 18 months will put eggs into and remove them from basket; 2 year olds will understand concept of putting two or three eggs in; 3 year olds understand concept of putting up to five eggs in; 4 through 5 years old will understand concept of putting up to ten eggs in.

Length of Activity:	Allow 5 minutes.
Materials:	Wicker or plastic basket with handle Colored plastic or rubber eggs
Introduction:	Begin activity by asking, "Who would like to help me count the eggs in my basket?"
Procedure:	As you have a child remove an egg from the basket, say its number name, for example, "one." Continue until all the eggs are out of the basket and counted. Then say, "Now it's time to put the eggs back into the basket." Count out loud with the children as a child or several children put the eggs back into the basket. Give each child a turn.
Closure:	At the end ask, "How many eggs did we have in the basket?"
Follow-up Activity:	Place other objects in the basket to be counted. For older children vary the number of objects in the basket, five one time and eight another time.

MATCHING SHAPES

Purpose:	To match a felt shape to a picture of that shape.
Skills/ Concepts:	To identify shapes (triangle, square, and circle). To match shapes.
Ages:	2 through 5 years old.
Length of Activity:	Allow 5 minutes.
Materials:	Card with triangle Card with circle Card with square Felt cutouts of a triangle, circle, and square
For Adult to Do Ahead:	Cut triangle, square, and circle out of one color construction paper. Glue shape to oaktag or cardboard. Cover with contact paper. Cut into three cards—one shape to a card. Cut same size triangle, square, and circle out of felt.
Introduction:	Ask, "Who would like to match some shapes?"
Procedure:	Place the three cards in front of you. Ask, "I wonder what shapes these are?" Help children to identify the shapes. Show the children the three felt shapes. Ask, "I wonder what shapes these are?" Hold up the felt circle. Ask, "Is there another circle on the table?" The child who answers can place the felt circle on the card. Proceed as above with the other shapes. Give each child a turn at matching the shapes.
Closure:	Conclude by saying, "Let's put the matching game in a box so we can play with it again."
Follow-up Activity:	Provide triangles, circles, and squares cut from one color of construction paper. Children can paste shapes onto another piece of construction paper. Hang the picture or place the picture in art folder.

FIELD TRIP TO THE GREENHOUSE/FLORIST

Purpose:	To visit a greenhouse or florist.
Skills/ Concepts:	To observe plant growth. To care for plants. To encourage language expansion.
Ages:	3 through 5 years old.
Length of Activity:	Allow 20 minutes—this is an activity to do when the children are rested and not hungry. Early morning is often best.
Materials:	One adult for every three children Cars with a selt belt for each child Permission slips signed by parents (see page xviii)
For Adult to Do Ahead:	Call the greenhouse at least a week in advance and let them know the number of children coming, age of the children, and number of adults accompanying the children. Some greenhouses will allow the children to start seed or small plants to take home with them.
Introduction:	Before loading the cars, tell the children that you are going to visit a greenhouse, florist, or nursery. Explain that a greenhouse is a place where people care for and sell plants. Name a few of the plants or flowers they will be seeing.
Procedure:	Take the field trip.
Closure:	When the children seem restless, it is time to go. Encourage the children to join you in thanking the staff; then buckle up and head for home.
Follow-up Activity:	Help the children make thank you cards to send to the greenhouse. Children can make their own drawings of the most beautiful flower they saw on the trip. Help sign each child's card, and then mail.

BABY FACE

Purpose:	To see and discuss the differences between a baby and a toddler and a toddler and a 5-year-old.
Skills/ Concepts:	To identify self. To learn that everyone changes as they grow. To encourage expansion of vocabulary.
Ages:	18 months through 5 years old.
Length of Activity:	Allow 1 to 2 minutes for 18 months through 2 years old; 5 to 10 minutes for 3 through 5 years old.
Materials:	Several pictures of each child from birth to present age, with identification on the back Picture frame tabs, available at drugstore Colored posterboard or construction paper, 1 sheet per child

For Adult to Do Ahead:	Mount pictures on posterboard or construction paper using the picture frame tabs.
Introduction:	Say, "Today we are going to look at pictures of each of you when you were younger."
Procedure:	As each child holds up his or her sheet of pictures, some questions might be
	Can you tell who this is?
	Is this a baby or a big girl/boy?
	How do babies act? (cry, smile, don't talk, gurgle, crawl, etc.)
	How does this picture look different from this picture? (point to same child but older) Elicit differences in hair, teeth, size of child and so on.
	Hang each group of pictures low on a wall or bulletin board where children can look at them when they want.
Closure:	Conclude by saying, "What beautiful pictures and what beautiful children."
Follow-up Activity:	Provide the children with dolls, blankets, and beds and suggest a game of "baby."

GROWTH CHART

Purpose:	To mark a child's growth visually.
Skills/ Concepts:	To follow directions. To develop a concept of tall/taller/tallest. To encourage development of attention span.
Ages:	18 months through 5 years old.
Length of Activity:	Allow 2 minutes to add to chart started in October.
Materials:	Brightly colored construction paper Black marker
For Adult to Do Ahead:	Cut tulip shapes from colored paper. Print each child's name on a tulip.
Introduction:	Begin by saying, "Let's check the growth chart and see if you have gotten any taller."
Procedure:	Stand with your back to the wall. "See how tall I am standing. Here is a tulip with my name. I am going to tape it to the chart." Invite each child to stand like "I did" against the wall. Mark the child's height on the tulip and tape to the chart at the proper height. Ask each child if he or she is taller than when the pumpkin was taped to the chart."
Closure:	Say, "Look how tall you are getting."
Follow-up Activity:	Choose 3 children of varying heights. Point out the difference between tall, taller, and tallest as they stand side by side.

CLEANING UP SPILLS

Purpose: To encourage children to be aware of and to clean up accidental spills.

Skills/ Concepts:
To soak up spills with sponge.
To wipe.
To use a small mop.
To use a broom and dust pan.

Ages: 2½ through 5 years old.

Length of Activity: Allow 5 minutes.

Materials:

Water	Rice
Large sponge	Child-sized broom
Child-sized floor mop	Dustpan
Pail	Brush
Wastebasket	

For Adult to Do Ahead: Use water and rice to make two separate spills on floor.

Introduction: Begin by saying, "I've found some water and some rice on the floor. Someone might slip on them, fall, and hurt themselves. What do you think we should do?" (clean them up)

Procedure: Show children how to use a sponge on small wet spills; then let them try soaking up water with sponge, squeezing excess into pail and soaking up water again. Demonstrate use of a mop on larger wet spills. Leave enough water for children to try. Have older children show younger children how to use a broom, dustpan, and brush on dry spills. Encourage children to try each cleanup activity. Remember they will be awkward their first few attempts.

Closure: Conclude by saying, "You have helped to make our classroom safe by cleaning up those spills."

Follow-up Activity: Offer pouring activities that include pouring water from pitcher to pitcher and rice from pitcher to cup. Be prepared for spills by having a sponge and dustpan handy.

BRUSH YOUR TEETH

Purpose: To review brushing teeth.

Skills/ Concepts:
To brush teeth after meals.
To use memory skills.

Ages: 18 months through 5 years old.

Length of Activity: Allow 1 or 2 minutes.

Materials: None needed.

Introduction: Ask, "Do you remember when you should brush your teeth?"

Procedure: Older children may respond, "After I eat" or "After lunch/supper/breakfast" or "Before I go to bed." Give verbal help if needed. Remind children that it is important to clean their teeth after they eat. If they don't have a toothbrush, they might rinse their mouth with water.

Closure: Conclude by asking, "When is it important to clean your teeth?"

Follow-up Activity: Read *Bill and Pete* by Tomie de Paola. New York: G.P. Putnam's Son, 1978.

MAY ACTIVITIES

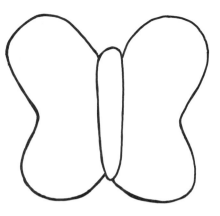

THEME: *Plants and Flowers*
SPECIAL DAYS: *May Day*
Mother's Day

ART:	Butterflies
	Clay Play
	Paperweights
MUSIC:	Planting Song
	Oats, Peas, Beans, and Barley
	Flowers
MOVEMENT:	The May Pole
	Heads, Shoulders, Knees, and Toes
	Follow That Line!
LANGUAGE:	Be a Clown
	The Butterfly
	Colors
NUTRITION	Food Groups—Vegetables
	Oatmeal Raisin Cookies
	Kitchen Rules
SCIENCE/ NATURE:	Flower Parts
	Let's Plant
	Floating Garden
MATH:	Cuisenaire Rods
	Tall and Small
	Seed and Plant Game
SOCIAL STUDIES:	Body Tracings
	Neighborhood Walk
	Let's Go to the Lake
HEALTH/ SAFETY:	Stop, Look, and Listen
	Kitchen Safety

BUTTERFLIES

Purpose:	To fingerpaint.
Skills/ Concepts:	To use fine motor skills. To develop tactile sense.
Ages:	2 through 5 years old (the younger toddlers may not enjoy fingerpainting; offer it again every few months to determine when they are ready).
Length of Activity:	Allow 2 to 5 minutes for fingerpainting, 2 minutes for pasting.
Materials:	Fingerpaint (chocolate pudding is good to use for little ones who still put their fingers in their mouths). Fingerpaint paper, white shelf paper, or white freezer paper An apron, smock, or old shirt for each child Newspapers Damp sponge
For Adult to Do Ahead:	Cover the table with newspapers.
Introduction:	Begin activity by saying, "Today, let's paint with our fingers instead of a paintbrush."
Procedure:	Help children into paint aprons. Show the children the damp sponges in front of each piece of painting paper. "Can you wipe the sponge on the paper?" (This makes the paint easier to spread.) Next drop a blob of fingerpaint on each paper. If a child seems shy or timid about spreading the paint, offer some verbal instruction and encourage watching a neighbor. "Can you spread the paint using your fingers? your thumb? your hand? How does the paint feel? Do you like the way it feels? Let's tape the paintings up so they will dry."
Closure:	End by asking, "Would you like to make a butterfly from your painting?"
Follow-up Activities:	Cut the accompanying butterfly shape from black construction paper. Some of the older children may be able to cut out the butterfly shapes themselves. Then cut two ovals from the fingerpainting. Children can paste the ovals on the black butterfly shape to make colorful wings. Recite the butterfly poem, see pages 184–185.

CLAY PLAY

Purpose:	To play with clay.
Skills/ Concepts:	To use fine motor skills while pinching, poking, rolling, and squeezing clay. To develop tactile senses.
Ages:	18 months through 5 years old.
Length of Activity:	Allow 2 to 15 minutes depending upon attention span of child.
Materials:	Clay (toddlers need soft clay or Playdoh, older children can use modeling clay)

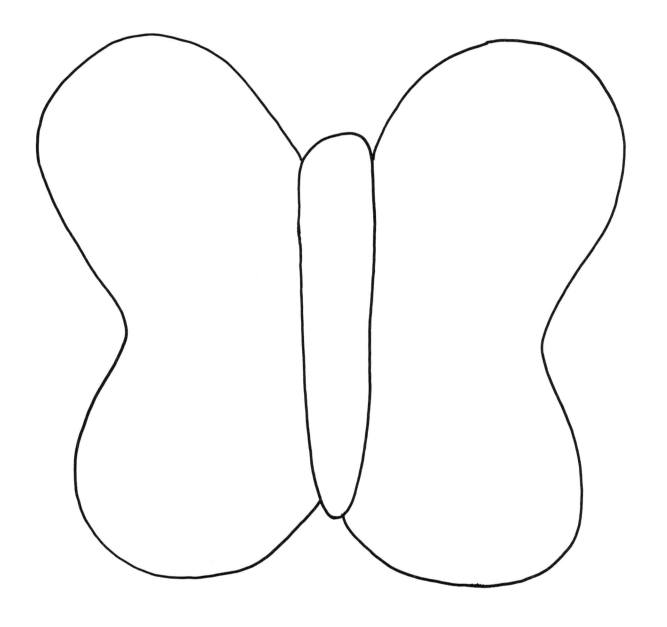

Introduction:	Show children the clay, and say, "This is clay."
Procedure:	Each child should have a piece of clay smaller than an egg. "Can you squeeze your piece of clay? Can you roll the clay?" Children will begin experimenting with the clay. Continue verbally describing what they are doing with their clay. "Can you make tiny balls with your clay? Can you pinch off a piece of clay? Eric is patting his clay."
Closure:	Ask, "Did you like to squeeze the clay with your fingers?"
Follow-up Activity:	Provide children with different items to experiment with while using the clay. Some good choices might include plastic knives, tongue depressors, cookie cutters, a small rolling pin, and teaspoons. An adult should always be in sight of a child playing with clay so that the tools mentioned are used appropriately.

PAPERWEIGHTS

Purpose:	To make a plaster of Paris paperweight.
Skill/ Concept:	To work with a sculpting medium.
Ages:	2 and 3 years old (with help); 4 and 5 years old (with verbal directions).
Length of Activity:	Allow 6 minutes (3 for adults, 3 for children); 10 to 20 minutes drying time
Materials:	Small aluminum pie pans from pot pies or small individual plastic applesauce containers (one per child) Vaseline or vegetable oil Plaster of Paris, see recipe Tin can, to mix plaster Small silk or plastic flowers Newspapers
For Adult to Do Ahead:	Cover the table with newspapers. Coat inside of applesauce containers with vaseline. Mix plaster of Paris just before it is to be used. It will harden quickly. Don't mix up more than you will use in several minutes. The older child will enjoy helping. Plaster recipe: 2 cups plaster of Paris 1–1¼ cups water Mix ingredients together. Do not over mix. The more plaster is stirred, the quicker it hardens. Plaster is ready when it is as thick as stew, which takes about 3–4 minutes.
Introduction:	Begin by saying, "We're going to make something special for your mother for Mother's Day."
Procedure:	Continue with, "This is plaster of Paris. Now it is a liquid, but soon it will harden. Before the plaster hardens, we are going to pour some into these containers and then press some of the flowers on the table into the plaster." Help younger children fill containers with plaster. Older children can spoon or pour plaster into container. "Which flowers would you like to use?" After children choose a few flowers tell them to push the stems into the plaster. The plaster should dry in 10 to 20 minutes. When plaster has set, pop the plaster out of the container.

Closure: Conclude with, "When the plaster has dried, we will take it out of the container."

Follow-up Activity: Make a Mother's Day card to go with the paperweight. Older children can use crayons or markers. Younger children can use a dried water color painting folded in half.

Read *Ask Mr. Bear* by Marjorie Flack. New York: Macmillan, Aladdin Books, 1932, 1960. (A story about a special gift for mother.)

PLANTING SONG

Purpose: To sing a song about planting a garden.

Skill/ Concept: To sing a simple song.

Ages: 18 months through 5 years old.

Length of Activity: Allow 1 minute.

Materials: Song

Introduction: Begin by saying, "I know a song about planting a garden."

Procedure: Hum the tune; then sing the words to the song. Invite the children to sing the song with you.

Closure: Ask, "What was that song about?" (gardens, seeds)

Follow-up Activity: Children can act out the song by pretending to dig in a garden, then plant seeds, then water the garden with a sprinkling can, and finally smile as they watch it grow.

Children can plant a marigold seed in dirt in a clear plastic cup, water it, and watch it grow.

Planting Song

Traditional
Words by:
JoAnne C. Calvarese

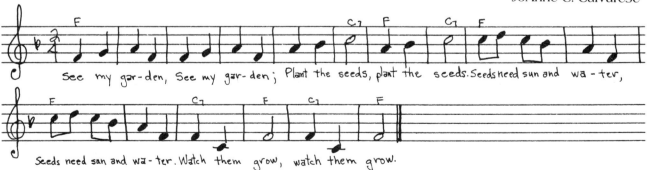

OATS, PEAS, BEANS, AND BARLEY

Purpose:	To sing a song about planting.
Skill/ Concept:	To memorize a song with verses.
Ages:	18 months through 5 years old.
Length of Activity:	Allow 2 minutes.
Materials:	Song
Introduction:	Begin by saying, "Let's sing another song about planting."
Procedure:	Tell the children, "This song tells about planting oat, pea, bean, and barley seeds." Sing the song for the child. "Can you sing the song with me?"
Closure:	Close by asking, "What seeds did we sing about in this song?"
Follow-up Activities:	Have children skip or walk around a chalk or masking tape circle as they sing the song.

Bring in some dried oats, peas, beans, and barley for the older children to see. This activity must be closely supervised so that these small vegetables do not get popped into ears, nose, or mouths. Displaying a few of each in clear plastic containers or glued to the inside of a small box keeps them from rolling around the room. |

Oats, Peas, Beans, and Barley

Traditional

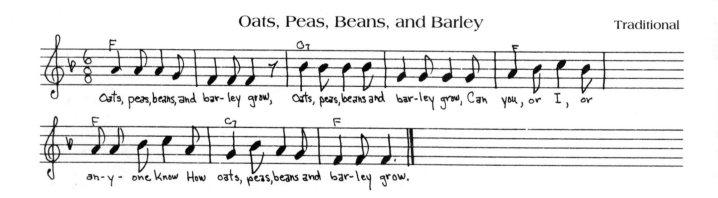

FLOWERS

Purpose:	To sing a song about flowers.
Skill/ Concept:	To memorize a song.
Ages:	18 months through 5 years old.

Length of Activity: Allow 1 minute.

Materials: Song
Picture of a field of flowers

Introduction: Begin by saying, "Soon there will be lots of flowers blooming." Show picture of the flowers. Talk about what is seen in the picture. Encourage the children to participate in the discussion.

Procedure: Hum the song. Sing the song. Invite the children to sing along with you a second time.

Closure: Close by saying, "The breeze was blowing the flowers. How do you think the flowers were moving?"

Follow-up Activity: As you sing the song again, pretend to be flowers blowing in the breeze.

Flowers

Words and music by:
JoAnne C. Calvarese

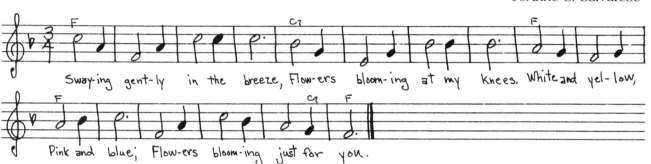

Sway-ing gent-ly in the breeze, Flow-ers bloom-ing at my knees. White and yel-low,

Pink and blue; Flow-ers bloom-ing just for you.

THE MAY POLE

Purpose: To celebrate springtime on May Day, which is May 1.

Skills/ Concepts: To develop gross motor skills of arms and legs.
To develop fine motor skills of hands.
To walk in a circle following another child.

Ages: 18 months through 5 years old.

Length of Activity: Allow 5 to 10 minutes.

Materials: Wooden pole
Crepe paper streamers, one per child
Staple gun
Music (recorder, flute, guitar, record, or tape)

For Adult to Do Ahead: Staple all streamers to top of pole and then cover with masking tape to reinforce. Sink pole in the ground. Prepare music.

Introduction: Begin activity by saying, "Today is the first day of May. It's called May Day. This pole with streamers is called a May Pole. Let's celebrate May Day by dancing around the May Pole."

Procedure: Have children stand in a circle around the May Pole each holding a streamer from the pole. Play waltzing music while the children walk around the May Pole following the person in front of him or her. They should continue walking round and round until the streamers have been completely wrapped around the pole (the tails will be hanging at the bottom of the pole).

Closure: Ask, "What colors are the streamers wrapped around our May Pole?"

Follow-up Activities: Make daisy or dandelion chains for necklaces or crowns.
Plant a tree or flowers to celebrate spring.

HEAD, SHOULDERS, KNEES, AND TOES

Purpose: To play a game that teaches four specific body parts.

Skills/ Concepts: To learn placement of head, shoulders, knees, and toes.
To develop listening skills.
To develop muscles through stretching.

Ages: 18 months through 5 years old (toddlers will be clumsy, move slowly, and miss some of the actions, but will enjoy stretching with the group and with practice will become more proficient).

Length of Activity: Allow 1 to 3 minutes (this can be used for stretching after a long story or quiet activity or just as a movement activity itself).

Materials: A tape recording or record of instrumental music
Tape recorder or record player

For Adult to Do Ahead: Ready tape recorder or record player.

Introduction: Begin activity by saying, "We've been sitting for quite a while now. Let's all stand up and stretch!"

Procedure: First, introduce exercise by slowly demonstrating touching head, shoulders, knees, and toes with two hands while naming each part as it is touched. Once children have caught on to the exercise, add music to make it more fun. Begin with a slow rhythm; then try music with different rhythms. Speed up and slow down. Children can take turns being the leader.

Closure: End by saying, "That was fun! Before we end, let's reach to the sky (stretch up) and then touch the ground (bend knees and reach toward the floor). Now with hands at our sides let's give a little shake (gently shake entire body). I feel great! How about you?"

Follow-up Activities: Play "Simon Says."
Sit or lie on the floor and take some deep relaxing breaths.

FOLLOW THAT LINE!

Purpose:	To play a following game. (This game can be played indoors or outdoors.)
Skills/ Concepts:	To develop large motor skills used in walking. To develop sense of balance. To develop foot-eye coordination. To follow a line.
Ages:	18 months through 2½ years old (may just enjoy following the line); 2½ through 5 years old.
Length of Activity:	Allow 2 or 3 minutes.
Materials Needed:	Wide chalk for outdoors, masking tape for indoors (Using colored chalk or tape provides another opportunity to learn the name of a color)
For Adult to Do Ahead:	Draw chalk line or lay down masking tape line. Start with a straight line, then later make it more difficult by adding turns and/or obstacles.
Introduction:	Say to the children, "Let's play a game called 'Follow That Line!' The trick is to walk along the line placing one foot in front of the other like this." (demonstrate) "Try to keep your feet on the line each time."
Procedure:	Have children walk one at a time along the line one foot in front of the other. Adding curving lines and obstacles each time the game is played will increase the difficulty of the game.
Closure:	Conclude by asking, "Who would like to try that again?"
Follow-up Activities:	Toddlers may wish to follow the line just walking regularly; older children may wish to draw their own chalk lines to follow. Play 'Follow the Leader!' with children taking turns.

BE A CLOWN

Purpose:	To learn about feelings.
Skills/ Concepts:	To recognize the facial expressions of happy, sad, angry, and surprised. To mime an expression. To use fine motor skills in making flannel board faces.
Ages:	2½ through 5 years old.
Length of Activity:	Allow 5 minutes.
Materials:	Flannel board Felt pieces, including round face with stationary eyes, nose, and hat; plus mouth and eyebrows to express happy, sad, angry, and surprised (see pictures below) Picture book of clowns from local library or bookstore
For Adult to Do Ahead:	Cut out the felt pieces for the various facial expressions.

happy   sad   angry   surprised

© 1990 by The Center for Applied Research in Education

Introduction: Ask the children, "Can you think of anyone in a circus who might look happy, or sad, or surprised all of the time?" (a clown) Give more clues if necessary.

Procedure: Lay out the eyebrows and mouths that go together. Children can take turns placing them on the clown's face and telling what expression the clown has. For example, "Can you make a happy face? What about a sad face? Now let's see an angry face. What about a surprised face?" (adult can make the face with younger children)

Closure: Ask, "Did you enjoy making clown faces?"

Follow-up Activities: Have a picture book of clown faces available for children to look at.
Invite an artistic adult to paint clown faces on children interested. Draw a picture of various expressions and let the child choose which one he or she would like to wear. Be sure to have a mirror handy—children love to look at themselves made up.

THE BUTTERFLY

Purpose: To teach a fingerplay that has rhyming words.

Skills/ Concepts: To introduce rhyming words.
To memorize a poem.
To use fine motor skills.

Ages: 18 months through 5 years old.

Length of Activity: Allow 2 minutes.

Materials: Poem.

Introduction: Begin by saying, "I know a fingerplay that has lots of rhyming words in it. Some words that rhyme are high and sky. Do they sound a little bit alike to you? Or how about two and shoe?" (emphasize similar sound) "They are also rhyming words."

Procedure: Butterfly By Charron C. Sundman

Butterfly	(Make fingers of one hand flutter.)
Flutter by	(Flutter fingers by your face.)
Flutter high	(Flutter fingers up in air.)
Up in the sky.	(Flutter fingers higher and away from body.)
Bye, Bye,	(Make fingers wave bye-bye.)
Butterfly!	(Flutter fingers again.)

Closure: Ask, "Did you hear the rhyming words?" (butterfly, bye-bye, high, sky)

| Follow-up Activity: | This song is good to use if you need to send children off to play, wash up, or dress for outdoors one at a time. Sung to the tune "One Little, Two Little, Three Little Indians." |

Butterfly, butterfly, where's my butterfly?
Butterfly, butterfly, where's my butterfly?
Butterfly, butterfly, where's my butterfly?
There, he landed on Thomas. (fill in name)

(Pretend to be searching for the butterfly while you sing the first three lines and then lightly let your fluttering fingers touch down on a child's shoulder.)

COLORS

Purpose:	To sing a song about colors.
Skills/ Concepts:	To develop listening skills. To recognize the colors red, blue, yellow, green.
Ages:	2 through 5 years old.
Length of Activity:	Allows 1 to 2 minutes.
Materials:	Colored cards or ribbons (red, blue, yellow, green) one color for each child Record or tape of Hap Palmer's "Learning Basic Skills through Music" (order through local record stores or through Educational Activities, Inc. Freeport, New York 11520) Record player or cassette tape player
Introduction:	Say to the children, "Today we are going to listen to a song about colors. We need to listen closely to the song so we will know when to stand up and when to sit down."
Procedure:	Distribute cards (or ribbons) making sure that each child recognizes the color he or she is holding. (Hint: For younger children, it is easier for all holding the same color to be grouped together so they can prompt each other to sit or stand.) Play record following directions for when to sit and stand.
Closure:	Hold up colored card or ribbon one color at a time and ask, "What color is this?"
Follow-up Activities:	Provide all four colors at the paint easel. 　　Fill a basket with eight small spools of thread: two reds, two blues, two yellows, and two greens. Encourage children to sort them by matching colors. 　　Decorate the room with bunches of balloons in the four colors above (one color to a bunch). Practice naming colors. Children get to take a balloon home. 　　Ask older children to look around the room and bring you something red. Continue with blue, green, and yellow.

FOOD GROUPS—VEGETABLES

Purpose:	To introduce the children to a variety of vegetables.
Skills/ Concepts:	To identify vegetables. To identify colors.

Ages: 18 months through 5 years old.

Length of Activity: Allow 5 to 10 minutes, depending upon interest of children.

Materials: A variety of vegetables such as lettuce, carrots, potatoes, peppers, cucumbers, celery, radishes
Basket

Introduction: Say to the children, "I love vegetables because they taste good and they help me stay healthy. Let's look at some of the vegetables I have in this basket. Can you tell me what they are?"

Procedure: Take vegetables out of the basket one at a time. Children will call out the name if they know it (or adult can name it and have children repeat the name of the vegetable). Encourage children to talk about the color, size, and shape of each vegetable as it is presented. Pass each vegetable around so that each child can feel its texture.

Closure: Lay the vegetables out on a table. Ask children once again to name the vegetables.

Follow-up Activities: Slice vegetables in half and provide paint and paper so children can make vegetable prints by dipping half in paint and then pressing it onto paper.

Thoroughly wash vegetables and process in an electric juicer or food processor. Serve the different juices in 3-oz. paper cups and encourage children to try them (carrot and celery work best when mixed with freshly squeezed apple juice).

OATMEAL RAISIN COOKIES

Purpose: To bake nutritious cookies for snack.

Skills/ Concepts: To measure.
To use fine motor skills through stirring and mixing.
To grease a cookie sheet.
To use a spatula.
To identify ingredients.

Ages: 3 through 5 years old.

Length of Activity: Allow 10 minutes.

Materials:

FOOD	UTENSILS
1½ cups flour	Two cookie sheets
½ teaspoon baking soda	Spatula
1 teaspoon cinnamon	Two mixing bowls
2 cups uncooked oatmeal	Two large spoons
1 cup raisins	Wax paper
1 egg	Measuring cup
¼ cup milk	Measuring spoons
⅓ cup oil	
½ cup honey	
1 teaspoon vanilla extract	
Shortening to grease pan	

For Adult to Do Ahead: Preheat oven to 325°F. Note: Keep children away from oven.

Introduction: Begin by saying, "It is not good for your body to eat too many sweets. What are sweets?" (cookies, candy, soda, sugared cereal) "Today I'm going to make some cookies that have some ingredients that are good for you. Who would like to help me?"

Procedure: With adult supervision, older children can

1. Measure out ingredients.
2. Mix flour, baking soda, and cinnamon. Then add oatmeal and raisins to this mixture.
3. In another bowl mix egg, milk, honey, oil, and vanilla until creamy.
4. Grease cookie sheet and drop batter by teaspoonfuls an inch apart on sheet.
5. Ask children if they know which ingredients are nutritious—good for them (oatmeal, raisins, egg, milk).

Note: At this point children can be sent off to another activity while adult bakes cookies.

Closure: Say, "Before we serve ourselves, let's offer some cookies to the younger children."

Follow-up Activity: Pour oatmeal from plastic pitcher to plastic cup or pitcher to pitcher.

KITCHEN RULES

Purpose: To learn the rules of working in the classroom kitchen.

Skills/ Concepts: To follow directions.
To develop listening skills.

Ages: 18 months through 5 years old (anyone who will be helping in the kitchen area).

Length of Activity: Allow 2 to 3 minutes.

Materials:
Posterboard   Clear contact paper
Magic Markers   Tacks or tape to hand poster

For Adult to Do Ahead: Write brief kitchen rule on one half of poster and draw a picture clue for each rule beside it on the other half. Cover with clear contact paper.

Introduction: Begin by saying, "It's important to have rules for working in the kitchen so that we can enjoy our cooking activities."

Procedure: Show children poster. Ask them what they think the pictures are saying. If there is a child who can read in the group ask him or her to read the simple rules; otherwise, have adult read them. Have children take turns pointing to the picture that goes with each rule. Sample rules include

WASH HANDS
WEAR AN APRON
TAKE TURNS HELPING
CLEAN UP

Note: Kitchen safety rules can be found on pages 195–196 in the Health and Safety section for the month of May.

Closure: Conclude by saying, "Now let's hang these rules up in the kitchen so that we won't forget them." (remember to hang them low at the child's level)

Follow-up Activity: Prepare a snack following rules.

FLOWER PARTS

Purpose: To learn the parts of a flower.

Skills/ Concepts: To identify stems, leaves, petals, and roots of flower.
To develop both fine and gross motor skills in assembling flower.

Ages: Toddlers will enjoy placing parts on the flannel board; 3- to 5-year-olds will learn the names of the flower parts with practice.

Length of Activity: Allow 2 minutes.

Materials: Felt for flower pieces
Flannel board

For Adult to Do Ahead: Cut the following flower parts from felt.

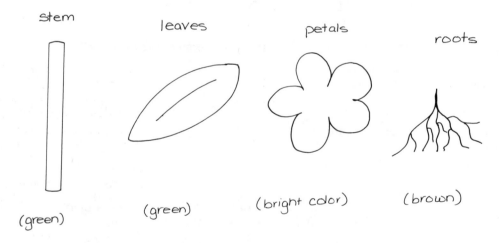

Stem (green)   leaves (green)   petals (bright color)   roots (brown)

Introduction: Begin by saying, "Let's make a beautiful flower."

Procedure: Lay felt pieces in front of children. "Can you help me make a flower from these pieces? Can you find the brown roots and put them on the board? Next we need the stem. It is green and is long and thin. Can you find the beautiful (pink) petals and put them on the board? Now there are how many leaves left?" (two) "What color are they?" (green) "They belong on the stem. Can you put one on each side of the stem? Look at the beautiful flower you made! Can you remember where the roots are? Where is the stem? Can you point to the petals? Can you count how many petals you see? Do you remember what these are called?" (point to the leaves)

Closure: Conclude by saying, "Let's leave the parts of the flower here beside the flannel board so you can make a flower whenever you want. Maybe you would even like to show another child how to make a flower with these felt pieces."

Follow-up Activity: Create a tear-and-paste flower. Older children can tear strips of green construction paper to use for stems and leaves. Tear colorful pieces of tissue paper to use for petals. Paste torn flower parts together on a sheet of paper starting with the stem.

LET'S PLANT

Purpose: To plant a garden.

Skills/ Concepts: To grow plants in soil (dirt, earth).
To learn that plants need water and sunlight to grow.
To use fine and gross motor skills in planting.
To enjoy an outdoor activity.

Ages: 3 through 5 years old.

Length of Activity: Allow 5 to 15 minutes.

Materials: Seedlings (may be purchased from a greenhouse or planted by you several weeks earlier, see p. 179)
A small section of yard to use for a garden or large planters or flower pots if yard is not available
Heavy plastic shovels or trowels
Box to carry seedlings.

Introduction: Say to the children, "We are going to plant our garden today."

Procedure: Continue with, "This is a seedling." (show children) "First, we need to dig holes in the soil to plant the seedlings." Help children dig holes which should be a little deeper and wider than the root ball of the seedling. "Now very gently place one seedling into each hole." (It is important for an adult to work with one or two children at a time so the seedlings will not be crushed and so the children's questions can be answered as they arise.) "Next I'll hold the top of the seedling up while you gently press the dirt around the plant to fill in the hole. Now let's plant two more seedlings."

Closure: Tell the children, "Plants need sunlight and water to grow. It's a nice sunny day today so all we need to do is water the plants." Children can do this with adult supervision using watering cans or a hose with a gentle sprinkler.

Follow-up Activity: Check plants every day with the children. Let them describe what they see. Help children water plants whenever the soil around them is dry.

FLOATING GARDEN

Purpose: To plant a garden in water.

Skills/ Concepts: To observe plant roots.
To identify plant's stem, leaves, roots.

Ages: 3 through 5 years old.

Length of Activity: Allow 15 minutes to set up and plan for daily observation.

Materials: House plants with well washed roots or plants sprouted
for summer garden
Foam meat tray (from supermarket), one for each plant
Aquarium or large clear glass bowl
Plastic pitcher
Sink or basin
Spoon
Plant food (for adult to use)
Exacto or sharp knife (to be used away from children)

For Adult to
Do Ahead: With an exacto knife, cut a slit 1½ to 2 inches long in foam meat tray. Cut a small hole at the end of the slit in meat tray. Place a colored tape line halfway up side of aquarium.

Introduction: Begin by asking, "Will you help me plant these plants?"

Procedure: Using a plastic pitcher, children can take turns filling the aquarium to the halfway mark (the colored tape line). "I need help washing the dirt from the roots of this plant." Children can take turns pouring water over roots as adult gently rinses dirt from roots. "Now we are going to place our plant on a little platform." Show children the meat tray. "We are going to put the plant stem into this little slit." Plant roots should be below the foam tray. Rest the plant in the small hole. "Can you place our plant in the water?" (after child completes this, ask) "Where are the plant's roots? (under water) "Where is the stem?" (point to stem) "Where are the leaves?" (point to leaves) "Our plant needs some special food to keep growing. I'll sprinkle the food on the water and you can gently stir the water with this spoon."

Closure: Encourage children to check the plant and stir the water each morning.

Follow-up
Activities: Older children can draw a picture of the plant stem. Use green fabric for leaves and brown yarn for the roots. Glue pieces into place.

Say to younger children, "Pretend you are plants. How would you act in the sunshine? in the rain? in the snow?"

CUISENAIRE RODS

Purpose: To build with Cuisenaire rods.

Skills/
Concepts: To use small muscle groups in fingers.
To use Cuisenaire rods.

Ages: 18 months through 2 years old (with supervision as children this age sometimes chew on the rods); 3 through 5 years old (can play with the rods by themselves once they are shown how to use them).

Length of
Activity: Allow 3 to 5 minutes.

Materials: Set of Cuisenaire rods
Basket to hold rods
Jelly roll pan

For Adult to
Do Ahead: Purchase Cuisenaire rods (at toy store or through learning game catalogs). If necessary, make rods (see p. xvi).

Introduction: Say to the children, "These are special blocks. They are called Cuisenaire rods. We are going to build with them."

Procedure: Continue with, "Let's make a design in this pan." Rods can be laid on their long edge. The edges of the pan will keep the rods together. As a pattern is built in the pan, talk about the different sizes of the rods, the different colors of the rods, and the shape of the pattern being built.

Closure: Say, "This is a wonderful pattern."

Follow-up Activity: Use the rods for sorting into groups of varying sizes or colors.

TALL AND SMALL

Purpose: To play a game using the terms "tall" and "small."

Skills/ Concepts: To learn size discrimination.
To use thinking skills.
To use gross motor skills.

Ages: 2 through 5 years old.

Length of Activity: Allow 2 minutes.

Materials: Poem

Introduction: Ask the children, "Can you make yourself very tall?" (stand on tiptoe) "Can you make yourself very small?" (squat)

Procedure: Say:

I am very tall	(Stand on toes.)
Now I am very small	(Squat.)
Sometimes I am tall	(Stand tall.)
Sometimes I am small	(Squat.)
Guess which I am now?	(Pick either standing or squatting.)

Children will tell you whether you are tall or small. Repeat several times.

Closure: Ask children, "Did you like being tall or small?"

Follow-up Activity: Have an adult stand beside a child and ask the children to decide who is tall and who is small. Try an older child and a toddler side by side and ask children who is tall and who is small. Then try a toddler beside a block and ask which is tall and which is small.

SEED AND PLANT GAME

Purpose: To play a sequencing game.

Skills/ Concepts: To identify seed and plant.
To discriminate sequencing growth visually.

Ages: 2 through 5 years old.

Length of
Activity: Allow 2 minutes.

Materials: White paper or posterboard
                  Colored pens or crayons
                  Clear contact paper

For Adult to   Cut paper or posterboard into three rectangles 5 inches by 7 inches (or use index cards
Do Ahead: this size). Draw a picture of a bean seed on one, the plant sprouting on the second, and
                  a large plant on the third (see below). Cover with contact paper.

 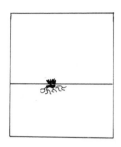 

Introduction: Begin by saying, "I have a plant game for you to play."

Procedure: Lay cards down on table facing child. "This is how a plant first begins." (point to the
                  seed) "This is a picture of a seed." Next point to the card of the sprouted plant. "The
                  seed has begun to grow. This card is second because it shows the plant while it is
                  sprouting." "Can you tell me which card would be the third card?" (the child will
                  probably be able to guess it is the remaining card) "Yes, the third card shows the plant
                  after it has grown."

Closure: Say to the child, "Let's mix the cards up. Can you put them in order for me starting
                  with the seed?"

Follow-up   Watch a real plant grow. See "Floating Garden" pages 189–190.
Activity:

© 1990 by The Center for Applied Research in Education

BODY TRACINGS

Purpose: To give children a sense of their size and shape.

Skills/   To place facial features.
Concepts: To use fine motor skills through coloring.
                  To learn about size.

Ages: 18 months through 5 years old.

Length of   Allow 15 to 20 minutes.
Activity:

Materials: Rolls of plain paper large enough to trace children's actual bodies (Hint: See local
                  newspaper or supermarket for donation of paper this size.)
                  Colored marking pens
                  Crayons
                  Mirror (optional)
                  Scissors

Introduction: Begin by saying, "Look around the room. Does anyone look exactly like you?" (If a child thinks so, point out visible differences such as height, color of hair, clothes worn, etc.) "I'm going to help you draw a special picture of yourselves."

Procedure: On the floor, unroll a 3- to 4-foot length of paper. Have first child lie down in center of paper. Using colored marker trace outline of child's body on paper. Write the child's name on paper. Cut that section off from the roll of paper. Ask child to use crayons to fill in facial features, hair, clothes, and so on. (Hint: Having mirror available often helps younger children; older children may add other details such as buttons, belts, shoelaces; toddlers with help may just add facial features.) Repeat with each child.

Closure: Conclude by saying, "Let's hang your pictures up." Pictures can be taped to wall or hung by clothespin from a clothesline strung out of reach of children. Hanging pictures may need to be lightly ironed with cool iron on back to keep from rolling up.

Follow-up Activity: Look at all the hanging pictures together. Encourage children to point out things that are alike and things that are different. Find the biggest and the smallest.

Play the song "What Are You Wearing" from Hap Palmer's album "Learning Basic Skills Through Music" (available where children's records are sold or through Educational Activities, Inc., Freeport, New York 11520).

NEIGHBORHOOD WALK

Purpose: To become acquainted with buildings, streets, and parks in the surrounding area.

Skills/ Concepts: To develop observation skills.
To develop description skills.
To develop color identification skills.
To cross the street safely.

Ages: 18 months to 3 years old (may wish to tour the playground and talk about how spring has changed it); 3 through 5 years old (can explore the neighborhood with adult supervision looking for signs of spring).

Length of Activity: Allow 15 minutes.

Materials: Proper adult supervision
Field trip permission slips (see p. xviii)

Introduction: Begin the activity by saying, "It's a beautiful spring day today. Let's go for a walk and enjoy it."

Procedure: Have children pair up holding hands with a buddy. As you walk along, stop occasionally to point out gardens, buildings, and signs. Encourage children to name colors, as well as describe what signs of spring they see (for example, green grass, flowers, leaves on trees). When crossing streets, use this opportunity to emphasize "Stop, look, and listen."

Closure: Say to the children, "Walking is very good exercise. I enjoyed my walk with you today. Did you enjoy it too?"

Follow-up Activities: Older children may enjoy drawing a picture of something they saw on their walk.
Younger children may enjoy painting with a color they saw on their walk.
Read *The Amazing Bone* by William Steig. Farrar, 1976.

LET'S GO TO THE LAKE

Purpose: To introduce children to activities that can take place at a lake.

Skills/ Concepts: To recognize and describe activities pictured.
To develop motor skill in using flannel board
To understand "in" and "beside."

Ages: 3 through 5 years old.

Length of Activity: Allow 10 minutes.

Materials: Flannel board and felt pieces described below under procedure section (see p. xv for assembling flannel board)
Pictures or picture book of lakes and activities at lakes (optional)—can be found in local library

For Adult to Do Ahead: Make flannel board.
Make felt pieces by cutting out pictures of activities listed below (or drawing them on paper) and glueing these to individual felt pieces.

Introduction: Say to the children, "Let's take a 'pretend' trip to the lake."

Procedure: Show children pictures of lakes. Then take out felt activity pieces one at a time. Ask children to take turns describing what they see. Ask them whether the activity would take place "in" the lake or "beside" the lake. Felt pieces might include the lake, a person swimming, people in a boat, a person fishing, people having a picnic, people sitting by a campfire, children tossing a ball, children digging in the sand, children sailing boats. Children can place felt pieces on board.

Closure: Ask, "Did you know there were so many fun things to do at a lake? Can we do any of those activities here?"

Follow-up Activities: Using a large washtub or small wading pool filled with water, let children sail small plastic boats.
IMPORTANT NOTE: CHILDREN PLAYING WITH WATER SHOULD BE SUPERVISED BY AN ADULT AT ALL TIMES.
Spread some blankets (inside or outside) and have a picnic lunch.

STOP, LOOK, AND LISTEN

Purpose: To learn a safety song about crossing the street.

Skills/ Concepts: To learn how to cross the street safely.
To memorize a song.

Ages: 18 months through 5 years old.

Length of Activity: Allow 2 minutes.

Materials: Song

Introduction: Begin by saying, "Do you know what you do *before* you cross a street? I'm going to teach you a song that will remind you."

Procedure: Sing song for children and then have them join you a second and third time.

Closure: Ask the children, "What are the three things you should do before you cross the street?" (stop, look, and listen)

Follow-up Activity: Play the Stop and Go game. Make a sign that is red with the word "STOP" written on one side and green with the word "GO" on the other. Children can take turns holding the sign. Other children line up and when the sign is green they start walking across the room or playground. When the sign is turned to red they must stop. When they reach the sign holder, a new sign holder is chosen.

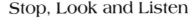

Stop, Look and Listen

Words and music by
Charron C. Sundman

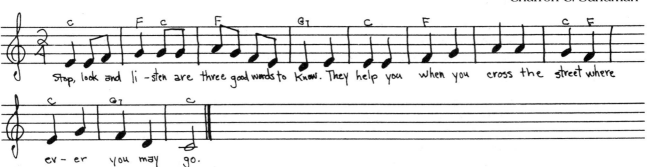

KITCHEN SAFETY

Purpose: To teach children safety rules for working in kitchen.

Skills/ Concepts: To learn listening skills.
To follow directions.

Ages: 2 through 5 years old.

Length of Activity: Allow 2 minutes

Materials: Posterboard
Colored marking pens
Clear contact paper

For Adult to Do Ahead: Write brief kitchen rules (see accompanying procedure) on posterboard with a descriptive picture beside each. Cover with contact paper.

Introduction: Tell the children, "When we work in a kitchen it is important to follow some safety rules so we won't get hurt."

Procedure: Using the safety rules poster, go over the rules with children. Encourage them to tell you what each picture means before you or an older child reads the rule associated with it. Some sample rules might include:

1. PLEASE STAY AWAY FROM STOVES AND OVENS.
2. PLEASE STAY AWAY FROM SHARP KNIVES.
3. PLEASE STAY AWAY FROM MATCHES.
4. PLEASE STAND ON THE FLOOR, NOT ON CHAIRS.
5. PLEASE CLEAN UP SPILLS.

Note: Knives and matches should be kept out of sight and out of reach of small children. However, in some homes these dangerous items can be reached by merely climbing on a chair. Including these in your kitchen safety rules can help avoid an accident at home as well as in a daycare or preschool room.

Ask the children if they know why each safety rule will keep them safe. For example, ovens and stoves are hot and could burn you; knives are sharp and could cut you; matches start fires and could burn you; you could lose your balance and fall off the chair; you could slip and fall on spills.

Closure: Conclude with, "Now that we've learned these kitchen safety rules, we can help prevent accidents from happening in our kitchen here *and* at home."

Follow-up Activity: Have a pots and pans parade using a variety of kitchen utensils for instruments. Pots and pans can be used as drums, a wooden spoon can be a drumstick, pot lids can be cymbals, aluminum measuring spoons rattle, and beans in a plastic margarine tub with a sealed lid can be shaken.

JUNE ACTIVITIES

THEME: *Transportation*
SPECIAL DAYS: *Father's Day*
                World Environment Day

ART:	Sand Pictures
	School Bus
	Clay Chimes
MUSIC:	The Train
	Trucks, Cars, and Buses
	Canoe Song
MOVEMENT:	Row Your Boat
	Riding Toys
	Airplanes
LANGUAGE:	Banbury Cross
	Cars and Trucks Maze
	Transportation
NUTRITION:	Cucumber Canoes
	Strawberry Milk Shakes
	Food Identification
SCIENCE/	Prisms
NATURE:	World Environment Day (June 15)
	Sense of Sight
MATH:	Right Hand, Left Hand
	Same or Different
	Is It Full or Empty?
SOCIAL	Here Comes the School Bus
STUDIES:	Let's Go to the City
	What Color Is?
HEALTH/	Seat Belts for Safety
SAFETY:	Wipe Your Face
	Picking Up Toys

SAND PICTURES

Purpose:	To create artwork using sand.
Skills/ Concepts:	To use fine motor skills. To recognize color. To use sand as an art medium.
Ages:	3 through 5 years old.
Length of Activity:	Allow 5 minutes.
Materials:	Colored construction paper White glue Paintbrush Clean white sand (purchase from florist or garden department) Poster or tempera paint
For Adult to Do Ahead:	Divide sand in plastic containers (old margarine bowls are great), one for each color. Add a small amount of paint to each container, cover and shake until sand is colored. Spread on paper to dry.
Introduction:	Ask the children, "What do you use to make a colorful picture?" Paint, markers, crayons. "Today we are going to use colored sand to make a picture."
Procedure:	Paint colored construction paper with watered white glue. Have children pick several colors of sand. Next have children take small finger fulls of sand (one color at a time) and sprinkle sand on the paper. Let the picture set for several minutes, then shake picture over a pan. The sand that landed on glue will stick to the paper and the rest will fall into the pan. Continue until all glue is covered.
Closure:	Conclude the activity by saying, "Let's look at the different pictures. You can each have a turn telling us what colors you used for your design."
Follow-up Activity:	Set up on a small tray two plastic bowls and a soup spoon. Children can practice spooning leftover colored sand from one bowl to the other.

SCHOOL BUS

Purpose:	To offer an art activity that complements a visit from the school bus (see p. 212).
Skills/ Concepts:	To use fine motor skills. To use memory skills.
Ages:	18 months through 5 years old.
Length of Activity:	Allow 2 to 5 minutes.
Materials:	Bus pattern (on following page), one for each child Crayons White and black construction paper Paste or glue Scissors for older children Cotton swab

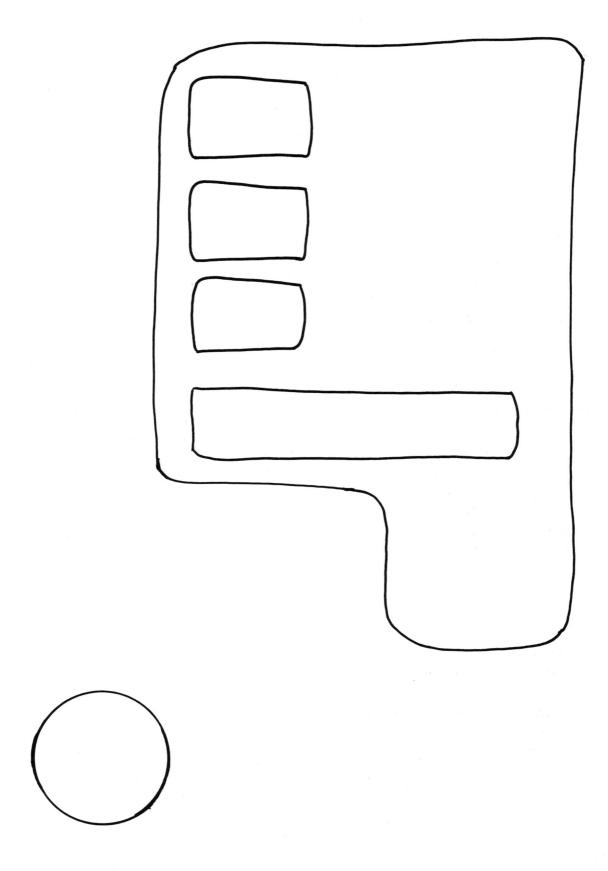

For Adult to Do Ahead:	Make a copy of the school bus pattern, one for each child. Cut out two tires for each child.
Introduction:	Begin by saying, "Today/Yesterday we saw a real school bus. Let's color a picture of a bus."
Procedure:	As children color the bus, talk about the visit the bus made. Ask questions about what they remember about the bus color, was it large, where did children sit, and so on. Older children may want to draw pictures of people in the windows of the bus before they cut out their bus and paste to white construction paper. Paste the black construction paper tires to the bus.
Closure:	Ask, "What color was the bus we saw? What color did you use for your picture of a school bus?"
Follow-up Activity:	Help children to set up chairs 2 by 2, with one in front to play school bus.

CLAY CHIMES

Purpose:	To make a present for Father's Day.
Skills/ Concepts:	To use fine motor skills. To differentiate the feeling of soft and hard.
Ages:	18 months through 5 years old.
Length of Activity:	Allow 10 to 15 minutes.
Materials:	Colored clay (see recipe below) Twine or sturdy macrame string Rolling pin Small sturdy tree branch for each child Cookie cutters
For Adult to Do Ahead:	Make clay. 2 cups baking soda 1 cup cornstarch 1¼ cups cold water

Mix in a 2-quart pan. Add water slowly to prevent lumps. Cook 6 minutes. When mixture looks like mashed potatoes, spread it on a cookie sheet to cool. Cover with a damp cloth to keep it moist. When cool, knead for 10 minutes; then divide into several containers. Older children may help with this part. Add several drops of food coloring (a different color for each container), and knead color into dough. Store in an airtight container.

Introduction:	Say to the children, "Father's Day is this Sunday. Today we are going to make a gift for your father."
Procedure:	Assist children in rolling dough out to about ¼- to ½-inch thickness. After children have picked the cookie cutters they wish to use, have them cut out several different shapes. Place shapes on cookie sheets. Using the end of a pencil, make a hole near the top of each shape for the string. Clay will harden in 24 hours at room temperature or place shapes on a lightly greased cookie sheet and bake 2 hours at 200°F. Cool in oven for 2 hours longer. When cool and hard on both sides, remove from oven. Attach varying lengths of twine to each shape. Tie the shapes to the branch a few inches from each other. Attach another 10-inch piece of twine to each end of the branch.

Closure: Say to children, "These chimes are beautiful. Let's take a set of chimes outside and watch the wind make them dance."

Follow-up Activities: Provide the children with wrapping paper and tape. Help wrap the chimes.
A simple card may be a picture drawn with crayon or markers and "signed" by the child.

THE TRAIN

Purpose: To sing a song about a train.

Skills/ Concepts: To repeat a song.

Ages: 18 months through 5 years old.

Length of Activity: Allow 1 minute.

Materials: Song

Introduction: Begin by saying, "Another way to travel is to ride on a train."

Procedure: Sing the song for the children. Invite them to join singing the song again.

Closure: Conclude activity by saying, "Now that we've sung a song about a train, let's read a story about a train."

Follow-up Activities: Make a train by lining up chairs, boxes, or carpet sample squares.
Read *The Freight Train* by Donald Crews. New York: Greenwillow, 1978.

The Train

Words and music by:
JoAnne C. Calvarese

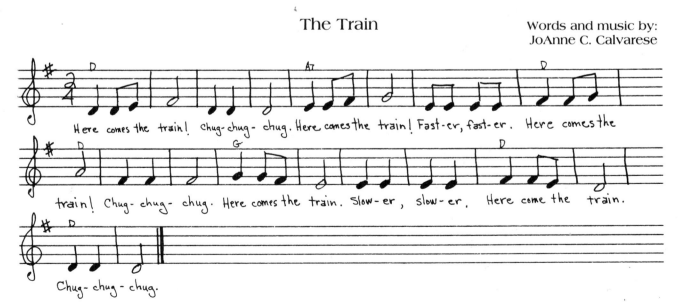

TRUCKS, CARS, AND BUSES

Purpose:	To sing a song about transportation.
Skills/ Concepts:	To sing a simple song. To reinforce safety in the car.
Ages:	18 months through 5 years old.
Length of Activity:	Allow 1 or 2 minutes
Materials:	Song
Introduction:	Begin by saying, "We have been talking about transportation, ways that we travel from place to place. I know a song about trucks, cars, and buses."
Procedure:	Continue with, "I am going to hum the song first." Hum song. "Next I will sing the words of the song." Sing the song. "Shall we sing the song again?"
Closure:	Conclude by asking, "What does this song tell us to do when we are riding in a car?"
Follow-up Activity:	Read *Truck* illustrated by Donald Crews. New York: Greenwillow, 1980.

Trucks and Cars

Words and music by:
JoAnne C. Calvarese

CANOE SONG

Purpose:	To learn a simple song.
Skills/ Concepts:	To repeat a song. To expand vocabulary.
Ages:	18 months through 5 years old.

Length of Activity:	Allow 2 minutes.
Materials:	Song Pictures of a canoe and a paddle
Introduction:	Show picture of a canoe. Ask, "Do you know what this is?" Answers might be boat, ship, or canoe. "This is a canoe. Canoes are used to travel in the water. The canoe is moved with a paddle." Point to the canoe and then to the paddle.
Procedure:	Continue with, "Let's sing a song about a canoe." Sing the song through by yourself. "Will you try singing with me?"
Closure:	Ask, "What was this song about?" A canoe or a paddle. "What is a canoe moved with?" A paddle. Leave the pictures of the canoe and paddle so the children may look at them.
Follow-up Activity:	Pretend to paddle a canoe as you sing the song again.

Canoe Song

by Margaret Embers McGee
1918

My pad-dle's keen and bright, Flash-ing with sil-ver. Fol-low the wild goose f'light, Dip-dip and swing.

2.   Dip-dip and swing her back,
     Flashing with silver.
     Follow the wild goose track
     Dip-dip and swing.

ROW YOUR BOAT

Purpose:	To sing a familiar song using body movements.
Skills/ Concepts:	To sing a simple song. To use gross motor skills.
Ages:	18 months through 5 years old.
Length of Activity:	Allow 3 minutes.
Materials:	Song
Introduction:	Tell the children, "A small boat moves through the water when a person rows with oars. Let's play a game and pretend we're rowing a boat."
Procedure:	Sit on the floor facing a child. Stretch legs out straight and have the child sit between your legs. (Two children will face each other with their feet touching.) "Can you

hold my hands? As we sing 'Row Row, Row Your Boat,' we are going to move back and forth very gently. When you move you will carefully pull your partner with you. Let's try." Sing the song as you gently pull your partner toward your body and then gently push your partner away from your body. Some children will repeat this activity again and again.

Closure: Ask, "Did you enjoy rowing a boat today?"

Follow-up Activities: Collect pictures of different types of boats. Help the children mount pictures on pieces of construction paper. These may be used for playing an identification game.
Join all the boat pictures together to make a boat book.

RIDING TOYS

Purpose: To list age-appropriate riding toys.

Skill/ Concept: To practice gross motor skills.

Ages: 18 months (wheel toy to push with feet)
2 years old (wheelbarrow)
3 years old or when child can alternate feet while climbing stairs (tricycle)
4 years old (scooter)
5 years old (bicycle)

Length of Activity: Allow time daily, as long as child wants.

Materials: See list.

Introduction: Begin activity by saying, "Let's use our riding toys."

Procedure: Children love to be moving and wheels are great to get around on. Check the list above for age-appropriate riding toys. If possible, provide a flat, smooth surface away from traffic.

Closure: Conclude by saying, "Let's park the riding toys before we dig in the sandbox."

Follow-up Activity: Ask children to name each riding toy as you point to it.
Make a book of riding toys by cutting pictures of them out of magazines or mail order catalogs and pasting to construction paper.

AIRPLANES

Purpose: To pretend to be an airplane.

Skills/ Concepts: To use gross motor skills.
To develop creative thinking.

Ages: 18 months through 5 years old.

Length of Activity: Allow 2 to 5 minutes (can be used as an indoor or outdoor activity).

© 1990 by The Center for Applied Research in Education

Materials: A picture of an airplane

Introduction: Show picture of the airplane. Ask, "Do you know what this is?"

Procedure: Continue with, "We are going to pretend we are airplanes. What can you do to make yourself look like an airplane?" Put your arms out to the side. "An airplane has wings. We can put our arms out to our sides and pretend we have wings. Does an airplane move quickly or slowly? Can you move like an airplane might move?" Join children in zooming and flying around the room or play yard.

Closure: Conclude with, "Let's land our airplanes. Did you enjoy flying around the room/yard?"

Follow-up Activity: Help children make folded paper airplanes to fly. Check your public library for how-to books on paper airplanes.

BANBURY CROSS

Purpose: To learn a nursery rhyme about riding a horse.

Skills/ Concepts: To memorize a nursery rhyme.
To identify pictures.
To use language skills.

Ages: 18 months through 5 years old.

Length of Activity: Allow 1 minute.

Materials: Pictures of horses and people riding horses, to be used on the flannel board

Introduction: Say to children, "Another way people travel is to ride horses."

Procedure: Show the children the pictures. Talk about what is in each picture. Children should place the pictures on the flannel board. "I know a nursery rhyme about riding a horse." Recite poem.

Ride a cock-horse to Banbury Cross,
To see an old lady upon a white horse.
Rings on her fingers and bells on her toes,
She shall have music wherever she goes.

Invite the children to join in repeating the poem.

Closure: Ask, "Do you think you would like to ride a horse?"

Follow-up Activity: Pretend to ride horses. Gallop around the yard or a large room.

CARS AND TRUCKS MAZE

Purpose: To use a game to talk about means of transportation.

Skills/ Concepts: To learn difference between a car and a truck.
To work in a small group.
To make and follow a maze.
To sort cars and trucks.

Ages:	2 through 5 years old.
Length of Activity:	Allow 5 minutes.
Materials:	Blocks Small cars and trucks, plastic, wooden, or metal Three buckets or baskets
Introduction:	Begin by saying, "We've been talking about transportation and vehicles we use to travel from one place to another. Let's look at two different vehicles today."
Procedure:	Show children the cars and trucks. "Can you help me put the cars into one bucket and the trucks into another bucket?" Help children lay out a two-sided maze or highway with the blocks. Children take turns to picking a car or truck and pushing it through the block maze.
Closure:	Say, "Let's divide into three groups." Divide children into groups. "Group 1 will put the cars away. Group 2 will put the trucks away, and group 3 will put the blocks away." After picking up say, "All of you did a very good job putting away the toys. Thank you for helping to keep our room neat and safe."
Follow-up Activity:	Add small trucks and cars to the clay table.

TRANSPORTATION

Purpose:	To identify vehicles used for transportation.
Skills/ Concepts:	To develop language skills. To identify vehicles.
Ages:	18 months through 5 years old.
Length of Activity:	Allow 5 to 10 minutes.
Materials:	Flannel board Transportation pieces for flannel board
For Adult to Do Ahead:	Attach large pieces of flannel to pictures of car, bicycle, truck, airplane, boat, and train.
Introduction:	Begin by saying, "When you want to travel a long distance, you usually ride there. Today we are going to talk about ways to travel."
Procedure:	Lay flannel board pieces out for children to look at. Ask children one at a time to pick up a specific piece and place it on the flannel board. Talk about where that vehicle travels, what color it is, who has ridden on one, and so on. For example, "Pete, would you please put the airplane on the flannel board. Where does the plane fly? What color is the plane? Have any of you ever flown in an airplane?" Continue with the other pictures.
Closure:	Conclude with, "We've talked about cars, planes, trains, and trucks. What if you're going to the house next door? What do you use to get there?" Your feet.
Follow-up Activity:	Have toy transportation vehicles available for imaginary play. Provide blocks or wood scraps to use as roads of airports. Place masking tape on the floor to be used as a road.

CUCUMBER CANOES

Purpose:	To make a nutritious snack in the shape of a canoe.
Skills/ Concepts:	To use fine motor skills for scooping, mixing, filling. To identify foods.
Ages:	18 months through 3 years old (will enjoy eating this snack); 4 through 5 years old.
Length of Activity:	Allow 10 minutes.

Materials:

Picture of a canoe	*UTENSILS*
FOOD (for 8)	Vegetable peeler
4 cucumbers, ½ per child	Spoons, plastic knife
1 cup cream cheese	Bowl
½ cup peanut butter	Measuring cups
	Plates

For Adult to Do Ahead:	Peel cucumbers ahead of time and cut in half.
Introduction:	Show the children the picture of the canoe. "This is a means of transportation for some people. It's a type of boat. Does anyone know what it is called?" Canoe. "Where would you use this canoe to travel?" Water, river, lake, and so on. "Let's make a canoe-shaped snack."
Procedure:	Show children a whole cucumber. Ask children to identify the cucumber. "Here are some cucumbers I peeled and cut in half. Can you help me scoop out the seeds?" Encourage children to scoop seeds into a bowl. Mix peanut butter, cream cheese, and cucumber seeds together in bowl, giving each child a turn stirring. Help each child fill a cucumber canoe with a spoonful or two of the cream cheese mixture.
Closure:	When "canoes" are completed say, "While our canoes are chilling in the refrigerator, let's wash the dishes we used to make them and wipe the counter clean."
Follow-up Activity:	Make canoes by cutting two crescent shapes out of vinyl wallpaper and taping them together along the bottom edge. Float in a sink or pan of water.

STRAWBERRY MILK SHAKES

Purpose:	To make a drink using fruit and milk.
Skills/ Concepts:	To identify foods. To introduce new vocabulary. To use fine motor skills for measuring, pouring.
Ages:	18 months through 5 years old.
Length of Activity:	Allow 5 minutes.

Materials:	*FOOD*	*UTENSILS*
	1 10-oz. pkg. of frozen whole strawberries or 1 pint of fresh strawberries 1 cup of milk 1 pint of strawberry ice cream or frozen strawberry yogurt	Measuring cups Blender or egg beater Large spoon Paper cups Straws, cut in half for small cups

For Adult to Do Ahead: Thaw frozen strawberries or wash and hull fresh strawberries. Cut fresh berries in half.

Introduction: Hold up a fresh or frozen whole strawberry. Ask, "Does anyone know what this is called? What color is it? Is it a fruit or a vegetable? Let's use these strawberries to make a delicious drink."

Procedure: Put strawberries and their juice into blender. Talk about what will happen to the strawberries in the blender. Cover and blend until smooth. Give each child a spoonful of ice cream to place in a cup. Place the rest of the ice cream in the blender. Cover the blender and blend until smooth. Pour mixture from blender over ice cream in cups.

Closure: Conclude by saying, "That was cool and delicious. We also used two foods that are good for us. Milk and strawberries are nutritious foods."

Follow-up Activities: Use blueberries or raspberries to make different flavors and colors of milk shakes.
Play a berry matching game. Draw or cut out pictures (two each) of strawberries, blueberries, raspberries, and blackberries. Have children match the berries in pairs and name the berries.

FOOD IDENTIFICATION

Purpose: To identify foods that have been introduced previously.

Skills/ Concepts: To develop memory skills.
To develop language.
To identify foods.

Ages: 18 months through 5 years old.

Length of Activity: Allow 2 to 5 minutes.

Materials: Pictures of various foods talked about in other chapters (might include food from the four food groups)

For Adult to Do Ahead: Cut out pictures and attach to construction paper cards. Place card between two pieces of clear contact paper.

Introduction: Begin by saying, "We've talked about a lot of different foods. I have some pictures of food to show you. Let's see if you can tell me what they are."

Procedure: Show the pictures one at a time. The children should take turns identifying them. Encourage the children to offer as much information as they are able. Older children will be able to continue the discussion by talking about what food group each food belongs to. Younger children will enjoy talking about the colors of the foods.

Closure: Conclude by saying, "Looking at all those pictures of nutritious food makes me feel hungry. Let's have a snack."

Follow-up Activity: Use the food picture cards for a sorting exercise. The cards may be sorted by food group or by color. Small boxes or baskets with visual color or food group cues will help children with sorting.

PRISMS

Purpose: To hang prisms for viewing.

Skills/ Concepts: To increase visual skills.
To increase vocabulary skills.

Ages: 18 months through 2 years old (will enjoy watching the light break into rainbows on a wall); 3 through 5 years old.

Length of Activity: Allow 1 minute.

Materials: Prism (available from ABC School Supply, Inc., 6500 Peachtree Ind. Blvd., P.O. Box 4750, Norcross, Georgia 30091)
String
Small hook or nail
A sunny day
A window

Introduction: Ask, "Have you ever seen a rainbow in the sky?"

Procedure: Then say, "We're going to make our own rainbow." Show the children the prism. "This is a prism. It is made out of glass. When light shines on the prism, the light appears as a rainbow on the wall." Attach string to each end of the prism. Hang prism from the hook. If children don't ask questions as they watch the prism, you might ask, "What do you see on the wall?" Rainbow or colors. "What colors do you see?"
Note: This activity is short, but it is one that can remain in the room for the children to watch and talk about.

Closure: Conclude by saying, "Let's leave the prism hanging so we can watch the rainbows dancing on the wall."

Follow-up Activity: Draw rainbows using pastel-colored Magic Markers. After children make lines on white construction paper, give them a paintbrush and a small cup of water. Painting the lines with water will make the marks run together.

WORLD ENVIRONMENT DAY (JUNE 15)

Purpose: To become more aware of the environment.

Skill/ Concept: To develop social awareness.

Ages: 2 through 5 years old.

Length of Activity: Allow 10 minutes.

Materials: Basket, bucket, or trash bag for trash

Introduction:	Say to children, "Today is a special day. It is called World Environment Day. On this day people make an effort to clean up their yards and neighborhoods."
Procedure:	Continue, "We are going on a walk. What might be some things we could pick up and clean in our yard or neighborhood?" Trash, paper, bottles, cans, rocks, and so on. Give a quick review of how to take a walk on page 193. "As we go on our walk, let's look for any of these things. We will take a bucket with us to put any trash into."
Closure:	Conclude by saying, "Look at all the trash we found. Do you think we helped clean up the neighborhood?"
Follow-up Activity:	Plant flowers in the yard. 　　Read *A Tree Is Nice* by Janice Udry. New York: Harper and Brothers, 1956.

SENSE OF SIGHT

Purpose:	To increase the awareness of the sense of sight.
Skills/ Concepts:	To use eyes to see. To identify colors. To identify objects.
Ages:	18 months through 5 years old.
Length of Activity:	Allow 3 minutes, as an indoor or outdoor activity.
Materials:	Room, yard, car filled with objects
Introduction:	Ask, "Do you know where your eyes are?" Help children locate eyes. "Can you close your eyes? Can you see anything? It's very dark when you close your eyes, and you can't see anything. Let's play a game using our eyes."
Procedure:	Proceed: "I spy with this little eye (point to your eye) something that is (pick a color or object)." If the children can't identify the object or color, say the rhyme again with another hint. Then say, "You see with your eye what I see with my eye. Would you like to try the rhyme?" Continue the game giving each child a turn to be the leader.
Closure:	Conclude, "We use our eyes to see things."
Follow-up Activities:	Do some simple eye movements with the children. "Can you blink like this?" "Can you close one eye at a time?" "Can you look up?" "Can you look down?" "Can you look to the side?" "Can you see your nose?" Older children enjoy leading this game. 　　Read the book *Sight* by J. M. Parramon and J. J. Puig. New York: Barron's Books.

RIGHT HAND, LEFT HAND

Purpose:	To learn a fingerplay that reinforces the concept of right and left.
Skills/ Concepts:	To memorize a poem. To learn right and left. To develop memory skills.
Ages:	18 months through 5 years old.

Length of Activity:	Allow 1 to 2 minutes.
Materials:	Construction paper Scissors Clear tape Poem
For Adult to Do Ahead:	Cut construction paper into 1-inch strips, one strip per child.
Introduction:	Say to children, "We are going to learn a poem about right and left. To help you remember which is your right hand I'm going to tape a construction paper bracelet around your wrist."
Procedure:	Tape a strip around each child's right hand. Then recite the poem

MY HANDS
by JoAnne Calvarese

This is my right hand,	(Hold up right hand.)
And what can I see?	(Cup right hand over eyes.)
I see my left hand	(Hold up left hand.)
Waving at me!	(Wave to yourself with left hand.)
My right hand,	(Hold up right hand.)
My left hand,	(Hold up left hand.)
Are happy to be Sitting in front of me	(Hold both hands in front of body.)
Here on my knee.	(Place both hands on a knee.)

Repeat poem several times if children seem interested.

Closure:	Conclude by asking, "Do you remember which hand is your right hand? Would you like to wear your bracelets a little longer?"
Follow-up Activity:	Play the selection "Put Your Hands Up in the Air" from the record *Learning Basic Skills Through Music,* Vol. I, by Hap Palmer. Educational Activities, Inc. Freeport, New York 11520.

SAME OR DIFFERENT

Purpose:	To introduce the concepts of same and different.
Skills/ Concepts:	To observe details. To develop language in describing differences and similarities.
Ages:	3 through 5 years old.
Length of Activity:	Allow 5 minutes.
Materials:	Transportation cards 5-inch by 7-inch index cards
For Adult to Do Ahead:	Draw a picture on each index card: two cars, two trucks, two planes, two trains, two boats. Each pair of cards should be exactly the same. (Pictures may be cut out and pasted to index cards.)

Introduction: Say to the children, "I have some picture cards. Some of the pictures look the same, some of them look different."

Procedure: Hold up a card with a car. Then hold up a card with a plane. Ask if the cards look the same or if they look different. Ask why they look different. Then put down the plane card and hold up a matching car card. Ask if they are the same or different. Ask why they are the same. Continue so that all cards are introduced and verbally identified by the group.

Closure: Say, "I'm going to put these cards in a basket on the shelf. You may take turns laying them out on the floor (table) and matching the cards that are the same by placing them side by side."

Follow-up Activity: Take children outside and help them to find things that are the same—swings, toys, shovels, pails, and so on.

IS IT FULL OR EMPTY?

Purpose: To show the difference between full and empty.

Skills/ Concepts: To learn the difference between full and empty. To learn visual discrimination.

Ages: 18 months through 5 years old.

Length of Activity: Allow 1 to 5 minutes.

Materials:
Shovels	Cups
Toy dump trucks	Sandbox or sandtable
Plastic bowls	

Introduction: Say, "Today we are going to talk about full and empty."

Procedure: Show the children an empty bowl. Ask, "Is there anything in this bowl?" No. "Yes, the bowl is empty. Help me fill this bowl up." Children should fill bowl to the top. Level it off and say, "Now this bowl is full. Who can make the bowl empty?" Continue filling and emptying the bowls, trucks, and cups.

Closure: Confirm: "When the bowl was empty there was nothing inside. When the bowl was full it contained sand."

Follow-up Activities: Practice filling and emptying measuring cups.
Pour or spoon the sand from one container to another.

HERE COMES THE SCHOOL BUS

Purpose: To have a visit from a school bus.

Skill/ Concept: To acquaint children with a bus.

Ages: 3 through 5 years old.

Length of Activity:	Allow 10 minutes.
Materials:	Picture of the type of bus that will be seen
For Adult to Do Ahead:	Contact a bus company and make arrangements for a visit. Tell the bus company representative the ages and number of children. Ask if the children will be allowed to get on the bus. A few suggestions and questions for the bus driver might include:

1. How you enter the bus
2. Where the driver sits
3. Where the children sit
4. What do you do after the bus starts moving

Introduction:	Announce to the children, "Today we are going to have a special visitor. ＿＿＿＿＿is going to come with a school bus." Show children the picture of the bus. Encourage the children to talk about the picture.
Procedure:	When the bus arrives, talk about what the children see: What color is the bus? Does the bus have wheels? Does the bus have windows? Doors? How many? Introduce the bus driver to the children. If the children are to get on the bus and sit, tell them, "We are going to get on the bus and sit in the seats." If the driver is going to give a short talk now would be a good time.
Closure:	Help the children thank the bus driver for bringing the bus.
Follow-up Activity:	Make thank you cards or pictures to send to the bus driver.

LET'S GO TO THE CITY

Purpose:	To acquaint children with the city.
Skills/ Concepts:	To develop perceptual skills. To develop social awareness. To expand vocabulary skills.
Ages:	18 months through 5 years old.
Length of Activity:	Allow 2 minutes.
Materials:	Flannel board Pictures of city scenes
For Adult to Do Ahead:	Collect pictures of city scenes. Attach large pieces of flannel to backs of pictures.
Introduction:	Show children a picture. "What can you see in this picture?" Buildings, cars, people, and so on.
Procedure:	Tell the children, "Many buildings built together are called a city. There are usually lots of cars, trucks and people in a city. Can you put this picture on the board? What do you see in this picture?" Help children identify what is found in each picture.
Closure:	Ask, "Which picture of the city did you like the best? Why?"

Follow-up
Activities: Draw buildings onto pieces of flannel and cut out. Children can use these shapes to build a city.

Provide children with blocks to be built into a city.

Read *Let's Discover the City* by Maria Ruis and J. M. Paramon. New York: Barron's Books.

WHAT COLOR IS?

Purpose: To increase awareness of self.

Skills/
Concepts: To develop thinking skills.
To develop language.

Ages: 18 months through 5 years old.

Length of
Activity: Allow 1 to 2 minutes.

Materials: Mirror

Introduction: Ask children, "Do you know where your eyes are? Do you know where your hair is? Can you show me where my hair is? Can you show me where my eyes are?"

Procedure: Show children the mirror and help them to identify the mirror. "Can you look in the mirror and tell me what color your eyes are?" Give verbal help if needed. "My eyes are blue and your eyes are brown." Continue game asking each child for hair color, color of shirt, color of sweater, and so on.

Closure: Ask the children, "Can you tell me what color your hair is? Can you tell me what color your eyes are?"

Follow-up
Activity: Using the mirror, give each child a turn to draw a self-portrait.

SEAT BELTS FOR SAFETY

Purpose: To teach good safety practices for riding in a car.

Skill/
Concept: To develop the habit of wearing a seat belt.

Ages: 18 months through 5 years old. (A child is never too young to begin learning good safety habits. This is a brief reminder to the child to help reinforce good safety at home.)

Length of
Activity: Allow 1 minute, with gentle reminders.

Materials: None needed.

Introduction: Ask the children, "When you go for a ride in the car, do you buckle up your seat belt?"

Procedure: Continue: "You should always buckle up your seat belt (or let your parent buckle up the seat belt on your car seat) when you ride in a car. Seat belts help keep you safe when you ride in a car."

Closure: Conclude: "Remind your parents to buckle up their seat belts for safety in the car."

Follow-up Activity: Sing the song "Trucks and Cars" on page 202.

WIPE YOUR FACE

Purpose: To encourage children to wipe their faces.

Skills/ Concepts: To learn to wipe face if it is dirty.
To learn to care for oneself.

Ages: 18 months through 5 years old.

Length of Activity: Allow 1 minute.

Materials: Damp paper towel or disposable wet wipe
Mirror

Introduction: Say to the children, "We've finished eating. Let's look in the mirror at our faces."

Procedure: Ask children to look at their faces to see if there is any food on them. Some children will need prompting to see the peanut butter, jelly, milk, juice, and so on. "Let's dampen a paper towel so you may wipe the food from your face." Offer assistance if needed. "Can you check in the mirror? How does your face look now?" If there is still food, help the child by giving verbal hints: "Wipe by your lips" or "Under your nose."

Closure: Say, "What a fine job of wiping your face."

Follow-up Activity: Remind children to wash their hands.

PICKING UP TOYS

Purpose: To use a song to encourage putting toys away.

Skills/ Concepts: To memorize a song.
To return toys to original place on shelves.
To use gross and fine motor skills.
To follow directions.

Ages: 18 months through 5 years old.

Length of Activity: Allow 1 to 5 minutes, depending on number of children and the extent of cleaning to be done.

Materials: Song

SUBJECT: HEALTH/SAFETY

Introduction: Begin by saying, "Look at all of the toys on the floor. What could happen if someone tripped over one of them?" They could get hurt. "Let's pick up our toys and put them away."

Procedure: Encourage children to sing the following song while they put their toys away.

PICK UP YOUR TOYS
(sung to tune of "Row, Row Your Boat")
by: Charron Sundman and Katie Doran

Help pick up your toys,
Pick up all the blocks,
Pick them up one by one,
Put them in the box.

Help pick up your toys,
Pick up all the books.
Place them all upon the shelf,
See how nice it looks.

Help pick up your toys,
Put them all away.
Now the floor is clean and safe,
We may go and play.

Closure: Tell children, "You did a really nice job of putting your toys away. Now our floor is clean and safe."

Follow-up Activity: Read the book, *The Berenstain Bears and the Messy Room,* by Stan and Jan Berenstain. New York: Random House, 1983.